D1236870

THE TRUTH ABOUT PET FOODS

Inquiry Press

The information contained in this book has been compiled for purposes of education. The views and conclusions expressed by the author and cited sources do not represent all-inclusive knowledge or unanimity of opinion, and should not be construed as specific medical advice.

Published by Inquiry Press
1880 North Eastman, Midland, Michigan 48642

Printed in the United States of America:

ISBN 0-918112-11-7

To Pets

*Reminders of the quiet strength and dignity
of unfettered creation*

Retaining gifts we have lost or never had

Masters of life in the moment and the art of simplicity

*Reflections of a world forgotten,
presynthetic, more complete*

*Where loyalty, love, forgiveness, acceptance, fun and truth
are neither measured nor withheld*

*Deserving of our wonder, respect and love –
and the health that can only come from nature obeyed*

CONTENTS

CONTENTS (continued)

CONTENTS (continued)

FIGURE LISTING

FIGURE LISTING (continued)

INTRODUCTION

First, let me caution that this is not a conventional book on pet health or nutrition. It is not about protein, milligrams of calcium, IU's of vitamin A, a special ingredient, vaccinations, yearly checkups or laboratory tests. If optimal health and nutrition that cannot be surpassed is your goal, these things are not the primary consideration. The key is far more simple and intuitive...if you will dare to be convinced.

I have spent over two decades studying and researching fundamental health issues from a practitioner-turned-skeptic viewpoint. This book reflects the progress of that investigation, and will confirm that suspicions you may have about the effectiveness of modern health care and nutritional approaches are warranted.

Einstein once said, when faced with reactions ranging from disinterest, to open and hostile opposition to his new ideas, "Fashion abides in every age without people realizing tyrants rule them." In our modern era where commerce seems to be at the root of everything, we must be highly cautious about what fashions we become convinced of, and then apply in our lives. Just because everyone is doing it, companies beguile you, experts insist it is so, or government says it's approved, does not make something true, or in our best interests. Seeking beyond what is popularized by the media and commercial interests, and being wary of convention are the first steps toward health.

But people in every culture, in every era, are convinced of the truth of popular opinion. Those who would challenge or veer from accepted dogma are labeled weird, eccentric, psychotic or evil, and historically have been ignored, anathematized, ostracized, persecuted or even killed. We must also always keep in mind that knowledge is a process, a path – not a destination.

Revolutions in thought are often resisted until the bitter end, when the sheer weight of evidence and experience collapses the old paradigm. Examples in science include the shift from Aristotelian to Newtonian physics, from Newtonian physics to Einsteinian, from the Ptolemaic geocentric universe (everything revolves around Earth) to the astronomy of Copernicus (Earth around the sun), from the phlogiston theory to modern Lavoisier chemistry, from a God-centered, religious pontification of reality to materialistic, mechanistic science, and from the presently-in-process shift from the reductionistic-materialistic-Newtonian-Cartesian (all questions will be solved by an examination of matter) paradigm to the quantum-relativistic-holistic paradigm (all questions are not solved by an examination of matter).

As unbelievable as it may seem to us here, now, with all our comfortable beliefs, most of our view of reality is skewed and will be eventually replaced with a better version. This should be welcomed since paradigm shifts move us (hopefully) closer to ultimate truth.*

Such change is not simply intellectual exercise or interesting history. It is critically linked to our well-being since bad ideas bring bad results. The old physics, chemistry, biology, sociology, politics and religion stultified progress in terms of comfort, safety, health and enlightenment. Modern life, a by-product of a long chain of paradigm shifts, scientific and social revolutions if you will, is a far cry from the difficult, precarious and short lives of Stone Age beings.

But there is no reason to get cocky or be complacent with the pragmatic accomplishments of modernity. Huge personal, social and international problems loom on a global scale, undiminished by an ever-rising flood of materialistic trinkets. We are Stone Age compared to what we will be if the ascent to truth proceeds.

Such a climb, however, requires open-minded inquiry and the willingness to change – in spite of the temporary discomfort usually accompanying change. Conformity is a close brother to popularity, quiescence, peace and acceptance. But when everyone smiles and agrees, progress weeps.

In this book, I will focus on a needed paradigm shift in pet feeding. Such a change becomes apparent when the myths underlying present feeding practices are exposed, and the link to disease, suffering and

---

* For further reading on important paradigm shifts, see: Kuhn T, <u>The Structure of Scientific Revolutions</u>, 1996. Frank P, <u>Philosophy of Science</u>, 1974. Feyerabend P, <u>Against Method</u>, 1993. Grof S, <u>Beyond the Brain</u>, 1986. Sheldrake R, <u>A New Science of Life</u>, 1995.

death identified. I know we're told that today's companion animals enjoy better health than they have ever had, live longer, that modern pet foods are carefully and scientifically balanced, and that modern medical measures cure disease and extend life. Yes, this is what we are told. But I'm going to try to untell it here. In reality, fundamental errors in nutritional and medical thinking have resulted in much harm and running in place with little, if any, meaningful advance.

In principle, the things I will discuss apply as well to human health. Thus, you will find me crisscrossing my discussion between humans and animals. In the context of health, there is little difference between the two. Both humans and animals are in the same modern setting and thus subject to similar dangers. It follows that both can enjoy relief through similar rethinking and remedies.

There is a veil obscuring the truth about pet foods. It is a tapestry of appliqués including faulty science, commercial greed, regulatory imperiousness, professional egoism, marketing legerdemain, consumer naiveté, desire for ease, and old paradigm romance. By and large, the accepted dogma about how to feed and achieve health is wrong, very wrong. It remains in place because reason does not usually rule the mind, rather bias and mythologies designed to protect status quo reign. Skepticism, not acquiescence, is critical in the search for wellness. The temporary suspension of disbelief is fine at the movie theater, but has no place in health and nutrition.

Set aside preconceptions and the grip of conformity for the short time it will take to consider what follows. Let's reason together. Perhaps a little revolution is in order.

SECTION I

PET FOOD MYTHOLOGY

Oh Let Us Never Ever Doubt
What No One Is Sure About

— 1 —

THE "FEED A '100% COMPLETE AND BALANCED' PROCESSED PET FOOD" MYTH

Well, that's what we're told, isn't it? Think about it, though. Our world is complex beyond comprehension. It is not only largely unknown, it is unknowable in the "complete" sense. In order for nutritionists and manufacturers to produce a "100% complete and balanced" pet food, they must first know 100% about nutrition. However, nutrition is not a completed science. It is, in fact, an aggregate science, which is based upon other basic sciences, such as chemistry, physics, and biology. But since no scientist would argue that everything is known

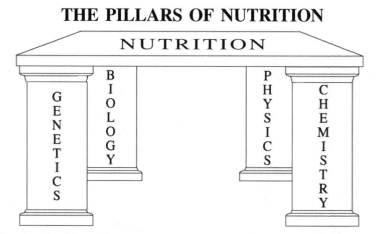

THE PILLARS OF NUTRITION

NUTRITION

GENETICS   BIOLOGY   PHYSICS   CHEMISTRY

Fig. 1. Nutrition rests upon the pillars of the basic sciences. But since no one claims 100% knowledge in these supporting pillars, how can 100% be known in nutrition? If 100% is not known in nutrition, how can nutritionists create a "100% complete" diet?

in chemistry, or physics, or biology, how can nutritionists claim to know everything there is to know about nutrition, which is based upon these sciences? This is the logical absurdity of the "100% complete and balanced" diet claim.

Claiming that anything is 100% is like claiming perfection, total knowledge, and absolute truth. Has pet nutrition really advanced that far? Does a chemist make such a claim? A physicist? Doctor? Professor? Did Einstein, Bohr, Pasteur, Aristotle, Plato, or any of the greatest minds in human history make such claims? No. Has the science of pet nutrition advanced to the point where everything is known about the physiology, digestion and biochemistry of animals, or that everything is known about their food? Certainly not.

In fact, although nutrition is rapidly being developed as a science, it has always lagged behind the other sciences. This is in part because it is a field of study that has not stood side by side with others in universities. Rather, nutrition has more or less been considered an incidental branch of homemaking or some other applied field such as animal husbandry. Additionally, because of its almost infinite complexity, the science of nutrition is not easily developed.

The fact of the matter is that the "100% complete" claim is actually "100% complete" guesswork. At best, one could say that such a claim is the firm possibility of a definite maybe.

Each time regulatory agencies convene to decide how much of which nutrients comprise "100% completeness," debate always ensues and

---

A "100% COMPLETE" PROCESSED DIET REQUIRES:
1. 100% complete knowledge of food.
2. 100% complete knowledge of nutrition.
3. 100% complete knowledge of #1 and #2 requires 100% complete knowledge of every science.

Since #1, #2, and #3 do not exist...
   the "100% complete" processed diet is a myth.

Fig. 2.

---

standards usually change (see Proofs, pages 74-85). This not only proves that what they claimed before was not "100% complete," but this should also make us highly suspicious about what they now claim to be "100% complete."

Additionally, consider this: in order to determine the minimum requirement for a certain nutrient – say protein – all other nutrients used in the feeding trials must be adequate. Otherwise, if vitamin E, for example, is in excess or is deficient, how would you know if the results of the study were because of the effects of protein or due to something amiss with the level of vitamin E?*

If the minimum requirements for all 26+ essential nutrients were all set and absolutely etched in stone, then there would be no problem. But they aren't. They are constantly changing. This means each time any nutrient requirement is changed, all test results for all other nutrients using the wrong minimum for this nutrient would then be invalid. Most nutritionists simply ignore this conundrum, feeling like cowboys trying to lasso an octopus – there are just too many loose ends. But they continue to perpetuate the "100% complete" myth, and excuse themselves by saying they make adjustments when necessary.

The point is, don't believe the claim on any commercially prepared pet (or human) food that it is "100% complete and balanced." It is a spurious unsupported boast, intended to build consumer trust and dependence on regulators and commercial products – not create optimal health in your pet.

---

* *J Am Diet Assoc*, 1996; 96(11):1156-64. *Acta Paediatr Scand Suppl*, 1982; 296:110-2. *J Nutr*, 2001; 131(4 Suppl):1331S-4S. *Prog Food Nutr Sci*, 1985; 9(1-2):1-33. *Ann Nutr Aliment*, 1976; 30(4):509-36.

— 2 —

THE "BUT IT'S ALL FIXED NOW" MYTH

What do manufacturers, nutritional scientists and regulators do when faced with the discovery that their "100% complete" processed foods haven't passed the red face test of not causing disease? First, they may deny and attack critics. Then, when faced with mounting evidence, research is focused on the problem. When the nutrient problem is identified, it is repaired – usually by "reformulation" with added synthetic nutrients – and the event is then heralded as a marvel of pet food science. The new repaired food is "100% complete." Yet the former, unrepaired food was also "100% complete." See a problem?

The industry doesn't. After all, the problem has been "fixed." Further, why should anyone expect perfection? Mistakes are made. Shouldn't we measure them by their willingness to discover the problem, admit error and make the necessary corrections?

Does an eventual explanation of causes justify results like disease, suffering and death? Correcting nutritional errors after disease results merits accolades only if the food is not being foisted on the public as "100% complete."

Things would be more forgivable if they weren't claiming perfection in the first place – and if they were not causing disease by so doing. "100% complete" means total, absolute perfection. Look it up. It's not like horseshoes and grenades where close is plenty good enough. 100% does not mean 99.99%. Complete does not mean incomplete.

Neither is it valid to argue that "100% complete" has a special loose definition qualified by matching a food to NRC minimal standards or feeding trial tests. The average person should be able to read a package and understand "100% complete" to mean just that, not a special case definition based on esoteric pet food industry argot and *caveat emptor.*

Real food consists of nutrients by the myriad, likely well over a hundred.* Some known, some not. Even if all the essential nutrients are in the starting materials, processing destroys or alters practically all of them.

There is also every reason to believe that only the more obvious tip of the nutrient/disease iceberg has been noticed and corrected. The hidden jagged edges of exclusively fed "100% complete" foods will continue to tear at the health bow of companion animals, robbing them of vitality in numerous subtle ways until they ultimately sink from decoys such as "infection," "old age," "degenerative disease," "genetics," "fate" or "unknown causes" (see Proofs, pages 74-85).

All is not well if "100% complete and balanced" (fixed) foods are fed exclusively. Although the pet food industry cleverly embroiders the truth and is charitable with themselves for past errors (and the thousands of animals diseased from reliance on the "100% complete" claim), the caring pet owner should not be. The lesson is, become cynical and skeptical, or the past will be prologue.

THE FOREVER BROKEN FIX

Fig. 3. Through the years nutritional problems in "100% complete" pet foods have been repaired. If something is 100%, no repairs should be needed. But repair will forever be needed because truly 100% complete processed foods are not possible.

---

* *Wysong Companion Animal Health Letter*, "The Whole Is Greater Than The Sum Of Its Parts," July 1996:1. *Am J Clin Nutr*, September 1995:621. *Tufts University Diet and Nutrition Letter*, May 1994:5.

— 3 —

THE "PET FOOD INGREDIENTS MUST BE APPROVED" MYTH

To assure safety and wholesomeness of pet foods, state and federal regulatory agencies proscribe or permit ingredients. Additionally, ingredients must be described on labels by precise nomenclature dictated by these alphabet (AAFCO, FDA, etc.) agencies.*

The problem is, those who sit on the committees deciding what can or cannot be approved may have commercial links (see Proofs, pages 74-85). They can push through ingredients that should not be in foods, and prevent the approval of those which either rub prejudices the wrong way or which may create unwelcome competition to their own interests. On the other hand, state regulators (a manufacturer must get approval from each individual state) may have little nutritional knowledge or academic credentials, but a lot of power.

Nutritionists who are consulted by regulators to help make decisions about ingredient approval are steeped in the reductionistic point of view. Since they believe nutrition boils down to percentages – % protein, % fat, % fiber, etc. – almost anything can be an approved ingredient provided these numbers are known. Where there are deficiencies, a few synthetic vitamins here, a few additives there (all properly "approved" of course), and all is well. The end result of this unholy marriage between commercial interests, prejudice, scientific naiveté, and regulatory dictatorship is the official AAFCO listing of approved pet food ingredients. Here are examples of what has been officially approved... and I'm not kidding:

---

* Association of American Feed Control Officials, <u>1998 Official Publication</u>.

- dehydrated garbage[1]
- polyethylene roughage
- hydrolyzed poultry feathers
- hydrolyzed hair
- hydrolyzed leather meal
- some 36 chemical preservatives
- peanut skins and hulls
- corn cob fractions
- ground corn cob
- ground clam shells
- poultry, cow and pig feces and litter
- hundreds of chemicals
- a host of antibiotic and chemotherapeutic pharmaceuticals
- a variety of synthetic flavorings
- adjuvants
- sequestrates
- stabilizers
- anticaking agents

On the other hand, if a manufacturer wants to be innovative and pack as much natural nutrition into products as possible, important ingredients are not approved. For example, even though it has been proven that the amino acid, L-carnitine, may be deficient in processed pet foods, it is not approved and cannot be used (see Proofs, pages 74-85). Proteoglycans such as glucosamine and chondroitin and other ingredients such as collagen, all of which have been proven to help prevent and alleviate arthritic conditions, are not approved.[1-2] Special natural foods that are particularly nutrient dense, such as pollen, composted sea vegetation, omega 3

---

1. Association of American Feed Control Officials, 1998 Official Publication.

2. Wysong RL, "Rationale for Contifin™, Glucosamine Complex™ & Arthegic™," 2002. *Wysong Health Letter*, "Chicken Cartilage for Rheumatoid Arthritis," 1994; 8(1). Clouatre D, Glucosamine Sulfate and Chondroitin Sulfate, 1999. Varma R, Glycosaminoglycans and Proteoglycans in Physiological and Pathological Processes of Body Systems, 1982. *Physiol Rev*, 1988; 68:858-910. *Ann Rev Biochem*, 1986; 55:539. *J Am Med Assoc*, 2000; 283(11):1469-75. *Br J Community Nurs*, 2002; 7(3):148-52. *Curr Opin Rheumatol*, 2000; 12(5):450-5. *Med Hypotheses*, 1997; 48(5):437-41. *Science*, 1993; 261:1727. *Chin Med J (Engl)*, 2000; 113(8):706-11. *Curr Opin Rheumatol*, 2002; 14(1):58-62. *Am J Clin Nutr*, 1998; 67(6):1286. *Am J Clin Nutr*, 1998; 67(2):317-21. *Arch Intern Med*, 1991; 151(8):1597-602.

Fig. 4. Regulatory authority and approval do not guarantee optimal health. Health is best served by knowledge and self reliance.

fatty acids, various biologically active phytonutrients (dozens of these have been discovered and their proven effectiveness has created a class of beneficial ingredients known as nutraceuticals) and even some organic ingredients cannot be used because they are not "approved."[1-2] There is

1. Association of American Feed Control Officials, 1998 Official Publication.
2. Wysong RL, Lipid Nutrition – Understanding Fats and Oils in Health and Disease, 1990. Wysong RL, "Rationale for Nutritious Oils," 2002. *Wysong Health Letter*, "Natural Foods Can Heal," 1992; 6(5). *Wysong Companion Animal Health Letter*, "Herbs that Heal," 1996(12). *Wysong Health Letter*, "An Herbal Medicine Chest," 1995; 9(9). *J Altern Complement Med*, 2000; 6(5):383-9. *Br J Sports Med*, 1982; 16(3):142-5. *Br J Urol*, 1989; 64:496-499. *Hua Xi Yi Ke Da Xue Xue Bao*, 1994; 25(4):434-7. *Nutr Rev*, 1999; 57(9 Pt 2):S3-6. *Mayo Clin Health Lett*. 1998; 16(8):7. *Rheumatology (Oxford)*, 2001; 40(12):1388-93. *Can J Cardiol*, 2001; 17(6):715-21.

no question of safety here – as regulators pretend – for these foods have been consumed for eons by animals and humans without ill effect.

Animal food regulatory absurdity becomes apparent when the very ingredients banned are sitting on shelves in grocery and health food stores fully approved for human consumption.

"Approved" ingredient regulations cannot be trusted. Banning nutritious natural ingredients and approving dehydrated garbage and feces makes it clear that the agenda of regulation is something different than encouraging optimal nutrition.

— 4 —

THE "DIGESTIBILITY, ANALYSES AND AAFCO FEEDING TRIALS PROVE 100% COMPLETENESS" MYTH

DIGESTIBILITY

These tests determine how much food is absorbed. Is food "B," because it is 95% digestible, better than food "A," which is 90% digestible? That would imply that if food "C" were 100% digestible, with zero fecal output, it would be the best food of all. Not so. Digestive tract health and the movement of food through the intestines depends upon a portion of food being indigestible.*

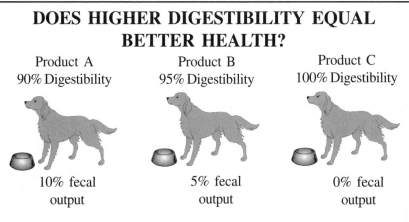

DOES HIGHER DIGESTIBILITY EQUAL BETTER HEALTH?

Product A	Product B	Product C
90% Digestibility	95% Digestibility	100% Digestibility
10% fecal output	5% fecal output	0% fecal output

Fig. 5. If higher digestibility is the goal, then a 100% digestible food would be the ideal. But 0% fecal output would cause disease, not health.

* *Br J Nutr*, 2001; 86(2):291-300. *J Nutr*, 1997; 127(1):130-6. Mindell E, <u>What You Should Know About Fiber and Digestion</u>, 1997.

Additionally, there is no generally accepted method for determining digestibility.* Such disagreement usually results when understanding is poor. Now then, if digestibility expert "A" disagrees with digestibility expert "B" and vice versa, we can disagree with them both and have the backing of an expert.

Digestibility tests attach simplicity to that which is incredibly complex. Measuring how much is absorbed compared to how much is lost or excreted says nothing about the *merit* of what is absorbed. Nutrition is a tissue-level biochemical phenomenon, not a simple subtraction between what is eaten and what is excreted.

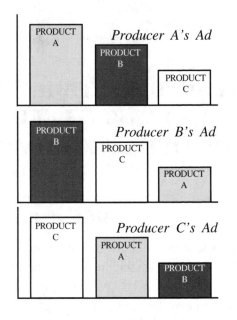

THE GAME OF DIGESTIBILITY ADVERTISING

Fig. 6. Producers attempt to lure consumers by touting high digestibility percentages. Problem is, each producer always shows their products win the competition. Since everyone cannot be winners, digestibility numbers are highly suspect.

FEEDING TRIALS

Feeding studies used to "prove" "100% completeness" are short-term, denying that nutrition can have an effect beyond the few weeks used in a feeding trial (see Proofs, pages 74-85). Undetected nutrient imbalance in youth has, for example, been shown to affect susceptibility to many

---

* *Anim Feed Sci Technol*, 2001; 89(1-2):49-58. *J Dairy Sci*, 2000; 83(10):2289-94. *Tufts University Diet and Nutrition Letter*, May 1994:5.

AAFCO IS NOT FOUND IN NATURE

Fig. 7. I'm starving – There's nothing around here with a "100% complete" AAFCO label.

chronic degenerative diseases which appear later in life (beyond the scope of a feeding trial).[1] Even the health of future generations can be affected through transference of nutritionally-induced genetic weakness (see The Pottenger Cat Study, pages 95-96).[2]

Current regulatory emphasis is on feeding trials, since some animals fed foods meeting NRC analytical guidelines suffered nutrient deficiencies. However, such deficiencies have also been experienced by use of pet foods which have passed AAFCO feeding trials (see Proofs, pages 74-85).

1. *Wysong Health Letter*, "Don't Let Apparently Youthful Health Fool You," 7(12):6. *J Am Coll Cardiol*, 1993; 22(2): 459-67. *J Am Med Assoc*, 1999; 281:727-35.
2. Pottenger FM, Pottenger's Cats: A Study in Nutrition, 1983. Price W, Nutrition and Physical Degeneration, 1982.

An AAFCO feeding trial requires a manufacturer to send food to a laboratory where it is fed to caged laboratory breeds for a period of 10-26 weeks. Hair coat, weight, body measurement, and color of the blood are then analyzed to determine nutritional perfection – "100% completeness."* It is like trying to measure the length of a virus with a yardstick. Such general measures do not fully reflect either nutritional adequacy or long term optimal health. "Caged" human prisoners of war have *survived* for years on little more than water and rice. Survival, or passing crude measures of nutrient deficiency, do not equal nutritional "completeness" (perfection).

Additionally, results from an unfortunate laboratory-bred puppy living on concrete or in a stainless steel cage, under fluorescent lights, breathing

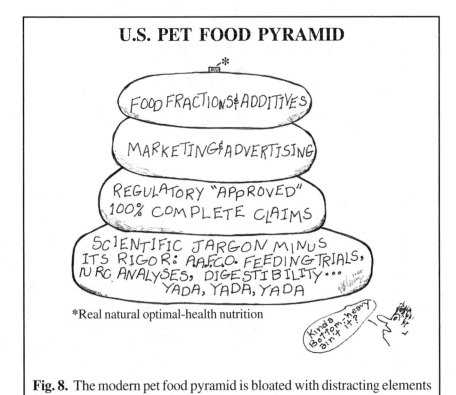

U.S. PET FOOD PYRAMID

FOOD FRACTIONS & ADDITIVES

MARKETING & ADVERTISING

REGULATORY "APPROVED" 100% COMPLETE CLAIMS

SCIENTIFIC JARGON MINUS ITS RIGOR: A.A.F.C.O. FEEDING TRIALS, NRC ANALYSES, DIGESTIBILITY··· YADA, YADA, YADA

*Real natural optimal-health nutrition

Kinda Bottom-heavy ain't it?

Fig. 8. The modern pet food pyramid is bloated with distracting elements having little to do with health-saving optimal nutrition.

---

* Association of American Feed Control Officials, 1998 Official Publication.

conditioned air, do not correlate to real animals in homes and back yards. Obviously not. If feeding trials worked, thousands of cats fed feeding-trial-proven diets with "100% complete" claims would not, for example, have died from taurine deficiency (see Proofs, pages 74-85).

None of this speaks to the unnecessary cruelty of imprisoning animals for months and years for feeding trials used to perpetuate a mythology.

ANALYSES

Nutrient analyses (reflected as "Nutrition Facts" on labels) can only prove that foods contain nutrients at levels that regulatory agencies say are necessary for the food to be "100% complete." Again, since no one knows what "100% complete" is, proving that a particular nutrient reaches a certain level is meaningless in terms of actually achieving optimal nutrition. Properly analyzed diets meeting guidelines have caused severe deficiencies (see Proofs, pages 74-85).

Measuring a food's merit using NRC levels such as percentage of protein, fat, fiber, ash and about a dozen vitamins and minerals tells only a partial story. There are over forty essential nutrients known and over fifty under investigation. How can making sure a food contains the appropriate amounts of only a dozen nutrients merit a "100% complete" designation?

What's more, testing to establish minimums is cursory and haphazard at best. For example, in the cat, phosphorus and manganese were NRC tested directly, but sodium, chloride, iodine, copper and selenium levels were merely extrapolated from values in other species.* In other words, a "100% complete" diet for cats could be based on something like sodium levels for aardvarks and selenium levels for newts. Maybe those aren't the species used, but no matter. An extrapolation is a guess regardless, and does not add up to "100% complete."

If producers wish to claim their food is X% digestible, or that it contains certain amounts of nutrients, or that it has been subjected to a certain feeding trial, that is fine. But don't you believe it when they take an incredible leap (actually a fall) in logic and then claim their food is "100%

---

* *J Nutr*, 1996; 126(9 Suppl):2377S-2385S, 2452S-2459S. *Pediatr Clin North Am*, 2001; 48(2):401-13. *Ann N Y Acad Sci*, 1975; 246:237-48. *Cancer Res*, 1992; 52(7 Suppl):2067s-2070s.

complete and balanced." It's like me claiming that because I can jump over the couch I can also jump over the moon.

Analyses, digestibility studies and AAFCO Feeding Trials are a futile life-support system for the hopelessly terminal "100% complete" claim. Don't be deceived. The "100% complete" claim is not good science. It is a shameless attempt at credibility by mere fraternization with the distinguished coattails of science. If science is the sun, the "100% complete" claim is Pluto.

Reliance on such dubious information distracts from important issues of natural nutrition and simply builds reliance on commercial interests.

I have not mentioned the waste of hundreds of thousands of dollars spent by manufacturers on testing and licensing to be able to make the "complete and balanced" claim. A huge regulatory and laboratory industry now exists to assure the perpetuation of the "100% complete" myth. Who pays for this? You do. This deceptive myth occupies an increasing economic space in your can or bag of pet food.

— 5 —

THE "MEETING AVERAGE REQUIREMENTS PREVENTS DISEASE" MYTH

An important advance in nutrition is the discovery that there is a difference between overt nutrient deficiencies (causing conditions such as rickets, anemia, blindness, etc.) and nutrition necessary to optimize health and prevent a host of more indirect, subtle and chronic diseases.*

SHOULD INDIVIDUALS TRUST AVERAGES?

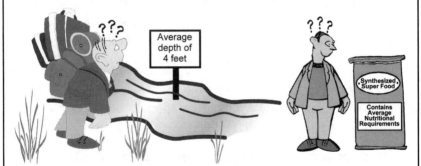

Fig. 9. Who would cross a stream that has an *average* depth of 4 feet with 100 pounds strapped to their back? Similarly, why would we strap ourselves with food designed for *average* requirements when we don't really know the depth of our nutritional requirements?

---

* *Wysong Health Letter*, "Essential Versus Optimal," Sept 1998:1-3. *J Nutr*, 1996; 126(9 Suppl):2309S-2311S. *Int J Vitam Nutr Res*, 2002; 72(1):46-52. *Petfood Industry*, July 1998:39.

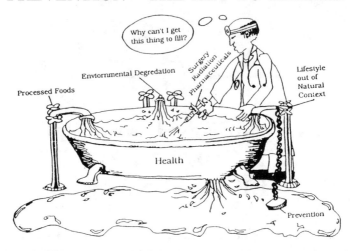

PREVENTION – THE KEY TO HEALTH

Fig. 10. True health can only be achieved by addressing all things that can impact health from a holistic, preventive standpoint. Symptom-based interventions will never solve underlying health problems.

Pet foods which are designed to achieve "average" levels of nutrition for prevention of classical nutrient deficiencies (so-called "100% complete" foods) fall short of this newer knowledge. They are most certainly not "100% complete." Being just barely good enough is not really "100% complete." Being just barely good enough nutritionally is like barely good enough parachutes or fire extinguishers. The risk is too great.

The confusion, even blindness, of researchers and regulatory agencies (however well intentioned) is apparent in the following incredible contradiction by authors with DVM, PhD and specialty board certification in veterinary internal medicine and nutrition:

> "These protocols (the authors are discussing AAFCO feeding trial studies) were designed to assure that pet foods would not be harmful to the animal and would support the proposed life-stage. These protocols were not designed to examine nutritional relationships to long-term health or disease prevention."*

---

* *Veterinary Forum,* Oct 1992:34.

In other words, a food could cause disease and destroy long-term health yet at the same time "not be harmful," "support life" and be classified as "100% complete"! So after a pet has been fed the "proven" food for a period of time equal to the duration of an AAFCO study (26 weeks), all bets are off. The "100% complete and balanced" food may then be starving or poisoning the animal with the blessings of the academic, professional, scientific, governmental and industrial pet food establishment (see Proofs, pages 74-85).

When researchers set nutrient requirements they use statistics. A bell curve is created which is a statistical distribution to determine what the requirement would be for the average majority. If an animal falls in the middle of the bell curve for every nutrient (each nutrient has its own bell curve) all may be well. But each edge of the bell curve also represents a number of animals for which the "average" dose is either too little (creating a deficiency) or too much (creating possible toxicity). There is a good chance that any specific animal (as opposed to a statistical average) will be on the edges of the curve for at least one of the nutrients.*

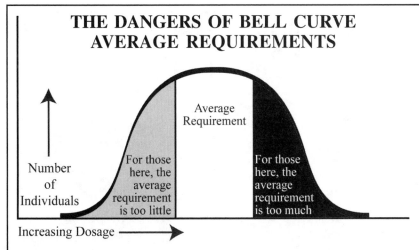

THE DANGERS OF BELL CURVE AVERAGE REQUIREMENTS

Average Requirement

Number of Individuals

For those here, the average requirement is too little

For those here, the average requirement is too much

Increasing Dosage ⟶

Fig. 11. Average nutritional requirements mean certain individuals in a population are at risk of deficiency or overdosage if they achieve these averages. No two creatures (other than identical twins) are stamped out of the same mold. All are biochemically and nutritionally unique – not "average."

---

* *Wysong Health Letter*, "Average May Not Be You," July 1998:3. *J Am Diet Assoc*, 1996; 96(8):754-5.

— 6 —

THE "INGREDIENTS COME FROM FARMERS' FIELDS" MYTH

F ood consumers see two things, the beginning and end – farms and packaged food products. The dangerous middle, food fabrication, is ignored. It's assumed that if corn, wheat, cheese, meat, etc. are on the label, then that's what's in the package. Not true.

WHAT WE IMAGINE IS NOT WHAT WE GET

PREMIUM PET
FOOD

All Natural

100% Complete

INGREDIENTS:
Corn, Chicken,
Rice, Beef, Fat

Shaped Like Real T-Bones

Fig. 12. Modern pet food, packaging and advertising would lead you to believe that what is in the package is straight from the farm. Its origin is really the chemist's lab and the food torturing industry.

THE DANGEROUS MIDDLE

THIS LOOKS GOOD

THIS IS WHAT
WE DON'T SEE

**Processing
(Food Torturing)**

Drying
Storing
Milling
Heating
Baking
Dehydration
Extruding
Freezing
Refining
Artificial Color
Artificial Flavor
Artificial Texture
Artificial Preservatives
Prolonged Storage

Processing Degradations

Racemized Amino Acids
Isomerized Fatty Acids
Dehydroascorbic Acid
Cis-Isomerized Vitamin A
Pyridoxyl Lysine
N-Glucosyl amines of
   Lysine and Methionine
Desulfurized Amino Acids
Quinone Pigments
Metalloproteins
Cholesterol Oxides:
  - Hydroxycholesterol
  - Alpha and Beta Epoxides
  - Cholestane Triol
  - Trienic and Dienic Fatty Acids
Heat Destruction Products of
  Vitamins A, B_1, B_3, and C
Succinylation & Acetylation of:
  - Lysine   - Threonine
  - Cysteine - Tyrosine
  - Histidine
Altered Physiochemical State
Lysoalanine & Lanthionines
Nitrosamines & Nitropyrenes

THIS LOOKS GOOD

PREMIUM
PETFOOD

Ingredients:
Corn, Chicken,
Oats, Fat

100% Complete
All Natural
Scientifically
Tested

Fig. 13. What happens between the farmer's field and the commercial package significantly vitiates healthful nutrition. Unfortunately, this dangerous middle is by and large ignored.

WHOLE WHEAT vs. FORTIFIED FLOURS

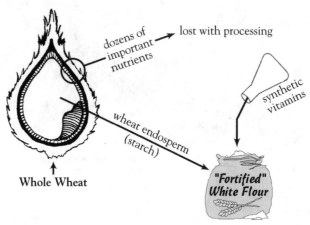

Fig. 14. Within whole wheat, particularly in the germ and outer layers, are many minerals, vitamins, enzymes, proteins, fats, and carbohydrates important for healthful nutrition. Ground whole wheat retains most of these nutrients, whereas fractionated white wheat flour does not. Synthetic vitamins are then added to impoverished white flour and this is, deceptively, called "fortification."

WHOLE RICE vs. BREWER'S RICE

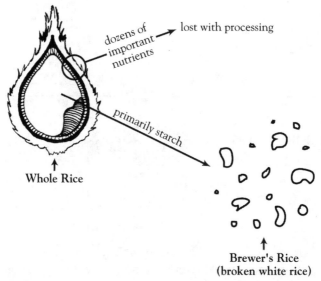

Fig. 15. Whole rice is highly nutritious. Once it is fractionated into white rice, unbalanced nutrition occurs, setting the stage for disease.

PROCESSED GOOP

Fig. 16. Food processors continue to shrink the natural diversity of food starting materials. It is economically advantageous for them to merely fractionate a few easily tilled grains and then modify them into a variety of "value added" products cleverly packaged and marketed.

Once foods are milled, fractionated, blended, extruded, pelleted, dried, retorted, baked, dyed, breaded, fried, sauced, gravied, pulped, strained, embalmed, sterilized, sanitized, petrified to permit endless shelf-life, and finally prettified, they become something entirely different from the wholesome starting materials.*

The vast majority of modern foods are inert and anonymous processing concoctions of a few base ingredients – white sugar, oil, flour and salt – all highly refined and processed and resembling not at all anything from nature. Not only are the resulting myriad products nutritional shells of the real thing, but processors have the audacity to call these products "value added."

* Wysong RL, Lipid Nutrition – Understanding Fats and Oils in Health and Disease, 1990. *Feedtech*, May 1997:39-43. *Arch Biochem Biophys*, 1966; 113:5.

This is not to say packaged products should not be processed. They must be, or the grains and legumes would be indigestible, and meats would spoil.

In our age of convenience, packaged products are here to stay. However, as with everything in the marketplace, there are good and bad products. All creatures are genetically designed for foods directly from nature, not for the chemical potpourri resulting from vigorous processing. Good, therefore, means as close to natural whole foods as possible. Bad means highly processed food fractions and synthetics.

PROCESSING APPROACHES

PROCESS	HEALTH APPROACH	VOLUME AND PROFIT APPROACH
1. Ingredient Storage	• Leave whole • Natural pest control • Oxygen excluded	• Preprocessed food fractions • Pesticides • Exposed to air
2. Grinding	• Low heat • Immediate use	• High heat/speed • Storage
3. Extrusion	• Careful control of heat, pressure and moisture	• High production
4. Ingredient Addition	• Those not requiring cook added after heat e.g. nutritious oils, vitamins, probiotics, enzymes	• All mixed • All cooked
5. Meats and Veggies	• Fresh	• Rendered • Precooked • Pre-dried
6. Fats and Oils	• Minimally processed • Minimally stored • Natural antioxidants • Nitrogen microbubble purging of oxygen	• Aggressively processed • Extended storage • Synthetic preservatives • Oxygen left in
7. Packaging	• Oxygen removed • Light barrier package • Nitrogen, CO_2 flushed	• Permeable bags exposed to oxygen and light
8. Storage and Transportation	• Fresh batch, fast delivery	• Warehousing
9. Innovation	• Continuing research and improvements to optimize nutrition and retain natural value • Leadership, not following market whims	• Research directed at consumer appeal, cosmetics, marketing, promotion of "100% complete" myth

Fig. 17. Food processing is more than mere business, it is an opportunity to do great good by preventing disease and optimizing health.

— 7 —

THE "INGREDIENT LABELS DEMONSTRATE FOOD VALUE" MYTH

Two very different products can have identical ingredient labels. One can be nutritionally far superior to the other.

The reason for this is that regulations only permit standard descriptions of each ingredient.* Thus, a manufacturer who is trying to create a truly high quality, nutritionally rich product cannot describe these efforts on the label by being specific.

The chart on page 40 demonstrates how a nutritionally superior food may cost a manufacturer 32 times what another manufacturer pays to produce an apparently identical product. Since ingredients must be listed using required terminology, the unique quality that may be present is hidden from the consumer.

To determine the true value of a commercial product, read the company's literature (not product labels) carefully.

---

* Association of American Feed Control Officials, <u>1998 Official Publication</u>.

PRICE AS A FUNCTION OF INGREDIENTS

INGREDIENT CLASS	Product A HIGH PRODUCTION & MAXIMUM PROFITABILITY INGREDIENT USED	PRICE	Product B HIGHEST QUALITY NUTRITION AND HEALTH INGREDIENT USED	PRICE
1. Soy	Soybean meal	$164/ton	Organic, whole, extruded	$340/ton
2. Rice	Brewer's rice	$128/ton	Organic, whole, brown	$950/ton
3. Vitamin E	Synthetic E	$10/lb	Natural E	$20.91/lb
4. Copper	Sulfate	$.50/lb	Chelated	$2.25/lb
5. Poultry	Meal	$403/ton	Fresh meat Low ash meal	$1000/ton $520/ton
6. Antioxidants	Ethoxyquin	$4.30/lb	Oxherphol*	$10.87/lb
7. Wheat	Middlings	$72/ton	Organic, whole	$320/ton
8. Oats	Grain	$78/ton	Organic groats	$500/ton
9. Soy Oil	Refined	$.39/lb	Whole, unrefined	$.57/lb
10. Salt	Refined	$95/ton	Whole	$213/ton
11. Fat	Beef Tallow	$.17/lb	High grade poultry	$.24/lb
12. Corn	Grain	$84/ton	Nutrient Dense	$95/ton
13. Peanut Hulls	Yes	$30/ton	No	
14. Rice Hulls	Yes	$1.50/ton	No	
15. Spirulina Platensis	No		Yes	$13.64/lb
16. Barley & Wheat Grass Powder	No		Yes	$8.50/lb
17. Probiotics	No		Yes	$90/lb
18. Enzymes	No		Yes	$4/lb
19. Chelamin**	No		Yes	$4/lb

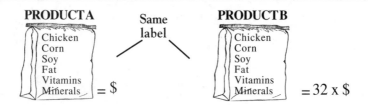

PRODUCT A
Chicken
Corn
Soy
Fat
Vitamins
Minerals = $

Same label

PRODUCT B
Chicken
Corn
Soy
Fat
Vitamins
Minerals = 32 x $

Fig. 18. Two apparently identical products can be vastly different in the cost of their ingredients and their impact on health. We can thank regulators for this misleading uniformity.

* Natural antioxidant preservative.
** Trace mineral supplement.

— 8 —

THE "MORE EXPENSIVE PET FOODS ARE BETTER" MYTH

Manufacturers are under no compulsion to charge based upon cost of production. Modern marketing results in more spent creating the *perception* of value, than actually is spent putting such value in the package. Refer again to Fig. 18 showing how foods appearing identical on the label may have a multiple-fold difference in cost of ingredients, but the charge to consumers may be the same. Inexpensively manufactured products may even have higher retail prices, and be hugely successful with the power of a large marketing budget.

Although it is true that a truly nutritious food is going to be expensive, it is not necessarily true that an expensive food is truly nutritious. Notice that it was expensive premium foods which killed thousands (see Proofs, pages 74-85).

DOES THE PACKAGE CONTAIN MARKETING OR INGREDIENTS?

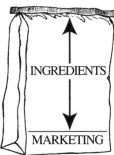

Fig. 19. "Premium," "super premium," "generic," and "natural" are marketing slogans. Anyone can make claims. If the company is truly doing something nutritionally significant, they will have literature that explains it fully. Question, probe and read to be sure the bag is full of nutrition, not marketing.

— 9 —

THE "PET FOODS ARE HUMAN QUALITY" MYTH

Notice that your pet food label lists such things as corn meal, meat and bone meal, soy mill run, wheat middlings, whey products, and the like. The descriptive words are different from what you would find in a grocery store because most pet food ingredients are food fractions left over after human food elements have been extracted. Or, they may be industry by-products, believed to be unfit for human consumption.* The slick advertising portrayal of pet food ingredients, as if they were just like what would appear on a Thanksgiving Day table, is misleading.

How can it be argued that meat and bone meal – which is basically all that is left of a cow after most of the edible organs and meat have been

---

TYPICAL ADVERTISING CLAIMS

"Our pet food is 100% complete and balanced, meets nutrient requirements of AAFCO, has passed feeding trials, contains nutritious vitamins, essential fat, minerals, fresh meats, dairy products and grain, is packaged in an Earth-friendly paper bag, needs no refrigeration, and is guaranteed to be fresh for one year."

Fig. 20. The portrayal of processed pet foods as if they were just like fresh home prepared meals is misleading.

---

* Association of American Feed Control Officials, 1998 Official Publication.

removed from the carcass – is equal to a T-bone steak purchased from the grocery store? Or how can chicken by-product meal alone – heads, feet and intestines – be equal to fresh, whole, store-bought chicken?

This is not to say by-products or discards from human food processing, correctly chosen, may not be nutritious, even highly so. Wild canines and felines will eat the viscera of prey (by-products) as the first preference.* But pet food marketers would prefer to have consumers think their products are made up of pork chops, chicken breasts and T-bone steaks, even though that could not possibly be what's in the package.

CHICKEN MAY NOT BE CHICKEN

"Chicken"
As found in many pet foods

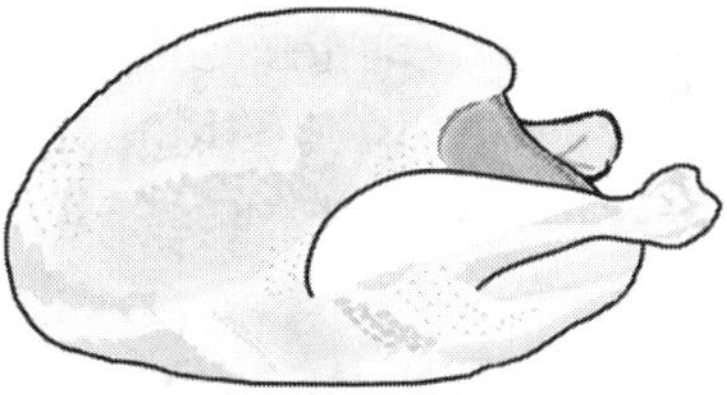

"Chicken"
As found in
a grocery store

Fig. 21. The word "chicken" is used loosely in pet foods. Pet food "chicken" is usually heads, feet and entrails, not the dressed chicken we see in grocery stores.

If you doubt this, check the price of such fresh meats at the grocer. Then compare pet food prices on a per-pound basis. You tell me how pet food "pork chops" – processed, packaged, marketed and shipped – cost a fraction of the fresh, non-processed, non-packaged counterpart in the meat counter.

Bottom line is that carnivores eat their entire prey.* You should feed your pet accordingly (see The Optimal Health Program, pages 195-208) and not be misled by the "human grade" ingredient pet food marketing game.

---

* Wysong RL, "Rationale for Archetype™," 2002. Tabor RK, The Wild Life of the Domestic Cat. Purves WK et al, Life – The Science Of Biology, 1992. Busch RH, The Wolf Almanac, 1998. Ewer RF, The Carnivores, 1973. *J Wildl Manage*, 1972; 36:3. *J Wildl Manage*, 1980; 44(3):583-602. *J Mammal*, 1977; 4:2. *Aust Wildl Res*, 1983; 10:3.

—10—

THE "BAD INGREDIENTS MUST BE AVOIDED" MYTH

This depends upon how "bad" is defined. Anything, natural or not, can be toxic ("bad") in suffi-cient doses.*

Avoiding the endless parade of bo-geyman ingredients is fruitless. First there are horror stories of the dangers of soy, then corn, then by-products, then wheat, ethoxyquin, sa-ponins, fat... and on and on. These stories begin with half-truths, grow to axiomatic law by mere repetition, and then are seized upon and legiti-mized in the form of commercial products pan-dering to the confused and misled public.

Allergies are the beginning point of much of this hysteria. But allergy or sensitivity can develop to any ingredient if fed unrelentingly as in exclusive feeding of processed pet foods. Why would anyone do something so foolish as feed the same food meal after meal,

Fig. 22.

---

*   *Wysong Health Letter*, "Nutritional Bogeymen," June 1996:1. *Wysong Health Letter*, "Natural May Be Toxic," July 1996:3. Ottoboni MA, The Dose Makes the Poison, 1984. Casarett LJ et al, Casarett & Doull's Toxicology: The Basic Science of Poisons, 2001. *Science News*, August 26, 1995:135. *Science News*, June 18, 1988:397. *Science*, 238:1634. *Tufts University Nutrition Letter*, 5(10):7. *Journal of Food Science*, 53(3):756. *Science News*, April 15, 1989:238. *Food Contaminants, Sources and Surveillances*, 1991:1. *Food Processing*, May 1996:52.

Fig. 23. The human tendency to seek easily identifiable enemies is capitalized upon by pet food marketers. It's easy. Find any piece of evidence incriminating a certain ingredient, demonize that ingredient, then produce a new "pure" food minus that ingredient.

day after day? Because real smart "experts" like regulators, nutritionists, veterinarians and manufacturers tell them to.

There is no magical "good" ingredient to be fed at every meal. Anything can be "bad," but any natural food fed in variety can be "good" and prevent both toxicity and allergy.*

Good nutrition is not the result of the presence or omission of singular ingredients. It springs from foods as close to nature as possible, fed in variety.

---

* *Wysong Health Letter*, "Food Allergies," May 1998:1. *Wysong Health Letter*, "Causes Of Allergy," October 1996:1. *Infect Dis*, April 1994:392. *Ann Allergy*, 1987; 58:14-27. *Compr Ther*, 1985; 11(6):38-45. *Nutri Rev*, 1984; 42(3):109-116. *Ear Nose Throat Journal*, 1990; 69:27-4. *Pediatric Clin NA*, 1-988; 35:995-1009. *J Allergy Clinical Immunology*, 1984; 74:26. *J Allergy Clinical Immunology*, 1995; 95:652-53.

—11—

THE "EXOTIC INGREDIENTS MEAN GOOD NUTRITION" MYTH

The fervor of the race for a niche, an edge, in the pet food market intensifies.

Since most pet foods are essentially made the same, the only place left to be "special" is on the ingredient list. So we now have foods with grapefruit, turnip greens, parsley oil, dandelion, split peas, thyme, apples, spearmint, marigolds, persimmons, broccoli, eyebright, quail eggs, and on and on. (Kind of starts to sound like lizard tongue, bat wing and eye of newt, doesn't it?) Although each of these ingredients prepared properly may have some food or nutraceutical merit, just mixing a smidgen into standard mixed "100% complete" processed foods just to create a fancy label is another matter. Without scientific evidence of value at the levels being used (which never seems to be there), such fad exotics can only create a false sense of nutrition.

Then there is the question of cost. If these ingredients were being used in a proportion that could have any meaning other than homeopathically (a branch of medicine based upon infinitesimally small dosage), they would put the price of the food out of reach of everyone but Bill Gates. For example, many such ingredients can range from between $10 to over $200 per pound. If such ingredients were used in meaningful amounts, a forty-pound bag of dry food could cost $100 or more.

But most consumers don't think this through. They get swept along by beguiling ingredients and evocative propaganda and don't put two and two together. Is it not strange that twenty pounds of the food they are buying for twenty dollars might cost $100 or more if they were to buy the fresh ingredients in the grocery store? That doesn't include the processing, shipping, packaging, infrastructure of a pet food corporation and advertising, built into the packaged product.

But no matter. You know, pet food manufacturing is kind of like astrophysics. No ordinary person can hope to fathom such esoteric science. After all, if they know everything there is to know about nutrition and its scientific underpinnings to create "100% complete" foods, it should be an easy matter to put $100 or more in a packaged product, sell it for $20 and make a profit.

Well, that's the long and short of the absurdity. What is most pathetic is that it is actually pulled off, with wave after wave of new pet food packaged brews barking whatever fad ingredient happens to be capturing the public's attention for the moment.

Enough delirium. The fact is, anyone, yes you too, can go to any number of manufacturers who have ready-made formulations sitting on the shelf. You can

Fig. 24. Some ingredients are listed on the labels purely for market appeal. If used in significant quantity, the price of the food would be beyond the reach of most consumers. So what's the point, other than deceiving buyers into thinking they are getting what they aren't?

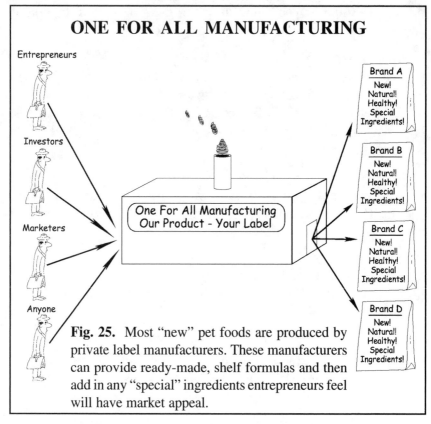

Fig. 25. Most "new" pet foods are produced by private label manufacturers. These manufacturers can provide ready-made, shelf formulas and then add in any "special" ingredients entrepreneurs feel will have market appeal.

ask them to rearrange the ingredient list a little and add a few pinches of a whole array of exotics you think will make your product irresistible to a gullible public. Why, you can even go to the store and buy caviar, send it to the manufacturer and have him squish one tiny egg in each ton of food he mixes. Now you can say your food has caviar in big red glossy letters in full-page ads in the most chic publications in the world. No problem. You're not lying. And, most importantly, you're on your way to becoming a caviar pet food mogul.

A better way to evaluate a food is to ask these questions:

- Who designed the product?
- What are their health, nutritional and scientific credentials?
- How long have they been doing this?
- What are the results of feeding over long term?
- What does the company believe?

- What is the informational and scientific quality of their educational/marketing materials?
- Are they manufacturing it or having it made at a toll producer?
- Do they seem principled, or merely profit oriented?
- ... All the other things you will learn in this book about how to evaluate foods.

Epilogue: Now for a bit of a confession. I am at least in part responsible for some of the above insanity. Many years ago when I first thought there was a need to develop alternative pet foods, most products were the same. The game was mostly percentage protein, digestibility and, of course, palatability. Ingredients didn't matter much if these objectives were achieved. My view was that ingredients did matter. Whole wheat was better than white flour, whole chicken was better than just heads and feet, and so forth, as you will learn throughout this book. I also discovered that there was significant science behind – and health benefits to – certain ingredients that could be used in micro amounts, such as probiotics, enzymes, phytonutrients, antioxidants and the like.

Partly because we were moderately successful in the market (to the degree we could educate and overturn deeply ingrained bias, tough job), and partly because other manufacturers (the big billion dollar guys saw us as a mere ripple in their tidal wave of financial success) could not defend well their inferior ingredients, some became concerned, not wanting to lose face. Others saw opportunity. The big guys eventually adopted some of our innovations, and some profiteers would start whole new lines, often shamelessly copying our products and adding a few exotics to be "different" and "better."

"Why not make exotic ingredient labels playing to increasing human concerns about nutrition and capture an emerging health conscious market?" they thought. What was lost in this singular quest for profit, however, was an underlying commitment to good science and health. The result: exotic ingredient labels with no true underlying scientific documentation or meaningful impact on health. Just words on yet more of an endless line of "100% complete" labels chasing markets. I had helped create a monster.

Sorry.

—12—

THE "DON'T FEED YOUR PET BONES" MYTH

Offering your pet raw, clean chicken wings or necks, or raw, clean beef knuckle bones, can virtually eliminate degenerative tooth and gum disease. This modern plague results from the constant consumption of mush and melt-in-the-mouth food trinkets.[1] The accumulation of tartar and the resultant septic gum disease bring on tooth loss. This oral/dental degeneration not only causes foul breath, but the cruel pain can affect appetite. Additionally, chronic mouth infection can seed organs with infection, resulting in degenerative organ diseases.[1-2]

You say, "But won't bones get caught in their throat?" And I say, "How did dogs and cats survive in the wild for eons?" They ate raw bones and meat exclusively. The dental disease we see in modern pets is virtually nonexistent in animals in the wild eating their natural, whole – and bony – prey.

Raw bones also provide important elements including minerals, protein, fats, proteoglycans, collagen, vitamins and enzymes in perfect proportions, exactly as nature intended. This is not to mention the exercise and entertainment pets enjoy from bone gnawing and chewing.

A Caution: Don't feed smaller cut bones such as from beef and pork which can be consumed too rapidly and may lodge in and around teeth. Moderation is the key. Excess bones (particularly if cooked) can cause severe constipation if suddenly introduced into the diet. The animals'

---

1. Wysong RL, "Rationale for Dentatreat™," 2002. *Vet Clin North Am Small Anim Pract*, 1998; 28(5):1129-45. *Veterinary Medicine*, 1989:97-104.
2. Hefferren JJ et al, Foods, Nutrition and Dental Health, Volume 1, 1981. *Microbes Infect*, 2000; 2(8):897-906. *J Am Geriatr Soc*, 2002; 50:430-433. *J Periodontology*, 2001; 72:50-56.

natural craving can cause them to overdo it in eagerness. Once a regular part of the diet, however, raw bone consumption will be self-regulating. Begin slowly. Offer fresh raw bones regularly. Start kittens and puppies right out on them. They can yield big dental and overall health dividends and greatly add to your pet's enjoyment. They can also help prevent boredom... and might even save some furniture and woodwork.

LOOKING FOR BONELESS NATURE

What's a guy to eat? All these things have bones in 'em!

Fig. 26. Popular pet feeding lore would have us believe carnivores were able to find boneless prey.

—13—

THE "DON'T FEED YOUR PET TABLE SCRAPS" MYTH

This is good advice only if you are putting processed junk food on the family's dinner table (see Proofs, pages 74-85). But if you are health conscious, trying to feed your family a variety of fruits, nuts, vegetables, whole grains, dairy products and meats, such food can only benefit.

Fig. 27. People do not apply common health sense to their pets.

Thousands of cats have suffered from a heart disease called dilated cardiomyopathy. This disease resulted from a deficiency of the amino acid taurine in commercial pet foods. No, these were not cheap inferior generic foods. They were premium diets which had been "proven" to be "100% complete and balanced" through feeding trials, laboratory analyses and digestibility studies (see Proofs, pages 74-85).

If cat owners had occasionally fed portions of organs and meats, the deficiency would have never resulted.[1] Untold thousands of cats would have been spared suffering, disease and death, and owners spared grief and medical costs.

The fact that manufacturers now add synthetic taurine to diets does not really solve the underlying logical problem of reliance on commercial products being "100% complete." Again, no one knows what "100% complete" is. Must we continue to learn the hard way?

Taurine deficiency is just the tip of the iceberg. Other recent discoveries include potassium deficiency, carnitine deficiency, zinc deficiency, riboflavin deficiency and chloride overdose (see Proofs, pages 74-85). There is every reason to believe that many chronic degenerative diseases such as arthritis, obesity, heart disease, cancer, immune disorders, allergies, and skin, eye and ear infections can often be related to chronic malnutrition.[2] Subtle deficiencies cast a long shadow on health and cannot be

---

1. Association of American Feed Control Officials, 1998 Official Publication.
2. Wysong RL, The Synorgon Diet, 1993. Wysong RL, "Rationale for Vitamins and Minerals," 2002. Wysong RL, "Rationale for Antioxidant Supplements," 2002. Wysong RL, "Rationale for Contifin™, Glucosamine Complex™ & Arthegic™," 2002. Wysong RL, "Rationale for Carvasol™," 2002. Wysong RL, "Rationale for Salad™," 2002. Wysong RL, "Rationale for Immulyn™," 2002. Wysong Health Letter, "Arthritis and Calcium, Folic Acid, Vitamin E, Zinc and Selenium," 1999; 13(10). Wysong Health Letter, "B Complex for Arthritis and Stroke Risk," 1995; 9(12). Wysong Health Letter, "Boron for Arthritis," 1993; 7(12). Wysong Health Letter, "Less is More," 1992; 6(9). Wysong Health Letter, "Obesity," 1997; 11(10). Wysong Health Letter, "Prevention and Therapy for Heart Disease," 1995; 9(2). Wysong Companion Animal Health Letter, "Folic Acid and Heart Disease," 1997(5). Wysong Health Letter, "Vitamin C and Heart Disease," 1997; 11(12). Wysong Health Letter, "Heart Disease: What Does and Doesn't Work," 1995; 9(5). Wysong Health Letter, "Selenium and Cancer," 1998; 12(1). Wysong Health Letter, "Vitamin D as an Anti-Cancer Agent," 1996; 10(12). Wysong Health Letter, "Cancer and Vitamin E," 1999; 13(11). Wysong Health Letter, "Vitamin E and Immune Response," 1997; 11(11). J Am Coll Nutr, 1994; 13:351. N Engl J Med, 1995; 332(5):286-91. Semin Arthritis Rheum, 27:180-5. J Am Med Assoc, 1996; 275:1828-1829. J Optimal Nutrition, 1994; 3(3). Can Med Assoc Journal, 1954; 71:562-568. J Am Med Assoc, 1996; 276:1957-63. Cancer, 1992; 70:2861. Lipids, 1998; 33(5):461-9. J Am Med Assoc, 1997; 277:1380-1386.

ARE PET FOOD SCRAPS
BETTER THAN TABLE SCRAPS?

Fig. 28. The very people who tell pet owners not to feed table scraps use them in the preparation of commercial foods.

detected in short-term feeding trials. Rather, they incubate over the lifetime of the animal to crop up in later years when little can be done to resolve the problem or (convenient to the perpetrators) identify the underlying cause – "100% complete" pet foods.*

* *Wysong Health Letter*, "Don't Let Apparently Youthful Health Fool You," 7(12):6. *J Am Coll Cardiol*, 1993; 22(2): 459-67. *J Am Med Assoc*, 1999; 281:727-35.

Not only do manufacturers imply that their foods are human quality, but they then caution pet owners against feeding table scraps or grocery non-processed foods. They can do it, but you can't?

Home cooking and feeding is just not good business. It runs contrary to the ultimate objective of marketers – 100% consumerism. We, the public, are to be mere profit centers – passive, compliant, uncritical, dependent and unthinking. Food industrialists will engineer, grow, cook and deliver your food, and, just like mom and dad, tell you what is best and beg you to eat it. As Wendell Berry put it, "If they could figure out a profitable way to prechew and force feed it they'd do that too."*

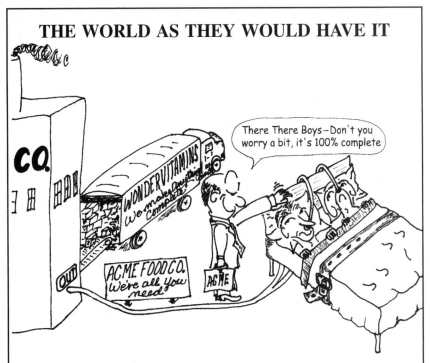

Fig. 29. If food producers could figure a way to force feed their products they just might do it. The pet food industry made a giant step in that direction with the "100% complete" diet. Although not physically strapped down, the consumer's mind has been shackled by confidence in, and reliance upon, that which is not true – the notion that producers have the requisite 100% complete knowledge of nutrition to enable making 100% complete processed foods.

---

* *The Sun*, January 2002.

Further, if commerce had things their way, society would be enclosed within walls containing only one-way valves where their food gadgets come in but no thinking can come out. Better yet, we and our pets should be strapped to the dinner table with stomach tubes coming direct from the factory and money conveyors going back. Actually, the AAFCO ingredient list has closed the loop even more completely with approval of feces and garbage as food. Tubes could run to "eat" and "exit" ends in a nice tidy closed circuit direct to and from industrialists.

As much as supplemental independent grocery store feeding is cautioned against, there must surely be some evidence of damage from this feeding practice. But other than occasional reports of problems brought on by feeding large quantities of cooked bones, or meat only, or liver only, or fish in excess, there is no such evidence. In 17 years of medical practice I did not see one such problem.

Of course, ridiculous excesses of anything can cause problems. Even oxygen and water can kill if overdosed. But feeding fresh foods, in variety, can cause only health – not disease. If you believe that the natural instincts of your companion animal mean anything, offer some clean, raw liver or meat and observe. Case closed.

—14—

THE "MEALS MUST BE BALANCED" MYTH

This idea springs from the "four food groups" style of nutrition taught in grade school. Problem is, it is taught seriously rather than as part of the fairy tale sessions right before kids curl up with their blankies for afternoon naps.

A Big Mac™ is a four food group meal...meat (fried burger), veggie/fruit (lettuce, pickle, onion), dairy (processed cheese), and grain (white flour bun). Optimal nutrition? Doubtful.

"Balance," "food groups" and "food pyramids" all complexify what is simple. Natural foods, fed in variety, create optimal nutrition, not slogans or words meant primarily to make everyone dependent upon processed foods. How do I know? Because that's what creatures ate for eons prior to nutritionists, dietitians and regulators. They did fine or no creature would now exist. Creatures cannot survive prior to their proper, optimal food.

Additionally, research has proven that not all nutrients need be eaten at the same meal or even on the same day. You do not even need all of the essential nutrients at every meal or every day for optimal health.[1] In fact, no nutrients at all for a time (fasting) has many health benefits.[2]

---

1. *Wysong Health Letter*, "Biochemical Individuality," July 1987:1. *Int J Cancer Suppl*, 1998; 11:66-8.
2. *Wysong Health Letter*, "Fasting Is Healthy," March 1996:3. *Wysong Health Letter*, "Fasting For Health," 8(10):5. *Wysong Health Letter*, "Healing By Eating Nothing," 10(1):3. *Am J Gastroenterol*, 1994; 89(2):267-70. *Science News*, March 5, 1994:147.

Nothing new here. It's the way nature is. In the wild, animals or humans would rarely have the "four food groups" at every meal, or every day. If you found some berries, that might be all you ate that day. Perhaps only meat the next. Then nuts a couple of days later. Then perhaps some eggs you were lucky enough to happen upon. Then nothing. (Probably a lot of that.) Same goes for animals. They ate what was there and did not go shopping for the missing food groups.

Additionally, the digestive system is best adapted to processing one thing at a time.* Fruits are not digested in the same way as fats or meats, for example. Mix them all together at every meal and the digestive system

KNOW YOUR FOOD GROUPS

THE DONUT GROUP

THE JOLLY RANCHERS GROUP

THE COFFEE & POP GROUP

THE SUGARED YOGURT & PUDDING CUP GROUP

Fig. 30. Nutrition should not be about arbitrary food groups. Health is best served by the variety of foods a creature is genetically designed to eat from nature, fresh as is.

---

* Wysong RL, The Synorgon Diet, 1993. *Am Nat,* 2000; 155(4):527-543. *Living Nutrition,* 2000; 8. Bass SS, Ideal Health Through Sequential Eating. Howell, Textbook of Physiology for Medical Students and Physicians, 1924.

is taxed. Foods are incompletely processed, resulting in the epidemic of digestive disturbances common to humans and domestic animals.

Here, again, the "100% complete" myth raises its ugly head. To be "complete" requires that the meal be "balanced" (as if words and claims make it so) since pets by the millions are condemned to such monofeeding. Problem is, as you now know, nobody is certain what true balance or completeness is.

Much better to use nature as the principle. Natural foods, fed in variety, create health. Anything else creates something less than that.

—15—

THE "PETS REQUIRE SPECIAL DIETS" MYTH

There are life-stage pet foods, large breed foods, breed specific foods and a host of foods targeting specific diseases. Promoters of such diets embellish advertisements with just enough technical flare to create the illusion that such foods spring from hard research and science. Here are some of the buzzwords to snare the uninformed and trusting public: "science," "research," "clinical," "doctor," "university," "trials," "studies," and the like. Lace this argot with a little pie chart here, a bar graph there, a scientific reference or two, and it all becomes very impressive.

In actual fact, you would be hard pressed to find any controlled study published in a peer-reviewed journal that has ever proven the value of any such diets over just good, varied home cooking. (This is not to suggest that such publications are the only place to find good evidence. But if the promoters of such foods are going to start throwing around "science," then they should be able to cite the medium of science – scientific journals. "Put up or shut up," comes to mind.)

Aside from this, do specific diets even make sense? Well, let's go to the great teacher and mother of us all – nature. Do puppies in the wild eat differently than adults, or seniors? Do different kinds of canines or felines eat different foods? Do big dogs or cats eat anything fundamentally different from what kittens or puppies eat after weaning? Are carnivores in the wild who get sick (a very rare thing in terms of the degenerative conditions we see plaguing modern pets) doomed if they can't find a diet to match their condition? The answer to all is an emphatic "no."

Creatures in the wild eat what they were designed to eat: raw, natural, whole foods exactly as found in nature. No fancy, fabricated, fortified, "complete and balanced" concoctions. Just the best science of all – nature.

True, some designed diets may help some animals in special situations much like some drugs will also help in special situations. But the problem is, such allopathic approaches are symptom-based, temporary Band-Aids fraught with contraindications and potential dangers in themselves, and do nothing to cure or address underlying causes.* It's like turning the fire alarm off while letting the fire continue to smolder in the closet.

Much better in these special situations to use diets with concentrated natural nutrition, augmented with fresh foods and natural supplements. This can stimulate the healing forces within, rather than drug-like attempts to force the body into submission.

The cause of most illness in modern pets (and humans) is modern living and processed diets. So can more similarly designed exclusively fed processed diets (the cause), be the cure? Not likely.

---

* *Wysong Health Letter*, "Pharmaceuticals Compel and Mask – But Do Not Heal," 1992; 6(5). *Wysong Health Letter*, "Probiotics May One Day Replace Antibiotics," 1992; 6(5). *J Am Med Assoc*, July 26, 2000; 284. Kohn L et al, To Err Is Human: Building a Safer Health System, 1999. *Tijdschr Diergeneeskd*, 1997; 122(2):36-9. *Science News*, March 7, 1992:159. *N Engl J Med*, 1999; 341:1249-55. *Arch Intern Med*, 1999; 159:71-8. *Br Med J*, 2000; 321:471-6. *J Am Med Assoc*, 2001; 285:1460-5. *Arthritis Rheum*, 2001; 44:1515-24. *J Am Med Assoc*, 2001; 286:954-9. *Diabetes Care*, 2001; 24:1711-21. *J Am Med Assoc*, 2002; 287:734-41. *Arch Intern Med*, 2000; 160:2897-900. *Pharmacology*, 2000; 20:1417-22. *American Family Physician*, 1997; 56(7).

—16—

THE "FOOD ALLERGIES ARE CURED BY ELIMINATING CERTAIN PET FOOD INGREDIENTS" MYTH

Food sensitivities and allergies are increasing problems. Many pet owners have animals tested to determine which ingredients cause allergic reactions. Once the laboratory report comes back, they then seek a food that does not contain the incriminated ingredient. Manufacturers cheerfully respond with new varieties of supposedly hypoallergenic foods.

The results of such an approach, however, are disappointing. The reason is that pet foods are not made up of singular ingredients. They are also not made up of the same things that laboratories use to test for allergies.

Pet foods can be comprised of as many as fifty different ingredients, all processed under rigorous conditions, including high temperature and hundreds of pounds per square inch of pressure. With such food "torture," the molecular makeup of the food changes. The starting materials are transformed into different ingredients. Fifty starting ingredients transform into hundreds of food fractions and chemical novelties.

Allergy testing laboratories use protein isolates. This is not the same as the end product of processing. Beef, chicken, corn and soy in a pet food are not the "beef," "chicken," "corn" or "soy" used in a laboratory.

Therefore, the only way to test an animal for sensitivity or allergy to a commercial pet food is to actually feed the food over a period of time to observe results (see Fig. 31).*

Attempting to treat allergies by removing an allergen – usually impossible to do – solves only part of the problem. Focus needs to be redirected to feeding foods which will enhance immune system health and prevent allergic reaction. Additionally, no food should be fed day in and day out. Variety is not only key to nutrition but also to prevention of toxicity and allergy.

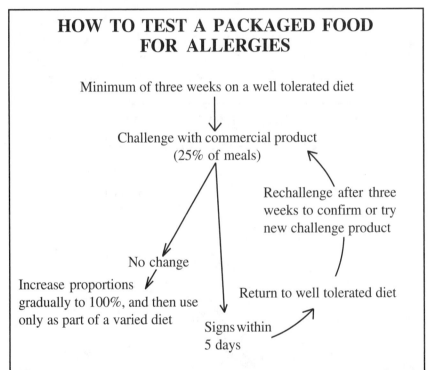

HOW TO TEST A PACKAGED FOOD FOR ALLERGIES

Minimum of three weeks on a well tolerated diet

Challenge with commercial product (25% of meals)

Rechallenge after three weeks to confirm or try new challenge product

No change

Increase proportions gradually to 100%, and then use only as part of a varied diet

Return to well tolerated diet

Signs within 5 days

Fig. 31. Since allergy tests do not test for the same allergens as found in mixed processed foods, the only way to determine food tolerance is to test feed it.

* *Wysong Health Letter*, "Food Allergies," 1998; 12(5):1-2. *J Vet Intern Med*, 2001;15(1):7-13. *J Am Vet Med Assoc*, 1993;203(2):259-62. *J Am Vet Med Assoc*, 1992;200(5):677-80. *J Am Vet Med Assoc*, 1991;198(2):245-50.

—17—

THE "USE A PET FOOD WITH NO PRESERVATIVES" MYTH

Fats and oils as they exist within natural living food are stable. Natural biochemicals, called antioxidants, prevent living food biochemicals from oxidation and rancidity. (It should be noted,

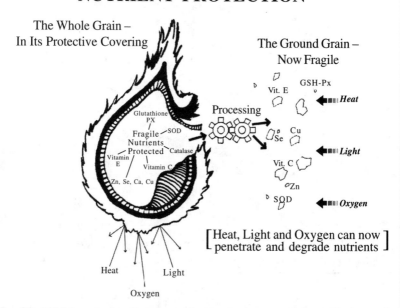

PROCESSING DESTRUCTION OF NUTRIENT PROTECTION

The Whole Grain –
In Its Protective Covering

The Ground Grain –
Now Fragile

Vit. E   GSH-Px

Heat

Glutathione PX

Processing

Fragile Nutrients Protected

SOD

Catalase

Cu

Se

Vitamin E

Vitamin C

Light

Zn, Se, Ca, Cu

Vit. C

Zn

SOD

Oxygen

[Heat, Light and Oxygen can now penetrate and degrade nutrients]

Heat   Light

Oxygen

Fig. 32. Within whole plants, nutrients are protected by a variety of natural antioxidants and other protectants. Once food is processed and fractionated, these protective elements are lost, exposing the fragile nutrients to degradation.

however, that even this mechanism can deteriorate, particularly in animals and humans being fed processed foods.) Internal fat rancidity can result in a host of diseases.* Once natural food ingredients are processed – by grinding, heating and otherwise disrupting their natural integrity – fats and oils are exposed to heat, light and oxygen and rapidly deteriorate.

Since pet foods are made up of such processed ingredients, fats and oils within their ingredients can quickly degrade. If these fats and oils are not protected, and they become oxidized, they will form potent toxins which, if ingested, can cause serious disease.* This is one of the reasons why a steady diet of "100% complete" processed foods serves as a pre-cursor to degenerative disease.

Therefore, it is important that processed foods have fats and oils properly preserved.* The popular headline "No preservatives" found on both pet and human food packages is therefore a Catch - 22. Fats and oils in such products, if not properly stabilized, can be more toxic than the synthetic preservatives they are excluding. Do not use processed products without fat and oil preservatives.

* Wysong RL, Lipid Nutrition – Understanding Fats and Oils in Health and Disease, 1990. *Wysong Health Letter*, "Oxidized LDL Antibodies," 1993; 7(5):3-4. *J Toxicol Environ Health*, 1981; 7(1):125-38. *Lancet*, 1992; 339(8798):883-7. *N Engl J Med*, 1992; 326(21):1444. Wysong RL, "Oxherphol™ Technical Information," 2002. Luck E et al, Antimicrobial Food Additives: Characteristics, Uses, Effects, 1997.

—18—

THE "PET FOODS MUST HAVE SYNTHETIC PRESERVATIVES" MYTH

A variety of natural substances can be effectively used as antioxidant preservatives. Oil-soluble forms of vitamin C, epimers of vitamin E, oleoresin extracts from herbs such as cloves, rosemary and sage, phosvitin found in egg yolks, capsaicin from chili peppers, citric acid from fruits, rice bran oil, ferulic acid from plants, beta carotene as found in richly colored plants, certain fruit components, and whey as found in milk products all can exert antioxidant protection for processed foods.* (Note: pet food preservatives protect nutritional fats and oils from rancidity, but not spoilage from other degradations such as insects, molds or bacteria.)

Feed foods as fresh as possible. A good rule of thumb is: Feed what spoils rapidly, but feed it before it does. Processed foods should be packaged in oxygen and light barrier packages and be preserved with natural antioxidants. But even these products should be consumed as soon as possible.

Don't be fooled by food scientists telling you that your pet food must have synthetic preservatives, or, on the other hand, by health food

---

* Wysong RL, "Oxherphol™ Technical Information," 2002. *Wysong Health Letter*, "Colon Cancer, Gas and Preservatives," 1999; 13(2):5-6. Risch SJ et al, Spices: Flavor Chemistry and Antioxidant Properties, 1997. *Mol Pharmacol*, 2000; 58(2):431-7. *Toxicology*, 1998; 130(2-3):115-27. *Int J Food Sci Nutr*, 2000; 51(5):327-39. *J Agric Food Chem*, 1999; 47(9):3541-5. *Biochem Biophys Acta*, 1992; 1124(3):205-22. *Prostaglandins Leukot Essent Fatty Acids*, 2000; 62(2):107-10. *Int J Food Microbiol*, 1999; 50(1-2):1-17. *Arch Latinoam Nutr*, 1998; 48(1):7-12. *J Agric Food Chem*, 2002; 50(7):2161-8. *J Dairy Sci*, 2001; 84(12):2577-83. *J Food Sci*, 1977; 42(4):1102-6. *Proc Biochem Soc England*, 1965; 97(3):28-9. Hunter BT, Consumer Beware! 1971.

enthusiasts touting products which have no preservatives at all. If a company is using natural antioxidants, ask the company for an explanation of how these products are used and seek packaging that is both a light and oxygen barrier. Freeze, in appropriate containers, any unused dry product that is going to be kept for any length of time.

—19—

THE "PET FOODS IN PAPER BAGS CAN HAVE SHELF-LIVES UP TO A YEAR OR MORE" MYTH

The length of time food remains edible is called "shelf-life." The race for ever-greater shelf-life has turned much of modern food processing into mortuary, rather than life science.

Rocks and cardboard keep well in paper bags for a year. Since when do highly nutritious foods do so? Pet foods are comprised of grains, dairy products, meats, oils, fats, vitamins and minerals, all of which – unless they are altered significantly, which nutritionally neutralizes them – deteriorate with time.

Notice what happens to foods which you know to be highly nutritious. Can you put a steak, some yogurt, cheese, bread, vegetable oil and cereal in a paper bag and leave it in your cupboard for six months or a

PUT THESE IN A BAG FOR A YEAR?

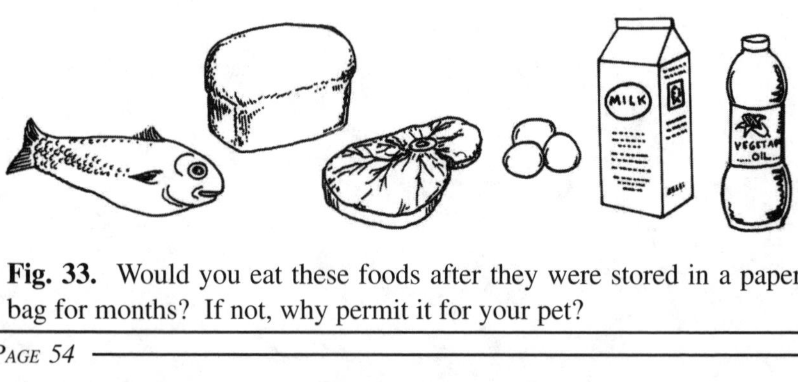

Fig. 33. Would you eat these foods after they were stored in a paper bag for months? If not, why permit it for your pet?

year and then find it suitable to eat? Hardly. Leaving such things exposed in this way for even a day is unwise. Real, nutritious foods are fragile, and easily deteriorate in the presence of oxygen and light.* If something in a paper bag lasts a year or more on a shelf, is it food or an embalmed food artifact?

Food processors are not magicians. Something must give to make meat, eggs, milk, etc. last in a paper bag. What gives is nutrition. Health is, in effect, traded for shelf-life.

Consumers must therefore use the same common sense about how their pet foods are packaged that they'd use about foods which they, themselves, consume. To properly preserve fragile nutritional value, foods must be carefully prepared from fresh whole ingredients preserved with natural antioxidants, and rapidly packaged in oxygen-free and light barrier packages. Small portion packing is best (that's not a fifty-pound sack), and unused portions should be tightly sealed, then refrigerated or frozen.

THE NUTRITIONAL IMPORTANCE OF PACKAGING

The Best Food Package
- Careful Processing
- Whole Ingredients
- Oxygen-Free Atmosphere
- Natural Antioxidants

A Poorer Choice
- Processed Food
- Food Fractions
- Oxygen Atmosphere
- Synthetic Antioxidants

The Worst Choice
- Processed Food
- Food Fractions
- Oxygen Atmosphere
- "No Preservatives" (No Antioxidants)

Fig. 34. Healthful food package design must address critical factors, such as the exclusion of oxygen and light from the packaging.

* Loken JK, <u>The Haccp Food Safety Manual</u>, 1995.

—20—

THE "ASK YOUR VETERINARIAN OR PET PROFESSIONAL" MYTH

I f you want expert advice on what to feed your pet, ask your veterinarian or pet professional...

And you live happily ever after. The end.

If life could be so simple.

In my 8-1/2 years of college learning to be a veterinary physician and surgeon, I had one course in nutrition.* And that concentrated on food animals, not pets. Then, all of a sudden in practice, I was supposed to be a nutrition expert. Clients relied on my advice. What profundity did I come up with? Feed a name brand, not a generic, and don't imbalance the foods by feeding table scraps. Not what you would call heavy advice, expert, or even responsible when I look back on it. But at the time I was quite proud of myself for coming up with such wisdom. (Actually, I didn't even come up with that. It's what my profs taught me to say. They were remarkably wise in this area also.)

In school I was focused on the technology of medicine. That is the emphasis in human and animal medical schools. Nutrition was kind of like homemaking, not science. And besides, all those "name brand" pet food companies had all the details figured out. All that pets needed to do was eat out of their bag (actually hand, as you are learning) and you could put nutrition out of consideration as a factor in health.

---

* Michigan State University College of Veterinary Medicine, Doctor of Veterinary Medicine (DVM) Professional Program, 1997. Michell AR, <u>The Advancement of Veterinary Science: Veterinary Education</u>, 1993.

Most other pet professionals know even less. But pet owners need to rely on the advice of someone, so they go to the obvious. Regretfully, the advice they receive – "feed '100% complete' processed foods exclusively" – if applied, condemns most pets to eventual disease and suffering, as you will learn in these pages.

Veterinary students do become familiar with some brands of pet food while in school. But this is not through critical evaluation, but rather because some manufacturers provide free products for the teaching hospitals along with polished marketing materials. Pet food companies are no dummies. Brainwashing infants (in this case, veterinary neophytes) is highly effective and will more than pay for itself when graduates move to practice and recommend all they know.

Veterinarians, pet store employees, breeders, groomers, trainers or kennel owners are not purposely misleading. It's all they know, or it's where the money is because they represent a particular brand.

Now, a veterinarian has an excellent background in the sciences to use as a base to gain some true nutritional understanding. A few do this, but not many. If you find one, pay attention. Pet professionals, unless educated well in the sciences, have a more difficult task and are more easily bamboozled by pet food technomarketing. They also often are led astray by getting fixated on lore regarding the benefits of a certain ingredient or the horrors of another. It gives them something to get passionate about when advising plebeians. Nevertheless, if they have an open mind, want the truth, and will work intellectually to get it, their advice can become worthy as well.

One must still be cautious because some veterinarians and pet professionals are "on the take." In return for their authoritative credentials and endorsements, they are given all kinds of perks. This need not be bad in and of itself, but it can skew even a professional's judgement.

For you to even know what is or is not good advice, you must engage your mind, learn a little, and be bent on the truth. Ultimately, in matters of health for yourself or your pets, you are the most reliable expert. If what you are told does not make sense and is not grounded in science, forget the credentials.

—21—

THE "PET FOOD REGULATION PROTECTS THE PUBLIC AND GUARANTEES HEALTH" MYTH

Fostering, condoning, promoting and regulating the "100% complete" claim that has killed and maimed untold thousands of pets (see Proofs, pages 74-85), and visits upon their owners emotional anguish and medical costs, is not public protection. It is more like tyranny, or state sanctioned mind control. (Apologies to all the level-headed regulators who just try to reasonably do their job and do not pretend that present pet food regulation of "100% completeness" is important.)

Strong words? Perhaps. Hyperbole? No. For the reasons set forth in this book, and the documented clinical evidence, health and "100% complete" exclusive feeding are clearly antithetical.

Should we expect regulators, nutritionists and the pet food industry to change any time soon in the face of contrary evidence? Don't count on it. The money is too wonderful, egos and security too important.

The burden is on you, Joe Public, to sharpen up, see the obvious, take control and not take it anymore.

This conspiracy by the powerful, although perhaps unintentional, is no big revelation. Life teaches us that we are our own best caretaker. After all, aren't you the most important person in your life? Don't you think experts and regulators have their own interests primarily at heart too? Should you really then trust your, or your pet's health to another?

No, neither trust nor money is the answer to health.

With that said, let me get down from my pulpit to have a little fun. Indeed, if the consequences of the "100% complete" claim and its regulation were not so serious, this could all be a real belly slapper.

The following are examples of how we at Wysong have been "regulated" through the years in response to efforts to improve nutritional quality. No exaggerations here. These are real live case histories from our files chronicling some of the unreasoning discriminatory efforts of some regulators.

Several agencies regulate pet foods either directly or indirectly. There's the USDA (United States Department of Agriculture), FDA (Food and Drug Administration), AAFCO (Association of American Feed Control Officials Incorporated), and each state has its own feed regulatory agency. All of this to control what is fed to your cat or dog! A little overkill (pardon the pun) wouldn't you say? I mean we're not talking powerful pharmaceuticals, addicting drugs or hazardous chemicals. Just food. You'd wonder what it is all these people do to fill their time. Well, I'll show you.

"ORGANIC"

We developed an organic, non-GMO (genetically modified organisms) food and were going to name the product "Organic."

After submitting labels for approval, regulators responded that we could not name it "Organic."

Further, we could not call the ingredients organic (even though they were) without impossible red tape, such as providing third party confirmations, affidavits, and proofs like needed in some kind of criminal case. We were trying to do something good and they treated us like we were planning a mass murder. Now if we wanted to use AAFCO approved, dehydrated refuse and scrap plastic (see pages 7-8) and call it "100% Complete," no problem.

Do you feel safer now that our killer "Organic" food is not on the market?

"FREE RANGE"

When we found sources of free-range meats and wanted to describe on labels that this was more humane, regulators said no.

Further, to even say "free range" on the label would require the same criminal-type onerous red tape provings as with "organic."

They disagreed that animals out in fields, on real ground, breathing fresh air and getting genuine sun were being treated any more kindly than those in close quartered feedlots standing in manure up to their knees, or in wire cages, pens or crates crammed inside buildings.

By such reasoning, regulators could argue that imprisonment for humans is not even punishment.

"OPTIMAL NUTRITION"

Regulators objected to our use of the phrase "Optimal Nutrition." They argued that if we used levels of nutrients above their "approved" levels, that would make our ingredients unapproved food additives.

In other words, if we were to discover that regulatory minimums were insufficient to prevent diseases such as arthritis, cancer, dental disease, heart and organ disease, and the like (which we, and scientists worldwide, have), we could not move our formulas to match this new knowledge. No, regulators would want us to stay at their minimums, condemning pets to preventable disease. Public protection?

"GENETICALLY MATCHED"

Consistent with the theme throughout this book that creatures require natural food to which their ancestors were adapted, we attempted to describe this on our labels by using the term "genetically matched." Regulators prohibited this unless we could provide proof by way of "scientific peer reviewed literature."

Problem is, there are some things so obvious, scientists would never spend the time or money to prove or publish them. For example, you can't find "scientific peer reviewed literature" proving the sun comes up in the morning, wind contains air, heavy things fall to the Earth, plants need sun or creatures need the natural food that genetically matches them. But we were supposed to hunt through libraries around the world for "peer reviewed" articles proving dogs and cats require natural meat and vegetable products, not things which they are not genetically matched to eat, like ground Formica table tops, shredded carpet, crushed tile flooring, dyes, herbicides, pesticides or used motor oil.

Help!

"FRESH MEAT" & "WHOLE INGREDIENTS"

The criminal-type provings (affidavits, third-party documentation) were also required for us to say we used fresh meats (rather than just prerendered dried meat ingredients), and whole ingredients (rather than food fractions such as brewer's rice, white flour, soy mill run, etc.). As you will see later in this section, grocery shelves are lined with approved pet products with claims which were obviously never so proven. Short of practically inviting the AAFCO committee and regulators from every state agency into our plant (we'd probably be responsible for five-star accommodations, first-class tickets and gourmet meals – which you can bet would have "fresh" and "whole" entrees) – to watch our every move and verify every ingredient, we were being prevented from truthfully stating what was in our products. Now if we were saying something like our food "contains strychnine at healthy levels," I could see regulatory intervention. But how, even if we were wrong, could "Fresh" or "Whole" – even in a regulator's wildest nightmare – create harm!?

"ALIVE"

Living creatures require living foods. One way we accomplish this in our dried pet foods is to enrobe the product after processing with active enzymes and living probiotic (yogurt-type) cultures. To describe this we wanted to state that these cultures were "alive." But no, since the public would be at such great risk (?), regulators wanted us to do the "scientific peer reviewed" do-si-do again.

Provide scientific literature proving bacteria are alive? How are you going to do that?

"SYNERGISTIC COMPLEXITY OF LIFE ITSELF"

Life is not a simple addition of a few elements. It is complex and interdependent beyond our ability to even comprehend. That's what makes life different from nonlife. By using whole, fresh, natural food ingredients, we recognize this complexity and its value to health. When we tried to describe this on our labels by using the phrase that healthful foods should contain the "synergistic complexity of life itself," regulators hit us with that "peer reviewed" proof thing again.

Now I defy you to find a scientific article that attempts to prove that life is synergistic and complex and not just a simple pile of carbon, nitrogen, hydrogen, oxygen, sulfur and calcium. But we were supposed to.

Do you think maybe they want us to spend our time roaming libraries rather than make products that challenge their tidy little, "add up chemicals and claim 100% completeness," fairy tale?

"PHYTONUTRIENTS"

Research has proven that certain plants and plant components can prevent and reverse disease.* To incorporate these elements fresh and unaltered into our foods, our products are enrobed with them after processing. But when we attempted to describe this on labels, regulators asked for "proofs." When proofs were supplied, they either did not respond or said the proofs were insufficient. You see, since regulators don't understand how fresh ingredients can be in a processed food, or that something other than a pharmaceutical can impact disease, they attempt to prohibit innovation and possible salutary effects. If we wanted to dye our foods iridescent purple, put jellybeans or raffle tickets in the package, that would be fine.

---

* *Wysong Companion Animal Health Letter*, "Herbs that Heal," 1996(12). *Wysong Health Letter*, "An Herbal Medicine Chest," 1995; 9(9). *Nutr Rev*, 1999; 57(9 Pt 2):S3-6. *Mayo Clin Health Lett*. 1998; 16(8):7. *Rheumatology (Oxford)*, 2001; 40(12):1388-93. *Can J Cardiol*, 2001; 17(6):715-21.

"UNIQUE"

When we stated our products were "unique," regulators said that was a no-no. They argued that because our label listed ingredients like in other pet foods, there was no uniqueness. But get this. Why do our labels appear this way? Because regulators force us to name our ingredients the same even though they are not (see Chapter 7, pages 25-26).

Aside from this, our formulations are totally unique (regulators have no idea what they are since they cannot force manufacturers to reveal this proprietary information), and our nutrient sparing packaging and processing are unique.

Go to the grocery some time and see whether other approved pet food products get to say things like "special," "best," "premium," "superior," or the like, all terms synonymous with unique.

"FORBIDDEN INGREDIENTS"

When we tried to incorporate some special nutrient dense ingredients, regulators said they were unapproved.

Examples include:

POLLEN – even though it is impossible to eat plant foods without eating pollen. Additionally, pollen can be found in grocery stores and has been consumed by people and animals for eons. It is, in effect, a plant kingdom egg and as such contains almost every nutrient known.[1]

SPIRULINA – available in stores and even consumed as a staple by some cultures. It too contains essentially every nutrient known. Regulators evidently feel vitamins and minerals should come from "approved" chemical factories rather than from real natural foods.[2]

---

1. *Wysong Health Letter*, "Natural Foods Can Heal," 1992; 6(5). *J Altern Complement Med*, 2000; 6(5):383-9. *Br J Sports Med*, 1982; 16(3):142-5. *Br J Urol*, 1989; 64:496-499. *Hua Xi Yi Ke Da Xue Xue Bao*, 1994; 25(4):434-7.
2. *J AOAC Int*, 2001; 84(6):1708-14. *Crit Rev Food Sci Nutr*, 1991; 30(6):555-73. *J Nutr Sci Vitaminol*, 1998; 44(6):841-51

TRACE MINERAL SEA SALT – processed salt (approved) with its important trace minerals removed, and additives combined, is a totally different creature than real trace mineral rich sea salt which regulators would not permit us to describe on labels.[1]

GEOLOGICALLY COMPOSTED SEA VEGETATION, SEA CUCUMBER, CHONDROITIN, COLLAGEN, PSYLLIUM SEED – all prohibited even though they have proven health benefits, are consumed with regulatory approval by humans and are natural foods.[2]

VITAMIN C – an innocuous vitamin proven to have great benefit in many species is prohibited because regulators who are not *au courant* think it unnecessary.[3]

"FORBIDDEN NAMES"

"PREMIE" – We designed this intermittent special diet to emphasize certain nutrients for the very young. Regulators said this was like a medical claim. In other words, they would not want the public to be "misled" into thinking that if they used Wysong "Premie" it would be like putting your kitten or puppy into an intensive care pediatric unit, or that any infant disease would be automatically cured. Thank goodness they saved you from having us pull that one over on you!

---

1. Wysong RL, "Rationale for Whole Salt™," 2002. *Price-Pottenger Nutrition Foundation Health Journal*, 1999; 21(2):574. *J Amer Coll Nutr*, 1987; 6(3):261-70.
2. *Wysong Health Letter*, "Chicken Cartilage for Rheumatoid Arthritis," 1994; 8(1). Wysong RL, "Rationale for Contifin™, Glucosamine Complex™ & Arthegic™," 2002. *Science*, 1993; 261:1727. *Chin Med J (Engl)*, 2000; 113(8):706-11. *Thromb Haemost*, 1991; 65(4):369-73. *Curr Opin Rheumatol*, 2002; 14(1):58-62. *J Am Med Assoc*, 2000; 283(11):1469-75. *Am J Clin Nutr*, 1998; 67(6):1286. *Am J Clin Nutr*, 1998; 67(2):317-21. *Arch Intern Med*, 1991; 151(8):1597-602. *Diabetes*, 1992:167.
3. Wysong RL, "Rationale for Antioxidant Supplements," 2002. *Wysong Companion Animal Health Letter*, "Cataracts," 1997(4). *Wysong Companion Animal Health Letter*, "Nutrients for Congestive Heart Failure," 1996(8). *Wysong Companion Animal Health Letter*, "Vitamin C for Respiratory and Sinus Disease," 1996(10). *Wysong Health Letter*, "Vitamin C and Asthma," 1995; 9(8). *Wysong Health Letter*, "Vitamin C for Ulcers," 1998; 12(5). *Wysong Health Letter*, "The End of Heart Disease," 1996; 10(5). *Wysong Health Letter*, "Decreasing Mortality with Vitamins E and C," 1996; 10(8). *Wysong Health Letter*, "Lead Poisoning and Vitamin C," 1999; 13(6). *Wysong Health Letter*, "A, C &E," 1993; 7(12). Goodman S, Vitamin C: The Master Nutrient, 1990. *Health Revelations*, June 1995:8. *Am J Clin Nutr*, 1996:190. *Am J Clin Nutr*, 1995:625S. *Am J Epid*, 1995; 141(4):322-324. *Cancer*, 1997; S0:1897-1903. *J Am Med Assoc*, 1999; 281:2289-93.

"STRESS/PERFORMANCE" – This special intermittent diet was high in protein and energy for animals with increased needs. Regulations said we couldn't use the name "Stress/Performance" because it implied a medical claim. You know, like if your cat or dog were exposed to stress, it would not experience it if you fed this food. Or if you had a Greyhound and fed the food it would automatically win all races. Right. That's just what we meant and what the public would think.

"GERIATR$_X$" – This intermittent diet was designed to emphasize special nutrients for the elderly. See the **R$_X$** symbol in "GeriatR$_X$"? Regulators said no way. That would tell the public that this food was a drug. Is that what you would think, that if you had an older animal with cancer, obesity, arthritis, heart disease, tooth loss, blindness or the like, all you would need to do is feed a food called "GeriatR$_X$"? Seems regulators don't give the public much credit for intelligence. Or do they? See with what names they expect you to use discernment (see pages 67-72).

"SYNTAX AND OTHER FELONIES" PUTTING YOUR PET IN PERIL

If you thought your old English teacher was tough, you should try writing a pet food label to be graded by regulators. Only here you either pass or fail. If you don't pass, your products can be banned and confiscated. For a small producer it could mean bankruptcy.

Here are examples of some things, which if not "corrected," could have sealed our fate long ago.

- The net weight had to be in kilograms, not just pounds.
- The word "complex" had to be beside a vitamin.
- Probiotics had to be quantitated in colony forming units, not cells (a colony forming unit is a cell, but no matter).
- Names of ingredients had to be in the same point size and letter style.
- Wording regarding AAFCO had to be precise.
- Nutrient analyses had to be positioned in just the "right" way.

How many lives have been spared by such picayune nonsense? Zero. How many have been lost due to the "100% complete" claim regulators love? Thousands.

It's like arresting jaywalkers while permitting murder and rape in the alley.

MORE PICAYUNE REGULATORY NONSENSE

Here's more.

- We can't state that we search for quality, rather than least cost ingredients.

- We can't state that processing destroys some nutrient value and therefore nutrients must be supplemented.

- We can't state that synthetic chemicals are not the source of best nutrition.

- We can't state that feeding Wysong reduces food intake (even though this is the experience of thousands of customers).

- We cannot say "quality" unless we use synthetic preservatives.

- They claimed Wysong foods have too much iodine if kelp (a seaweed) is an ingredient. (Yet they have never tested our foods for iodine, nor are they privy to our formulations.)

- We can't say our foods contain proteoglycans (important for joint health).* Proteoglycans are in all meat products. It is therefore impossible to produce a product that does not contain this if meats are in the formula.

- Glucosamines, one of the proteoglycans particularly beneficial for joint health, is not permitted in cats. Yet a cat in the wild would never eat a meal without consuming glucosamines.*

---

* Wysong RL, "Rationale for Contifin™, Glucosamine Complex™ & Arthegic™," 2002. *Physiol Rev*, 1988; 68:858-910. *Ann Rev Biochem*, 1986; 55:539. Varma R, Glycosaminoglycans and Proteoglycans in Physiological and Pathological Processes of Body Systems, 1982. *J Am Med Assoc*, 2000; 283(11):1469-75. *Br J Community Nurs*, 2002; 7(3):148-52. *Curr Opin Rheumatol*, 2000; 12(5):450-5. *Med Hypotheses*, 1997; 48(5):437-41. Clouatre D, Glucosamine Sulfate and Chondroitin Sulfate, 1999.

- We can't say that when we enzymatically digest a meat to make it more digestible that this is a meat product.

- We can't make any reference to the quality or grade of an ingredient – something that has everything to do with health. But we could talk all we want about color, shape, texture, mouth feel and aroma – things that have nothing to do with health.

OTHER PET FOOD LABELS

This is a random sampling from pet food labels and advertisements approved through the years by state regulatory agencies. We do not necessarily disagree with the following producers' right to say what they say – as long as Wysong can say the things we wish to say. If Wysong comes under painstaking scrutiny, so should everyone else.

This critique is not meant to criticize the producers cited (they are merely taking liberty with words for marketing purposes), but rather to demonstrate a regulatory double standard. So permit me here to be the regulatory devil's advocate. I'll censor these foods as ours have been, taking every word literally and permitting no poetic or marketing license.

BONZ™* – I can't say "Bonz" without it sounding like "bones." That's no accident. Yet when you open the box, you see no real bones. They claim: "Is good for a dog's teeth." What is "good for"? Proven? Peer reviewed? Where are the regulators?

MILK-BONES FLAVOR SNACKS™* – They are neither bones nor milk, but regulators don't seem to care here. "Your dog's 6 favorite flavors" – how do they know? Don't dogs have individual tastes? "A flavor no dog can resist" – is this every dog in the universe? Palatability is extremely individual. To say "no dog can resist" is without "peer reviewed" proof. "A hearty snap of cheese flavor that will tickle your dog's taste buds" – how exactly do a dog's taste buds become tickled? "Your dog will bark with delight" – is this a guarantee? Will the neighbors sue? Where are the regulators?

MILK-BONES™* – "Cleans teeth" – what does "clean" mean? Peer reviewed proof? "Freshens Breath Naturally" and "Nothing freshens your dog's breath better than Milk-Bone Dog Biscuits." Isn't a real bone natural, not a "Milk-Bone"? Veterinary dentists would argue that a complete tartar scraping and dentistry, followed by rinsing of the mouth, would certainly freshen most dogs' breath better than Milk-Bones. This second statement, in fact, may lead consumers to believe that dentistry is not necessary for dogs. A medical claim? Where are the regulators?

MILK-BONE DOG TREATS™★ – They are shaped like bone segments with a reddish center, and claim "with Real Bone Marrow." At a glance, we discover that it is the ingredient "meat and bone meal" to which they must be referring as "real bone marrow." In fact, meat and bone meal contains only insignificant fractions (if any) of marrow. Naturally it has some marrow in it, but the red dyed stuff in the middle is not just marrow. Where are the regulators?

SNAUSAGES™★ – "The Ideal Snack" – unless the definition of "ideal" has changed, this cannot be true, since they contain artificial/chemical and by-product ingredients. Can it be proven that they are "ideal"? They can say "ideal" (unproven) but we can't say "unique" (proven)? Where are the regulators?

JERKY TREATS™★ – Proclaims "Contains real meat" as if the consumer is to believe that is unusual, as opposed to the "fake" meat in all other treats? Where are the regulators?

TAST-TEE CHUNKS™★ – "They will have any Rover rolling over." Really? Probably pretty safe since nobody names their pet "Rover" anyway. Peer reviewed proof? Where are the regulators?

JERKY BITS™★ – "You and your dog will flip for ALPO Jerky Bits™." Not only your dog flips, but you do too. Is the flip a one-and-a-half, or a backward with a full twist? What if a human were to break his or her neck while doing one of these flips? Who pays for damages? Pity the insurance carrier. Where are the regulators?

CHEW-EEZ™★ – "Chew-eez™ gets your dog's teeth cleaner than Milk-Bone." Well, now hold everything. If this is true, somebody lied to us when they said nothing was better than Milk-Bones for my dog's teeth! I'm confused. How can both be approved and licensed? Where are the regulators?

TOP CHOICE™★ – Here the front panel claims "Better Than Hamburger," and "Chopped Beef Burger for Dogs." Better tasting, better nutrition, better smelling? Exactly how better? The second claim "Chopped

Beef Burger for Dogs" should read "Chopped Soybean Meal and High Fructose Corn Syrup Burger for Dogs" since these are the first two ingredients. Where are the regulators?

PUPPY CHOICE™★ – "Easy for puppies to digest." Peer reviewed? Proof? Because it is soft and mushy (easy to chew), does that make it easily digestible? Where are the regulators?

GAINESBURGERS™★ – "The canned dog food without the can." If there is not a can, it is not a canned food. Where are the regulators?

CYCLE 1™★ – "Because of its special formulation…" – special? How? What is special? Special for the consumer and pet, or special for the producer? They can say "special," but Wysong can't say "unique." Where are the regulators?

GRAVY TRAIN™★ – Another one claiming "Is ideal…." What is ideal? They get to say "ideal," but we can't say "unique"? C'mon. Peer reviewed proof? Where are the regulators?

KEN-L RATION CANNED FOOD™★ – This packaging tells us it is "America's first dog food," and is "a trademark of quality and commitment." First? Does being first (if this is really so) automatically imply merit? Was the "first" food good or bad? Are they still using this "first" formula from so many years ago? Where are the regulators?

TENDER CHOPS™★ – "Each succulent little chop tastes and looks like the center cut of the savory real meat chops dogs love." Will Fido love it because it looks like a meat chop? If I tasted it, would I agree that this grain-based product tastes like a "real meat chop"? Where are the regulators?

O.N.E.™★ – "Highly nourishing." What does "highly" mean? Compared to what? "Leading pet nutrition center in the world" – well, I'm sure they think so. "Visible results in just 10 days." This daring statement sounds like a health promise. Peer reviewed proof? Where are the regulators?

CYCLE 3™★ – "Fitness Food," which implies that fitness will surely result and sounds very much like a health claim. They can say "fitness" and we can't say "performance"? They also state "Nothing but good food," and yet the number one ingredient is wheat middlings. Other ingredients include rice hulls and BHA (butylated hydroxy anisol). Where are the regulators?

COME 'N GET IT™★ – This food is "Bursting With Taste." How does taste burst? I'm not going to taste it to see, and I can't get my dog to answer me when I ask him. They also claim to be the "Only dry dog food which offers 4 different flavors," but Flavor Snacks™ had my "dog's 6 favorite flavors" in the box! Regulators can't count apparently. Where are they?

LUCKY DOG™★ – Well, the "leading pet nutrition center in the world" announced, "You could find $100 inside this bag." What does that have to do with nutrition? Where are the regulators?

CHEWY MORSELS™★ – "Extra nutrition." What is "extra"? They can say "extra" but we can't say "optimal"? Nutrition that is extra is excreted or deposited like fat. If extra is important, do all their other products have extra? They continue, "No other puppy or adult food does more for your puppy," but their original Puppy Chow™ is still being sold. How can they offer it if it is inferior? Chewy Morsels is also proclaimed to "produce small, firm stools." Is this proven by peer review? Where are the regulators?

TENDER MEALS™★ – "The only soft-moist cat food good enough for Morris." Isn't Morris on the payroll? Wouldn't his opinion be biased? Are all other soft-moist foods in the universe not "good enough"? Where are the regulators?

ALLEY CAT™★ – "Good for cat's teeth and gums" and "Easy to digest." Did regulators demand peer reviewed scientific proof? I doubt it. Where are the regulators?

CHEF'S BLEND™★ – This cat food has "twice the meat taste." Twice the meat taste of what? Corn? Clay? Where are the regulators?

THRIVE™★ – "Thrive is the *only cat food* with chicken, fish, meat, milk, cheese, and egg protein." (Emphasis theirs.) Did regulators check all other cat foods? They missed at least one we know of (ours), which contains all those proteins plus more. Where are the regulators?

JOY PUPPY FOOD™★ – "There's no other puppy food as digestible as JOY Puppy Food." Perhaps Gaines, with their digestible Puppy Choice, would argue. Anyone could argue for that matter. So, can Joy prove their claim? Have they provided peer reviewed proof? Where are the regulators?

FIT & TRIM™ – "For a healthy aging process." Is it to be inferred that the aging process of my dog will be guaranteed healthy? He won't get ill? Not at all? Less? Will he really live a longer and healthier life? Are these foods FDA approved? They can make this health claim but we can't use the name GeriatR$_x$? Where are the regulators?

r/d™ – "With 40% fewer calories than grocery store brands" – which brands? "Three times more fiber" – than what? Water? They don't say. They claim an "optimum supply of vitamins, minerals, and protein" – what does this mean? How can they say optimum but we can't? Finally, their trademarked byline in this particular ad: "Nutrition as an aid in the management of disease™" sounds very much like a health claim. Is this a drug? Which diseases? Where are the peer reviewed proofs? Where are the regulators?

FELINE GROWTH™ & FELINE MAINTENANCE™ – In an advertisement of bold health claims we find: "…for the prevention of Feline Urologic Syndrome...optimum growth...proven to help kittens mature into strong, healthy cats...ideal food...optimum balance...extremely effective...This is the preventive health care difference between Science Diet™ cat foods and competing brands…only the highest quality ingredients are used to assure palatability and provide the optimum nutritional balance…" "Optimum...health care...ideal...effective...highest quality" – those are words regulators would lynch us for. Where are they?

CHUNKS™ – "All meat for protein." Meat is muscle, yet these products contain poultry by-products with viscera, heads, and feet (according to AAFCO), and corn, which also contains protein and is not a meat. "Never soy products" is claimed, implying that there is something wrong with soy products – but what is wrong and what is the proof? Where are the regulators?

BENCH & FIELD™ – Regarding pictures of their food not swelling when in water as compared to extruded foods swelling; is the implication that all dogs, which eat extruded foods (probably about 50 million in the U.S. alone), will get bloat if they don't eat Bench and Field? Do any dogs that eat extruded foods get bloat because the food swells in water? Peer reviewed proof? Where are the regulators?

Again, none of the above is meant to find fault with other manufacturers. They should be given such marketing license. The public is intelligent enough to separate fanfare from reality. This does, however, demonstrate a double standard when, instead of being cute or offering raffle tickets in our packages, we attempt to make serious health innovations.

What has brought pet food regulation to this sad state? It began when the public, with their quest for ease, and fixes for their consumer addiction, wanted a "100% complete" meal in a bowl. Actually, it may have begun when manufacturers discovered how to create food products with shelf-life and saw dollar signs. I'm not sure which was first, but the end result, people feeding these foods of convenience only, begged for regulation. There's too much danger and so regulators emerged to assure "100% complete" foods were just that. Problem is, they never stopped to examine the underlying premise. They simply assumed nutrition was at a scientific end point (absurd, of course) and went from there.

Similarly, if you assume yellow, white, brown, or black skin signifies inferiority, discrimination is fine and proper. If you assume disease is just one of those things that happens to you, then you don't practice prevention. If profit is the only objective of industry, then spending money on antipollution measures is a waste. The validity of starting premises must always be examined first, and closely, before public policy is enacted. That's how freedom is kept and tyranny held at bay. Problem is, the "100% complete" premise has not been critically examined by regulators (or for that matter, by most nutritionists, veterinarians, or the public).

So what should regulators do? First, forbid the spurious, unproven and unprovable claim of "100% completeness." Then, permit all manufacturers to say what they want about their products, as long as it is truthful and cannot cause harm. Leave discernment to buyers.

★ Bonz™, ALPO Jerky Bits ™, Chew-Eez™, Come 'N Get It™, Chef's Blend™, O.N.E.™, Lucky Dog™, Chewy Morsels™, Alley Cat™, Thrive™ and Fit & Trim™ are trademarks of Nestlé Purina PetCare; Milk-Bones Flavor Snacks™, Milk-Bones™ and Milk-Bone Dog Treats™ are trademarks of Kraft Foods Inc.; Snausages™, Jerky Treats™ and Tender Meals™ are trademarks of H.J. Heinz Company; Tast-Tee Chunks™, Top Choice™, Puppy Choice™, Gainsburgers™, Cycle 1™, Gravy Train™ and Cycle 3™ are trademarks of Gaines Pet Foods; JOY Puppy Food™ is a trademark of JOY Dog Food; Ken-L Ration Canned Food™ and Tender Chops™ are trademarks of Ken-L Ration; r/d™, Feline Growth™ and Feline Maintenance™ are trademarks of Hill's Pet Nutrition, Inc.; Chunks™ is a trademark of The Iams Company; Bench & Field™ is a trademark of Bench & Field Pet Foods, LLC.

In the alternative, prohibit all claims just like the World Health Organization (WHO) did with baby formulas. The analogy is practically perfect. Breast milk is what babies genetically expect. It is raw, natural and truly complete (provided mom is not eating too crazy). But no, nutritionists know better. A baby's tummy would never know the difference between a chemist's lab or food processor's concoction and the real thing. So along with the "Coca Cola-nization" of the third world, commerce further "solved" their starvation with synthetic formula.* The results were so disasterous the WHO interceded.

Singularly fed processed pet foods are just as synthetic and just as disasterous.

So I will follow the WHO/UNICEF code on the marketing of breast milk substitutes with an analagous pet food code that would truly make a difference in pet health.

WHO/UNICEF CODE	ANALOGOUS PROCESSED PET FOOD CODE
1. No advertising of breast milk substitutes.	1. No advertising of exclusively fed processed pet foods (EFPPF).
2. No free samples to mothers.	2. No free samples of EFPPF to pet owners.
3. No promotion of products through health care facilities.	3. No promotion of EFPPF through veterinary clinics.
4. No company mother-craft nurses to advise mothers.	4. No EFPPF company sales people to advise pet owners.
5. No gifts or personal samples to health workers.	5. No gifts or personal samples of EFPPF to veterinarians, staff or veterinary colleges.
6. No words or pictures idealizing artificial feeding, including pictures of infants, on the labels of the products.	6. No words or pictures idealizing EFPPF, or pictures of animals on the products.
7. Information to health workers should be scientific and factual.	7. Information to veterinarians should be factual and scientific.
8. All information on artificial feeding, including the labels, should explain the benefits of breast-feeding and the costs and hazards associated with artificial feeding.	8. All information on EFPPFs, including labels, should explain the benefits of fresh, raw, natural feeding and the costs and hazards of artificial EFPPF feeding.
9. Unsuitable products, such as sweetened condensed milk, should not be promoted for babies.	9. Unsuitable products containing predominantly food fractions and additives should not be promoted for animals.

---

* Lonsdale T, "Pet Foods' Insidious Consequences," 1993.

—22—

MEDICAL/SCIENTIFIC PROOFS AND DOCUMENTATION

Science, Volume 237, pages 764-8

Myocardial failure in cats associated with low plasma taurine: A reversible cardiomyopathy

P.D. Pion, DVM; M.D. Kittleson, DVM, PhD; Q.R. Rogers, PhD; J.G. Morris, PhD

Summary: "**Thousands of pet cats die each year with dilated cardiomyopathy**, the cause of which is unknown. Although taurine is present in millimolar concentrations in the myocardium of all mammals, taurine depletion has not previously been associated with a decrease in myocardial function in any species. In this study, low plasma taurine concentrations associated with echocardiographic evidence of myocardial failure were **observed in 21 cats fed commercial cat foods** and in 2 of 11 cats fed a purified diet containing marginally low concentrations of taurine for 4 years."

Diet used: "Complete and balanced" premium processed pet foods.*

Dr. Wysong's comments: "Thousands" of cats have died from this nutritional disease caused by eating "100% complete and balanced" foods. Not one, or a half dozen – thousands! The "100% complete and balanced" claim is therefore not only in error, it is an insidious fraud with the potential to cause great harm.

• •

Journal of the American Veterinary Medical Association,
Volume 199, pages 731-4
Comparison of procedures for assessing adequacy of dog foods

Thomas L. Huber, PhD; Dorothy P. Laflamme, DVM, PhD; Linda
Medleau, DVM, MS; Karen M. Comer, DVM, MS; Pauline M.
Rakich, DVM, PhD

Summary: "Dog foods with similar claims for nutritional adequacy were
tested by chemical analysis and the American Association of Feed
Control Officials' growth trial. All foods were similar chemically (the
same percentages of nutrients), however, dogs given one regionally
marketed food had **lower growth rate and food efficiency** as well
as suboptimal PCV and hemoglobin values during the growth trial.
Pups fed this diet also had **clinical signs typical of zinc and copper
deficiencies**. We conclude that American Association of Feed Control
Officials' approved feeding tests provide valid assessment of pet food
quality, and procedures involving only chemical analysis or calculated
values may not."

Diets used: Various "complete and balanced" premium processed pet
foods.*

Dr. Wysong's comments: The reason foods showing the same chemical
analysis can create different nutritional results is that chemical analysis
is not surety. As a means of measuring optimal health it is crude.
These were approved "100% complete" pet foods causing nutritional
disease. How can the authors claim that feeding trials prove adequacy
better than NRC analytical values when:

   a) foods "proven" by feeding tests have killed thousands (see
   above)?

   b) feeding trials are the basis for establishing invalid, according to
   the authors' conclusion, NRC chemical analytical or calculated
   values?

The bottom line is that "100% complete" is not that at all, regardless
of the "test" being performed.

Feline Practice, Volume 20, Number 1, page 30

Practice Bulletin: Commentary on topics of interest from government, industry and the profession

Summary: "**Feeding pets table scraps can lead to health problems**, according to the AAHA. In most cases, a balanced diet of quality pet food provides the nutrients the cat or dog needs. The pet's diet should not include table scraps – a primary cause of obesity. Table scraps can be hazardous because the fat content of human food is often too high. Pets also may become finicky eaters and refuse more nutritious pet food."

Dr. Wysong's comments: The idea that table scraps are harmful is an assertion for which there is no proof. How exactly are table scraps fed fresh worse than the scrap ingredients used in pet foods? There is far more evidence of damage from "100% complete" diets than table scraps. High carbohydrates in processed foods, not fat in table scraps, cause obesity. If pets are fed carbohydrate table scraps (like the carbohydrates in pet foods), yes, obesity may be promoted. If pets are fed fresh meats, bones and veggies, particularly before cooking, they will be receiving nutrition superior to pet foods and will not become obese. Pets become finicky if fed quality table scraps because pets evidently know where good nutrition is.

• •

Journal of the American Veterinary Medical Association,
Volume 201, pages 267-74

Clinical findings in cats with dilated cardiomyopathy and relationship of findings to taurine deficiency

Paul D. Pion, DVM; Mark D. Kittleson, DVM, PhD; William P. Thomas, DVM; Mary L. Skiles, DVM, MPVM; Quinton R. Rogers, PhD

Summary: "37 cats with moderate to severe idiopathic myocardial failure (dilated cardiomyopathy) were evaluated... taurine deficiencies were documented in most of the cats... These findings support the conclusion that most cases of dilated cardiomyopathy in cats have **a common etiopathogenesis related to diet and as such are preventable**."

Diets used: "Complete and balanced" premium processed pet foods.*

Dr. Wysong's comments: I strongly agree. Indeed, diet can either cause or prevent disease. This is what research decades old has clearly shown. Belief in the "100% complete" myth is the greatest of all threats to modern pet health.

• •

Journal of the American Veterinary Medical Association,
Volume 202, pages 744-51

Development of chronic renal disease in cats fed a commercial diet

S.P. DiBartola, DVM; C.A. Buffington, DVM, PhD; D.J. Chew, DVM; M.A. McLoughlin, DVM, MS; R.A. Sparks, DVM

Summary: Cats which were **fed a commercial food exclusively** since they had been kittens developed chronic renal disease.

Diet used: "Complete and balanced" premium processed pet foods.*

Dr. Wysong's Comments: More proof that "100% complete and balanced" processed foods can create disease.

• •

Journal of the American Veterinary Medical Association,
Volume 191, pages 1563-8

Potassium depletion in cats: Hypokalemic polymyopathy

Steven W. Dow, DVM, MS; Richard A. LeCouteur, BVSc, PhD; Martin H. Fettman, DVM, PhD; Thomas L. Spurgeon, PhD

Summary: "Generalized weakness of acute onset, apparent muscular pain, and persistent ventroflexion of the neck were observed in 6 cats. These clinical findings were associated with a low serum potassium concentration and high serum creatine kinase activity... The owners reported that all 6 cats had been **fed a commercial diet exclusively** for periods of at least 6 months before onset of muscle weakness."

Diet used: "Complete and balanced" premium processed pet foods.*

Dr. Wysong's Comments: More proof that "100% complete and balanced" premium processed pet foods can create disease.

Journal of Nutrition, Volume 129, pages 1909-14

Chloride requirement of kittens for growth is less than current recommendations

Shiguang Yu, PhD; James G. Morris, PhD

Summary: "...we recommend a minimum chloride requirement of 1.0 g Cl/kg diet for growing kittens. This value is considerably less than the recommended chloride requirement of the National Research Council of 1.9 g Cl/kg diet, or the allowance of the Association of American Feed Control Officials of 3.0 g Cl/kg diet. Because the bioavailability of chloride is high, the **previous estimates appear excessive.**"

Diets used: "Complete and balanced" premium processed pet foods.*

Dr. Wysong's comments: According to the latest research, the chloride requirement set by the National Research Council is double what it should be, and the AAFCO level is three times what it should be. More evidence that "100% complete" diets based on NRC and AAFCO standards are not properly balanced and may have toxic overages of nutrients.

• •

Journal of Nutrition, Volume 126, pages 984-8

The riboflavin requirement of adult dogs at maintenance is greater than previous estimates

J.L. Cline, PhD; J. Odle, PhD; R.A. Easter, PhD

Summary: Requirement for vitamin B_2 (riboflavin) used to create "complete and balanced" pet foods **is in error.**

Diets used: "Complete and balanced" premium processed pet foods.*

Dr. Wysong's comments: The requirement of the important B vitamin riboflavin has been wrong. Since "100% complete" diets are based on an incorrect level of riboflavin, they are not complete at all. Additionally, this invalidates the official requirement levels for all other nutrients since the base diets used to test all other nutrients were incorrect.

Nutritionists ignore this not-so-little perplexing problem. (See page 4 for further explanation.)

• •

University of Pennsylvania School of Veterinary Medicine
Compendium on Continuing Education
Common questions about the nutrition of dogs and cats
David Kronfeld, DVM, PhD

Summary: "NRC subcommittees... have **aimed at minimal requirements rather than optimums**... A veterinarian offering advice about nutrition is caught in a bind. **For legal sanctuary**, one should abide by the recommendations of the NRC which have been incorporated into regulations of the FTC, AAFCO and FDA, hence assumed the force of law."

Dr. Wysong's comments: Thus, minimal nutrition receives the imprimatur of law. Even professionals, who might know better, must conform by advocating disease-causing "100% complete" minimal diets. Why? Because NRC, FTC, AAFCO, FDA make it "legal."

• •

Journal of the American Veterinary Medical Association,
Volume 203, pages 1395-1400
Changes and challenges in feline nutrition
David A Dzanis; Quinton Rogers, PhD; Donna Dimski, DVM;
Tony Buffington, DVM, PhD, MS

Summary: "...a feeding trial **can miss some chronic deficiencies or toxicities.**" / "AAFCO profiles... provide false security... I don't know of any studies showing their adequacies..." "Some foods that pass the feeding trials still **won't support animals over the long term**... Cats that eat one food their whole lives are more likely **to suffer from nutrient excesses as well as deficiencies**... As the maintenance protocol lasts only 6 months, the effects of **an excess might not cause a problem for several years.**" / "The **cats that didn't become ill** (from eating 100% complete pet foods) were those that

were going outside and catching mice... Our colleagues in Europe rarely diagnose this disease (hepatic lipidosis)... Cats there are indoor-outdoor animals, catching and eating mice and birds... I diagnose hepatic lipidosis mostly in indoor cats (*fed "100% complete" pet foods*)." / **"The recommendation to feed one food for the life of an animal gives nutritionists more credit than we deserve... the greatest risk of diet-related problems is to cats fed one diet all their lives."**

Dr. Wysong's comments: Could it be more clear? Consumers who buy the "100% complete" myth and exclusively feed processed foods risk disease.

· ·

Clinical Nutrition

Evaluation and use of pet foods: General considerations in using pet foods for adult maintenance

Francis A. Kallfelz, DVM, PhD

Summary: "**Dog foods can be proven** to be 'complete and balanced' by one of two mechanisms: 1. The manufacturer can prove by analysis that the product contains the minimum required levels of all essential nutrients, as specified by the National Research Council (NRC) for maintenance, growth, and so forth. 2. The manufacturer can show by feeding trials (as specified by AAFCO) that the product supports maintenance, growth, and so forth."

Dr. Wysong's comments: No uncertainty here! But as can be seen by research and field results, the ONLY thing "proven" is that "100% complete" foods, consistent with NRC and AAFCO requirements, can cause disease and death.

· ·

Veterinary Clinics of North America Small Animal Practice, Volume 19, pages 527-37

Nutrition and the heart

R.L. Hamlin, DVM, PhD; C.A. Buffington, DVM, PhD, MS

Summary: "Nutritional deficiencies (e.g., carnitine in dogs, taurine in cats) resulting in cardiomyopathy, and nutritional excesses (e.g., calories leading to obesity, sodium leading to hypertension) have emerged as important considerations in cardiology. These dietary factors may become particularly exaggerated in altered physiological and/or pathological states (e.g., pregnancy, old age, primary cardiovascular disease). Unfortunately, **we do not have complete information on requirements for essential nutrients**, nor do we know the precise role nutrition may play in the production of so-called old-age diseases or on the interactions among other organ systems (e.g., kidney, liver) and the heart."

Diets used: "Complete and balanced" premium processed pet foods.*

Dr. Wysong's comments: Since these astute (and honest) scientists admit that nutrient requirements are not known, what business does the industry have tagging "100% complete" ballyhoo on pet food labels?

• •

Journal of the American Veterinary Medical Association,
Volume 198, pages 647-50

Myocardial L-carnitine deficiency in a family of dogs with dilated cardiomyopathy

Bruce W. Keene, DVM, MS; David P. Panciera DVM, MS;
Clarke E. Atkins, DVM; Vera Regitz, MD; Mary J. Schmidt, BS;
Austin L. Shug, PhD

Summary: **Dilated cardiomyopathy and heart failure** were observed in a family of boxers. Supplementation of L-carnitine resulted in clinical improvement.

Diet used: "Complete and balanced" premium processed pet food.*

Dr. Wysong's comments: More proof that "100% complete and balanced" premium processed pet foods can create disease.

• •

United States Patent No. 5030458, 1991

Method for preventing diet-induced carnitine deficiency in domesticated dogs and cats

Austin L. Shug, PhD; Bruce W. Keene, DVM, MS

Summary: "Pets, particularly the carnivores, **are at great risk for developing L-carnitine deficiencies.** As Table 1 indicates, dog and cat foods are extremely low in free L-carnitine levels as compared with that found in raw ground beef. Most **pets are maintained strictly on commercial pet food diets and are thus kept chronically deficient in L-carnitine**... the plasma L-carnitine concentration of a normal, otherwise healthy dog, previously maintained on a commercial pet food diet*, is substantially deficient in carnitine as compared with the plasma carnitine levels found in other mammals."

Diets used: "Complete and balanced" premium processed pet food.*

Dr. Wysong's comments: The very act of pet food processing destroys or eliminates important nutrients such as L-carnitine. Not only can foods be called "100% complete" and be void of L-carnitine, AAFCO will not even permit L-carnitine to be supplemented because they haven't "approved" it yet!

• • • • • • • • • • • • • • • • • • • •

Veterinary Forum, Volume 9, pages 34-5

Research in the pet food industry: an overview

George F. Collings, PhD; Tim Allen, DVM;
Michael Hand, DVM, PhD

Summary: "These protocols were designed to assure that pet foods would not be harmful to the animal and would support the proposed life-stage. These protocols were **not designed to examine nutritional relationships to long-term health or disease prevention.**"

Dr. Wysong's comments: How can something designed to assure no harm, not also assure long-term health or disease prevention? Is lack of health or disease not harm? Consumers buying AAFCO protocol "proven," "100% complete" diets assume – and rightly so – that 100% means just that, not something less that will cause or permit nutritionally related disease.

• •

Veterinary Forum, Volume 9, pages 26-8
Perspectives on nutrition
Francis Kallfelz, DVM, PhD

Summary: "It really is **important that animals be fed optimal diets rather than just minimal diets**... Small animal nutrition is to a large extent **dominated by nutritionists working for pet food companies.**"

Dr. Wysong's comments: "Minimal" diets are those designed to achieve the "100% complete" claim. Shouldn't "optimal" be equated with "100% complete"? Is there something fishy when the scientists used to "prove" that animal owners should feed processed pet foods exclusively are on the pet food industry payroll?

• •

American Journal of Veterinary Research, Volume 62, pages 1616-23
Effects of dietary fat and L-carnitine on plasma and whole blood taurine concentrations and cardiac function in healthy dogs fed protein-restricted diets

S.L. Sanderson, DVM, PhD; K.L. Gross, PhD; P.N. Ogburn, DVM, PhD; C. Calvert, DVM; G. Jacobs, DVM; S.R. Lowry, PhD; K.A. Bird; L.A. Koehler; L.L. Swanson

Summary: "Dietary methionine and cystine concentrations at or above AAFCO recommended minimum requirements did not prevent decreased taurine concentrations. The possibility exists that **AAFCO recommended minimum requirements are not adequate** for dogs consuming protein-restricted diets."

Diets used: "Complete and balanced" premium processed pet foods.*

Dr. Wysong's comments: The "possibility" that AAFCO minimum requirements are inadequate is more like surety for not only taurine, but for dozens of other nutrients. Otherwise, why would modern pets by the millions consuming "100% complete," AAFCO-approved pet foods suffer from the gamut of nutritionally related degenerative and immune-compromised diseases?

• •

Petfood Industry, May/June 1998, pages 4-14
New functions of vitamins and minerals are constantly being discovered
Richard G. Shields, Jr., PhD

Summary: "As new functions are identified for existing nutrients, it is possible that **requirements to optimize these new functions will change** as well... There's increasing acceptance that **an optimal range rather than a minimal requirement is appropriate.**"

Dr. Wysong's comments: So if regulatory minimums are not appropriate, and requirements change (which they always do), what business does the pet food industry have claiming foods that meet minimal requirements to be "100% complete"?

• •

Journal of Animal Science, Volume 75, pages 2980-5
Effect of increasing dietary vitamin A on bone density in adult dogs
J.L. Cline, PhD; G.L. Czarnecki-Maulden; J.M. Losonsky; C.R. Sipe; R.A. Easter, PhD

Summary: "The effect on bone density of feeding various concentrations of vitamin A in a canned dog food product was investigated... Diets were fed up to 1 yr. Computed tomography was used to determine bone density... There were no differences ($P > .10$) in tibia bone or marrow density in any of the dogs fed the various concentrations of vitamin A... These results indicate that **concentrations of vitamin A three times the recommended maximum safe amount (71,429 IU/1,000 kcal ME) are not detrimental to normal bone health in dogs.**"

Dr. Wysong's comments: The original safe amount of vitamin A was set at 10 times the requirement. Now we learn that even three times greater amounts than this are safe. Not only may they be safe, but higher levels of vitamin A may be important for health, since there is a good chance that the minimum requirement is too low if the maximum is too low. In any case, it is clear that the standards used for "100% completeness" are at best good, but likely bad guesses.

• •

Veterinary Business, Volume 2, page 1

Nutritional mismanagement of gastro-intestinal tract diseases

G. Guilford, DVM, PhD

Summary: "It is important to emphasize that the calculations made in the formulation of a diet make a number of **arbitrary assumptions** and the **potential for significant error is high**."

Diets used: "Complete and balanced" premium processed pet foods.*

Dr. Wysong's comments: "Arbitrary assumptions" cannot, of course, add up to "100% complete."

• •

Waltham International Focus, Volume 3(1), page 9

Protein requirements of dogs

J.V. Johnson, PhD

Summary: "The ideal level of protein intake for dogs is **still a matter of debate** amongst nutritionists, veterinarians and breeders, with the recommendations varying two- to three-fold.."

Diets used: "Complete and balanced" premium processed pet foods.*

Dr. Wysong's comments: If something as fundamental as protein requirements is not etched in stone, how is a "100% complete" fabricated diet possible?

---

* These results do not imply that the brands in these studies would be the only ones to cause such problems. Any processed, manipulated, fraction-based commercial food, fed exclusively, may risk disease.

SECTION II

FEEDING FOR HEALTH

Health Is Nature Obeyed

—23—

PUTTING IT ALL TOGETHER

There is a dangerous mindset that permeates much of the pet food industry – including manufacturers, nutritionists, health professionals, academicians, and government officials. Without careful examination, they have *en masse* embraced the notion that

Fig. 35. The same common sense people apply to themselves and their children must be applied to pets. Pet nutrition is not a special case situation requiring the intervention of food processors or nutritionists.

everything is okay if pets are fed exclusively processed products out of bags or cans for their entire lives.

Would you accept the advice of a pediatrician who told you that you should feed your child only what is in a bag or a can every day, every meal, for the child's entire life and never supplement anything to it? No raw carrots, no apples, no salad, eggs or milk? I hope not! Then why accept such advice regarding your pet?

The absurdity and danger of this philosophic approach is evident when we consider where we and our companion animals stand today in the stream of time. Let's compare the time since humans have been eating processed foods and feeding them to their pets, with the time prior to that when humans and animals existed in the wild eating fresh, whole, natural foods as they were plucked from the vine, so to speak. Consider a time line where the last 200 years since the Industrial Revolution would be one inch. In contrast, the time estimate for life on the planet prior to that Industrial Age, prior to processed foods, would be 276 miles.

The question is, which setting do you believe we and our pets are more likely adapted to? That time represented by the one inch, or the 276 miles? The answer is obvious and makes it clear that we have been extracted from our natural environmental context and thrust into something entirely new. These relatively sudden changes in our nutrition, life-style,

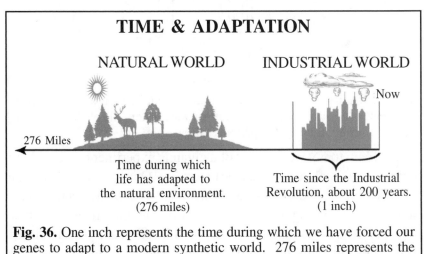

TIME & ADAPTATION

NATURAL WORLD   INDUSTRIAL WORLD

Now

276 Miles

Time during which
life has adapted to   Time since the Industrial
the natural environment.   Revolution, about 200 years.
(276 miles)   (1 inch)

Fig. 36. One inch represents the time during which we have forced our genes to adapt to a modern synthetic world. 276 miles represents the time our genes were incubated and shaped by the natural world. We must return to our genetic roots to achieve optimal health.

and environment, subject biological systems to undue stress and are at the root of many of today's degenerative diseases.

Just as a fish, if pulled out of its natural genetic water context, and placed onto the ground, will agonize and then die, so too will we and our companion animals succumb if subjected to an unnatural context. By not eating natural foods, not living a life-style closer to that for which we were designed, or not living in an environment that is cleaner and more pure, we become fish out of water facing the same end.

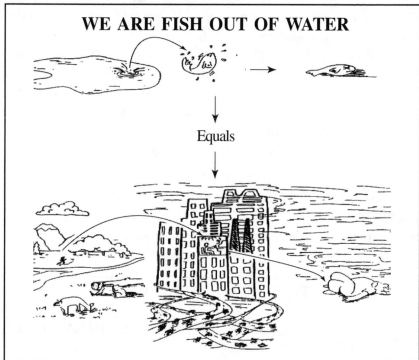

WE ARE FISH OUT OF WATER

Equals

Fig. 37. If a fish is taken out of its natural context, water, it will experience "dis-ease" (disease) and die. If humans are taken out of their natural context, nature, they will experience disease and die.

In effect, today we are part of a gigantic experiment. We and our companion animals are in a genetic time warp. Our genes are back in the 276 miles, the pre-Industrial Age, but we find ourselves in an entirely new environmental setting, the one inch: Artificial light, processed foods, sedentary living, little exposure to the sun, polluted air and pesticide-laden ground or chemically sterilized municipal water. We are in exile from biological reality.

THE GRAND EXPERIMENT

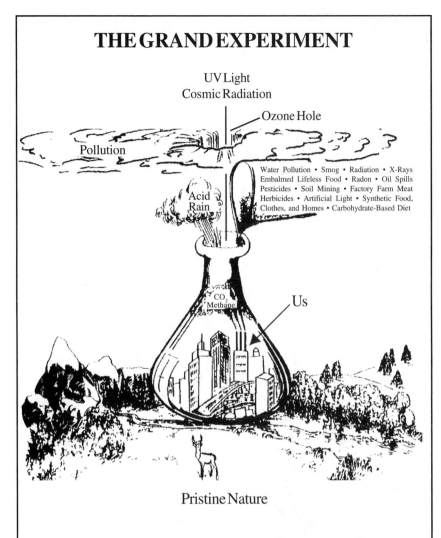

Fig. 38. The modern synthetic world in which we find ourselves is a gigantic experiment in which we are the unwitting subjects.

By understanding this simple concept, we can make appropriate moves in our own lives, and the lives of our companion animals, to restore nutrition to the way it was meant to be. At the same time we must make every effort to restore a more natural environmental context.

WHAT IS FOOD?

If modern nutritional science cannot tell us what is the best food, what are we to do? When the details become confused, look to the obvious. Food is the living material produced by planet Earth that has sustained life from its beginnings. Food predates the eater. This, then, would be the almost-too-simple key criterion. The food species must predate the eating species – it has been that way since time began. No species ever existed without food sources already available to sustain it. Modern food technologists have this confused. They argue that their new modern marvels are the best

GENETIC EXPECTATIONS

Genomes Expect This

But Get This

Fig. 39. All organisms are genetically fine tuned to a natural environment and foods they can eat raw directly from nature. Our new synethetic world is a genetic stress manifest in the host of modern degenerative diseases.

foods – that food can come after and actually be created by the eater. How did humans and animals survive through the millennia prior to the

WHICH CAME FIRST, THE CHICKEN OR ITS FOOD?

Food First?   **or**   **Chicken First?**

Fig. 40. Food is that which nourishes and sustains life. Food, by definition, must preexist the life forms which depend upon it. Which came first, the chicken or its food (a new version of an old conundrum)? The food had to have been there first or life would not have been possible. Natural food fits this definition. New forms of "synthetic" foods are new arrivals from a geobiologic perspective and thus do not fit the definition of food.

roller mill, the extruder, the oven, the microwave, the canner and popper? All life from the beginning of time has been sustained by eating the fresh raw natural foods from the natural environment.

Natural real foods are the foods that are inextricably linked to the life they support. There are subtleties in an apple, a carrot, a filet mignon that we only begin to understand. A simple potato contains over 150 chemically distinct entities, not just starch.[1] The modern processed diet is the "new guy on the block" and certainly cannot lay claim to being true food.

PANCREATIC SIZE

Species	Pancreas Weight as a Percentage of Body Weight
Wild Mice	0.32%
Mice on a Processed Diet	0.84%
Rats on a Raw Diet	0.165%
Rats on a Processed Diet	0.521%

Fig. 41. Enzyme-devoid processed foods cause enlargement (disease) of the pancreas.[2]

Life forms have spent eons adapting to natural foods, thriving on their nutrients and developing protective mechanisms against toxins. To suddenly consume the new modern processed concoctions presents to the body new chemicals, toxins and altered nutrients to which it has not had time to adapt. We, and our pets, are therefore part of a giant experiment, the results of which perhaps only our grandchildren will fully know.

Evidence demonstrating the superiority of the natural archetypal diet over the modern, purified, fractionated, processed fare is compelling. For example, studies by Dr. Pottenger over 50 years ago showed the

1. Lisinska G et al, Potato Science and Technology, 1989.
2. Wysong RL, "Rationale for Panzyme™," 2002. Howell E, Enzyme Nutrition, 1986. Aebi H, Nutrition and Enzyme Regulation, 1980.

DIET-RELATED TOOTH ALIGNMENT

 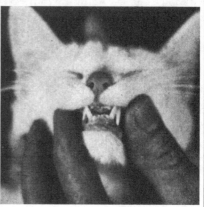

Tooth alignment in a cat raised on a natural, raw meat-based diet.

Severe tooth malalignment in a cat raised on processed food.

Fig. 42. The ten-year Pottenger Cat Study, in which over 900 cats were included for several generations, showed that even dentofacial structure is severely and negatively affected by replacing the raw, natural diet with cooked foods.

superiority of non-heated, natural food for cats (Fig. 42 & 43).[1] Anthropological studies worldwide have demonstrated that updated diets eaten by primitive people result in lost health once industrialized society introduces the modern processed marvels of white sugar, white flour, white salt and white oils (the four white poisons).[1-2]

The goal should be to mimic, as closely as possible, the archetypal (the original, primitive) diet and use ingredients that are nutrient-dense (containing naturally high levels of all nutrients) and unaltered "from the vine." It is, of course, not possible to achieve this goal perfectly other than by releasing the pet into the wild. Short of this, however, there is much that a pet owner can do in their own kitchen, as well as in the selection of a pet food, that recognizes the limitations of knowledge and builds foods accordingly.

1. Pottenger FM, <u>Pottenger's Cats: A Study in Nutrition</u>, 1983. Price W, <u>Nutrition and Physical Degeneration</u>, 1982.
2. *Tidsskr Nor Laegeforen*, 2000; 120(1):78-82. *Sante*, 2002; 12(1):45-55. *Nutr Rev*, 1999; 57(11):341-9. *Arch Mal Coeur Vaiss*, 1997; 90(7):981-5. *J Nutr*, 2001; 131(3):866S-870S. *Med J Aust*, 1993; 159(4):266-70.

NATURAL VS. TECHNICAL

"Natural" has become an overused and misused term. Since it was discovered that having the term on a label would increase sales, companies have increasingly given it preeminence in their marketing vocabulary. Thus "natural" fruit juice has been found that only contains 5% real fruit juice, "natural" cookies may consist primarily of sugar, and "natural" pet food is virtually indistinguishable from the "unnatural" kind. Of course

THE POTTENGER CAT STUDY	
Cats Fed *Raw* Meat, *Raw* Milk & Cod Liver Oil Diet	Cats Fed *Cooked* Meat, *Cooked* Milk & Cod Liver Oil Diet
Generally healthy, with good tissue tone, firm membranes, and excellent fur	Common heart problems, vision abnormalities, arthritis, infections, inflammation, paralysis, meningitis, hypothyroid, abnormal respiratory tissue, inferior fur
Striking uniformity of size	Generations with varying sizes
Maintenance of normal skeletal features from generation to generation	Malformation of the face, jaws, and teeth
Consistent calcium and phosphorous levels in bones	Steady decline in calcium content, becoming "spongy" by the third generation
Resistant to infections, fleas, and other parasites	Affected by numerous parasites
Intestinal tract measured an average of 48 inches long	Intestinal tract measurements of 72-80 inches, with decreased tissue elasticity
Friendly, predictable, energetic	Females irritable and violent, males docile and sexually passive

Fig. 43. The Pottenger Cat Study showed that simply replacing cooked foods with those that were raw noticeably improved the health of the cats.

Continued on page 96.

THE POTTENGER CAT STUDY (continued)

Cats Fed *Raw* Meat, *Raw* Milk & Cod Liver Oil Diet	Cats Fed *Cooked* Meat, *Cooked* Milk & Cod Liver Oil Diet
Reproduced several homogenous generations, few miscarriages	Experienced difficulty in becoming pregnant, frequent spontaneous abortions (25% first generation, 70% second generation), many mothers and kittens died during delivery
Over 3 years, 63 kittens born with an average weight of 119 grams	Over 3 years, 47 kittens born with an average weight of 100 grams
Over 3 years, 4 kittens born dead	Over 3 years, 16 kittens born dead
Average weight of 1008 grams at 14.5 months	Average weight of 636 grams at 14.5 months
No kittens suffered from hypothyroidism	Many kittens had significant thyroid deficiency
Kittens developed 6 normally spaced incisors	Kittens usually developed 3-4 irregularly-spaced, uneven, and crowded incisors
Most common causes of death were old age and injuries suffered in fighting	Common causes of death included pneumonia, empyema, diarrhea, failure to nurse, and infections of the kidneys, lungs, and bones
	After being on this diet for 12-18 months, females were never again able to give birth to normal kittens
	If fed this diet for more than two years, a mother cat will usually die during delivery
Fig. 43 (continued).	There were never more than 3 generations, with no cats surviving beyond the sixth month, and none able to produce viable offspring

anything can be called "natural" since atoms are natural and everything is made of atoms. This stretches definitions but at least demonstrates that the word can lose meaning and be manipulated to seduce consumers.

There is also the feeling that what is produced by technology is superior, more complicated, more scientific, more proven than the natural (using the word in its original sense). However, technology is simply based upon discovery of the laws and substances of nature. Technology is a crude and dim view of the infinite technology of nature. Nature is the ultimate technology.

A NUTRITIONAL SYLLOGISM:
1. Food comes from nature.
2. Life comes from nature.
3. Things equal to the same things are equal to each other.
   Natural life requires natural food.

Fig. 44. Because food in its original sense is natural, and life itself is natural, a loose syllogism exists which argues that life requires natural food.

Though reductionistic technology (focusing on parts and pieces – such as % protein, % fat, % vitamin A, etc.) may discover some nutritional diseases and cure them with synthetic vitamins, there is little reason for applause. Nutritional diseases are caused by reductionistic technology in the first place, that is by fractionating (reducing) foods through food processing. The cause is credited with the cure.

THE POWER OF PARADIGMS

It is true in any science (which commercial pet feeding is, kind of), that once a theory achieves the status of general acceptance as a paradigm, it will not be declared invalid unless a better alternative is available. In this case, such an alternative is available – varied feeding including home meals. But since this would mean economic loss to the industry, it cannot be enthusiastically embraced. Lack of congruence between the "100% complete" paradigm and the real world (such as a host of degenerative and nutritional diseases) is not sufficient to cause change. These are seen as mere foibles, idiosyncrasies to be solved by future modification, excuses and other circularly reasoned articulations.

SELF-JUSTIFICATION LEADS TO
A VICIOUS CIRCLE

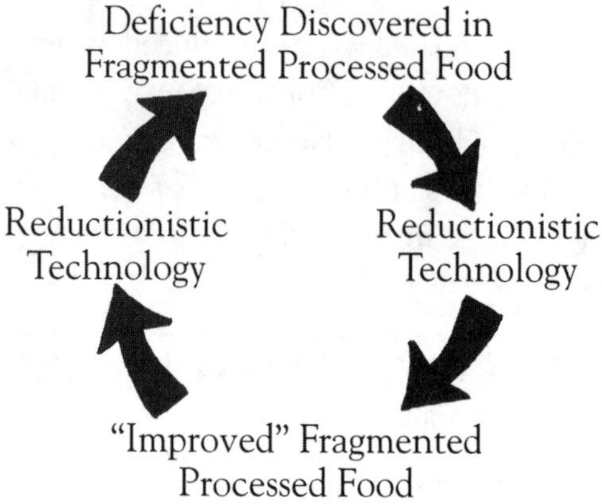

Deficiency Discovered in
Fragmented Processed Food

Reductionistic
Technology

Reductionistic
Technology

"Improved" Fragmented
Processed Food

Fig. 45. Fragmented Processed Food depends on Reductionistic Technology for product development. Reductionistic Technology depends on the Fragmented Processed Food Industry for economic support. Discoveries of deficiencies in products and suggestions for improvement are made by Reductionistic Technology. Reductionistic Technology is seen as policeman and creator rather than a cause of departure from wholesome natural foods and nutritionally inadequate products.

Pet food scientists are problem-solvers working within an intellectual straightjacket of blind acceptance of the "100% complete" paradigm. They have considerable investment in the preservation of its absurd assumptions. In part, this is due to understandable human motives hinged to time and energy in training, work product and academic achievements closely tied to the very paradigm that should be at issue.

Unfortunately, science is not a fundamentally creative venture. Novelty is not desirable unless it fits the preordained rules of the game. The rule in modern pet food is "100% completeness" and it is the premise from which all problem-solving nutritional activity springs. The pet food scientists will play with countless combinations, permutations and dosages of isolated nutrients, but never question whether that is really something they should be doing if optimal health is the ultimate objective.

THE "TURN-IT-OVER" PHENOMENON

Commercial interests and the desire for convenience have done much to create a "turn-it-over" society. Turn your health over to a doctor, turn disputes over to a lawyer, turn education over to schools, turn human feeding over to processors, and turn pet nutrition over to pet food manufacturers. When financial interests are at stake, individuals cannot be assured that their best interests are being taken care of since usually the primary motive of professionals and producers is profit. Serious matters such as health and nutrition must be returned to their rightful owner, the individual.

As for commercial pet foods, what should be done? Clearly the "100%" claim should not be permitted. In its place should be honesty in labeling. A manufacturer should be able to say anything which is true – ingredient descriptions, processing methods, packaging innovations and

WHAT WE HAVE BECOME

BUY OUR MICROWAVABLE
INSTANTIZED
WONDERFULLY COLORED
SUPER PROCESSED
ARTIFICIALLY FLAVORED
HYDROGENATED
EMBALMED
MEAL-IN-A-BOX
PERFECTLY SAFE
ACCORDING TO
GOVERNMENT
TESTS...
BLAH
BLAH BLAH

Fig. 46. We have become dependent and propagandized consumers, mere profit centers for commercial interests.

even nutritional test results if performed – but should not be permitted to assert unproven conclusions such as "100% complete and balanced." With honest and true labeling, consumers can become more fully informed and make more intelligent decisions.

This book is not to suggest that processed foods cannot be fed with benefit. What is important is that they not be singularly relied upon and that discernment be used in choosing brands.

There is no big secret as to what good nutrition is. We all intuitively know. You don't need a doctor or nutritionist to guide you, nor do you need to know how many calories, or milligrams of vitamin A, are in each meal.

Fresh natural food and variety are the cornerstones. It's what any thinking person does for their family. So why not do it for pets as well?

Fresh foods from the grocer, wholesome table scraps, dry, canned and frozen pet foods and supplements (designed properly) constitute the ideal diet. It's not about finding the cheapest food, the one your pet likes the most, % protein, absence of bogeyman ingredients or commercial ballyhoo by the manufacturer.

In the following section and in the Optimal Health Program (see pages 195-208), I outline the best health and feeding program. True, it involves more than filling a bowl with convenient, easy-pour, super-bow-wow cutlets. It's just as in life; nothing good comes easy. So too in health, effort is required.

Although there may be some added immediate cost, the long-term dividends more than balance the ledger. Correct feeding will mean less food (a savings), and diseases possibly averted can prevent medical costs. This is not to mention avoiding the family trauma of having to contend with the suffering of a beloved pet.

Pets put on the Optimal Health Program experience dramatic results. We receive continuing testimonies of turnarounds in health and even resolution of medical problems which had previously gone unresolved with "special" diets and medical care (see Appendix B).

If you follow the program and don't see immediate results, that's expected too. The best nutrition also fixes the unseen – the chronic degenerative diseases incubating within that are hidden from view until it is too late. Caring for your pet properly and feeding right is like changing the oil in the car. You may not experience an immediate reward but you *know* you are preventing catastrophe later.

So, make good nutrition a moral obligation: do what is right because you *know* it is.

For the reasons noted in this book, and many more, I've come to believe that restoring our more natural environmental context, including our food, can relieve more pain and suffering and bring better health than any other means. It is incredible that a trillion dollar medical care industry by-and-large ignores the preventive flowers blooming at their feet and instead single-mindedly pursues invasive technology and pharmaceutical agents which attempt to force the body into submission. (Unfortunately, they have a vested interest in your pain and suffering.) Nutrition and healthful life-style are the blossoms that can do so much more – and more pleasantly – than drugs and surgery.

We live in an age when reliance on experts is unavoidable to some degree due to our busy life-styles and specialization. Maybe you can't or don't want to learn how to fix the car, computer or toilet, but there is no real choice with health. You alone have your best interests at heart. The more informed, open-minded, rational and self-reliant you become, the better will be the health dividends for the whole family – including the four-legged members.

—24—

FEEDING HEALTHILY

Cooking – frying, baking, boiling, heating in any manner – severely alters food. Most significantly, high heat *kills* the food in the sense that valuable enzymes are destroyed, and vitamins, minerals, amino acids, essential fatty acids and various other micronutrients are altered, depleted, or lost completely. Worse yet, heat can initiate chemical reactions, which can turn perfectly wonderful foods into toxins such as carcinogens.*

The old adage "an apple a day…" is more important now, perhaps than ever before, since we could literally go a lifetime eating packaged pseudo-foods and never touch upon the health-enhancing nutrition available only through raw foods such as the fresh apple. Fortunately, with increasing awareness and cynicism toward packaged products, many people are feeding themselves and their families more carefully by seeking fresh vegetables, fruits, meats and whole grain products.

But what happens to the family pet? Are cats and dogs – mammals like us – so physiologically different from us that they don't have the same need for freshness in the diet? Common sense would tell us that they aren't different at all. But what about the pet food manufacturers' strong caution against supplementing their "balanced and 100% complete" foods with anything else, for fear of upsetting the delicate balance of their

---

* Wysong RL, Lipid Nutrition – Understanding Fats and Oils in Health and Disease, 1990. *Wysong Health Letter*, "Nutrient Loss During Processing," 1997; 11(11):1. *Wysong Health Letter*, "Processing," 1989; 3(1). *Wysong Health Letter*, "The Fragility of Vitamins," 1997; 11(10). *Wysong Health Letter*, "Ubiquitous B Vitamin Deficiency," 1997; 11(12). *Wysong Health Letter*, "Dangers in Cooked and Cured Meats," 1994; 8(6). *Wysong Health Letter*, "Glycosylation," 1990; 4(1). *Wysong Health Letter*, "Potato Vitamin Loss," 1992; 6(12). Wysong RL, "Biotic™ Means Life," 2002. *J Am Med Assoc*, 1990; 263(1):35. *Environ Mol Mutagen*, 2002; 39(2-3):112-8. *J Food Sci*, 1992:1136. *Feedtech*, May 1997:39-43. *J Agric Food Chem*, 2002; 50(6):1647-51. *J Toxicol Environ Health*, 1981; 7(1):125-38.

"nutrition-in-a-bag"? Nonsense. Fresh and raw foods are as crucial to a pet's body as they are to ours.

Fresh foods should be supplemented to all pets' diets. No processed can or bag can possibly – regardless of what the outside of the package says – provide the total nutrition your pet needs. It is up to you to go beyond packaged foods. The following will get you off to a good start.

Although some foods should not be fed completely raw, there are dozens of enzyme/vitamin/mineral-rich raw foods which will delight your cat or dog. What follows are suggestions for easy, raw food supplementation for your pet. More involved recipes are included in Chapter 26. This dietary change for your pet – from the processed, denatured, bagged and canned foods you have been feeding – will bring remarkable results you will witness firsthand. Such obvious benefit is the clear marker that you are doing what is right.

THE BASICS

The following section includes some shameless references to Wysong products. Sorry, I hate this part (perhaps leaving you with the impression that all I want to do is sell you something). But this is what our company has done to put words into deeds. If you are affronted, cover your eyes when you see "Wysong," and take heart in the fact that alternative ideas will follow that permit you to achieve optimal health for your pet without ever buying anything made by Wysong.

DAIRY
Milk: the more whole and less processed, the better. In states where raw whole milk is available, this and other products derived from it are preferred (for a scientific discussion of the merits of raw whole milk, see The Wysong Book Store Catalog, page 255).* Some animals are unable to tolerate milk, particularly as they get older, because they are unable to digest milk sugar, lactose. Thus, milk may result in loose stools for these animals. However, mixing with live,

---

* Campbell Douglass W, The Milk of Human Kindness...Is Not Pasteurized, 1985.

active culture yogurt (or Wysong Pet Inoculant™) and diluting with purified water (combined with Wysong WellSpring™) does help many animals tolerate dairy products.

Other excellent dairy products (made from raw whole milk if possible) are cheeses, cottage cheese and yogurt. When choosing yogurt, avoid the sugar/jam varieties and buy whole milk plain, or make your own (see The Wysong Book Store Catalog on page 255 for "how to" help in making yogurt). To be beneficial, live yogurt cultures have to be added after heating – look for the words "active yogurt cultures" on the package. All dairy products can be fed alone, mixed together, mixed with Wysong foods, or with other fresh whole foods.

MEATS

The ideal "meat" product would be the entire natural prey your pet's ancestors once hunted. This is not practical today, but nevertheless feeding meat should mimic this model as closely as possible. In the wild, carnivores eat the viscera (organs and their contents), muscle meat and bones.

Fresh grocery store raw meats, including chicken, turkey, beef, pork and lamb, should be cut into small ¼"-1" pieces if they are difficult for your pet to chew. This is unlikely, however, unless there is dental disease present. If cleanliness of the meat is in question, rinse it well, cleanse with Wysong Citrox™, and supplement with Call of the Wild™, which helps balance high meat meals and contains a special Wysong fruit extract that inhibits food-borne pathogens.

Organ meats, such as liver, kidney, heart and poultry giblets, should be used in combination with the muscle meats mentioned above in a ratio of approximately one part organs to five parts meat. Such fresh meat combinations should be a regular fresh food added to your pet's diet.

Cooked meats and table scraps may be fed with benefit. This is still superior to what is present in most commercial pet foods. Don't forget, vary meals, and balance will take care of itself. Lightly broiled or baked meats are best, and charcoaled, fried and deep-fried are worst. Wysong also offers All Meat canned varieties – Beef™, Chicken™, Turkey™,

Duck™, Rabbit™ and Venison™ – which can be used as a source of minimally cooked meats and organs. Wysong frozen Tundra™ foods and Archetype™ dried are all-meat, fully-prepared, non-cooked alternatives that you may also rotate into the diet.

GRAINS

Sprouted grains are raw and whole, make excellent additions to your pet's diet, and are eagerly accepted when combined with other foods. (See The Wysong Book Store Catalog on page 255 for books on home sprouting.)

Cooked grains should be a much smaller portion of your pet's diet. Raw, organically grown rolled oats or raw barley flakes, soaked in raw milk overnight (or Wysong Mother's Milk™ or pasteurized milk with Wysong Pet Inoculant™ added) result in a treat many pets will relish. Popcorn can be fed popped and soaked as above, as well. Cooked porridges of oats, brown rice, millet, amaranth, or quinoa can also be used occasionally.

Small amounts of leftover table scraps such as cereals, sandwiches, and homemade rolls and breads are beneficial additions to your dog or cat's diet, provided they are prepared carefully and with whole grain natural ingredients.

VEGETABLES, FRUITS AND NUTS

Believe it or not, many pets relish these foods. Simply grate, very finely dice or puree any fruit, vegetable or nut that you yourself would eat. Your pet may eat most eagerly if you are sharing the treat and eating the same raw fruits or vegetables at the same time. A small amount is best to begin.

Raw cashews, pecans, walnuts, macadamia and Brazil nuts, etc. (not the salted, cooked-in-oil variety) are excellent foods and most pets eagerly accept them. Soak and rinse pecans, almonds and walnuts for 12-24 hours to increase their digestibility. Make sure nuts are crushed or mashed quite thoroughly. If swallowed whole, they will not be properly digested.

Tofu is an excellent soy protein food which is relatively bland but pleasant, allowing you to easily blend it into other foods. A better alternative is Wysong Whole Soy™, which is the whole soybean, short-time heat processed. These granules can be mixed or sprinkled on any meal.

GRASSES

The reason cats and dogs frequently eat grass is because they crave and enjoy it – especially if they are feeling ill or are on a processed, dead diet. It is as simple as that. In the wild, pets will actually graze on grasses, roots and sprouts as they find them.

Many seeds, such as wheat, barley, buckwheat and sunflower, are available for sprouting, and you should experiment to see which varieties are most readily accepted. Alfalfa sprouts may be fine occasionally, but harbor potential toxins.

To offer your pet fresh, clean grasses, soak organic wheat seeds for 24 hours in pure water, spread out on top of a covered tray of dirt, and keep in the dark until the sprouts are about an inch long. Then introduce them to the sunlight until they start to turn green. When ready to "harvest" from your windowsill, these grasses may be cut and mixed with food, or simply offered to the pet for grazing and chewing. This is a treat you may wish to share since this is an excellent addition to human foods as well.

USING THE BASICS

Any of the above-mentioned basics can be fed on a daily basis at a ratio of one to three parts per day of Wysong foods, or alternated with Wysong foods. As a specific example, if you have a dog which usually eats four cups of Wysong food per day, you may wish to offer ½ cup of yogurt, ½ cup of raw meat, and two to three cups of Wysong food. The next day, you may wish to give ¼ cup of grated carrots, ¼ cup of grated cheese and a whole diced apple with Wysong food. Or, you may feed only the "basics" above one day, and Wysong the next.

When you feed yourself or your children with nature's raw foods, set an extra "place at the table" for your pet. If dicing fruits or chopping salad vegetables for the family, get into the habit of making a cat or dog "salad," custom-made for your pet, at the same time. Variety, imagination and creativity hold the key to unlocking your pet's maximum health. More specific feeding ideas follow in Chapter 26.

WHOLE IS BEST:
WHY THE SUM OF SOME OF THE PARTS
DOES NOT EQUAL THE WHOLE

Within nature's foods, in their whole and original state, lie many mysteries. Food scientists and nutritionists can only boast an elementary hint of the intricate inner "checks and balances" which nature built into all foods. To separate off and use only a fraction of any food – even just part of a simple grain of wheat (that's what white flour and refined salt are, for example) – upsets this "checks and balances" system and is a nutritional mistake.

Because the three major components of food – protein, fats and carbohydrates – account for the bulk or weight of food, many nutritionists and scientists believed that this was all that was needed for good nutrition. Such presumptuous conclusions lie at the root of today's plague of degenerative diseases.*

---

* Remarkably, such food disassembly is viewed as progressive and scientific. Here, again, we find starting premises not properly examined.

The bad starting premise is reductionism. Because exploration of ever smaller components in nature (reductionism) through chemistry, physics and biology have led to so many remarkable and pragmatic advances, it's assumed such an approach can be applied everywhere. (If you like a hammer and use it exclusively, you treat everything as if it were a nail.) Although reductionistic examination of ever-smaller pieces may help explain why an engine does not work, or how to synthesize a new plastic, or the nature of a toxin produced by a pathogenic bacterium, it cannot answer broader, more fundamental and important questions about nature.

For example, analysis of the minute metallurgic components of bomb shrapnel does not answer why the bomb was dropped, killing and maiming the people in the city. A study of the atoms in biochemicals does not reveal how life began. Or, to our specific subject, a study of the chemical components of food does not explain health.

You see, there is nothing about interactive forces between subatomic particles (about as small as science has thus far been able to explore) that answers the bigger questions. Quantum mechanics says nothing about why some foods create health and others make disease.

Whole systems have features not explained by an examination of the parts. The features of a knot in a nylon rope are not explained by exploring electron spin in nylon molecules. Creative genius is not explained by an examination of electrical conduction along myelin sheaths in the brain. Neither organic chemistry nor origin of life biopoietic experiments explain why humans came to be self-aware. And testing isolated nutrients does not reveal whole food merits.

The whole is greater than the sum of its parts. This is a perplexity that only a few scientists admit. Unfortunately, the life sciences, in particular modern medicine and nutrition, remain in the reductionistic Dark Ages.

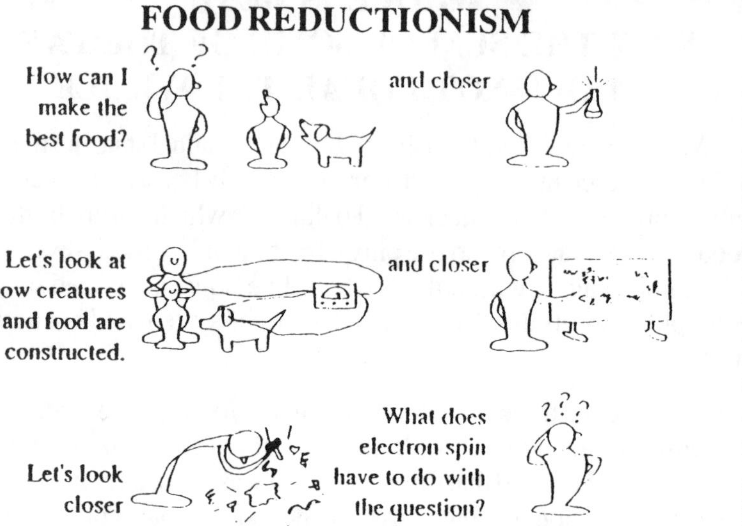

FOOD REDUCTIONISM

How can I make the best food?   and closer

Let's look at how creatures and food are constructed.   and closer

Let's look closer   What does electron spin have to do with the question?

Fig. 47. Reductionism – looking at ever smaller parts and pieces – cannot answer the ultimate questions about how to achieve best nutrition and health. The answers are holistic because life is holistic.

Whole food has many biological advantages over processed foods, but one obvious advantage is the fact that whole foods are digested much more slowly than processed foods. This allows time to properly assimilate nutrients, using the food's own inherent enzymes. It would be very difficult to consume five or six raw oranges or apples in under a minute, but the same amount of sugar stripped from them, approximately 5 teaspoons, can be consumed in a couple of swallows of a processed drink. Sugar in its natural form is released slowly into the body, whereas processed sugar is absorbed into the blood in a matter of minutes. The body becomes overloaded, does not have time to utilize or adequately produce its digestive enzymes, and the sugar must be metabolized by the liver from whence it is dispensed to fat stores throughout the body.*

---

* Atkins RC, <u>Dr. Atkins' New Diet Revolution</u>, 2001. *Am J Clin Nutr*, 1999; 69(4):647-55. *Am J Clin Nutr*, 1999; 69(3):448-54. *Br J Nutr*, 2002; 87(2):131-9. *Equine Vet J*, 2001; 33(6):585-90. *J Nutr*, 1999; 129(7 Suppl):1457S-66S.

Many food fractions are used in generic, and even in so-called "premium," "prescription" and "super-premium," pet foods. This makes them all pretty much alike, and yet most consumers believe there is a broad range of nutritional as well as dollar value available. In fact, when the basic formulas are compared, there is very little difference.

One manufacturer of a "premium" line of pet foods suggests using home cooking temporarily for certain health conditions, but unfortunately lists inferior ingredients for their recipes such as cooked white rice, white bread, dried brewer's yeast, granulated sugar, and canned vegetables! These types of inferior, dead ingredients will not produce good end results, no matter how they are combined. This also reflects an erroneous nutritional philosophy, which sure enough appears in their packaged foods as well.

For best health, ingredients should be in their whole, natural form, and only as a food fraction if there is special nutritional value, such as vitamins, minerals, enzymes, essential fatty acids, or phytonutrients.

IDEAL PET FOOD FEATURES

- **WHOLE, ORGANIC:** Fresh, whole, organic, and non-GMO ingredients as available – not just prerendered by-products and grain fractions.

- **FRESH:** Fresh meats, whole ingredients as starting materials – not just inexpensive, preprocessed food fractions that are nutrient depleted and aged.

- **GENETICALLY MATCHED:** Designed to mimic archetypal carnivore diets – not just grain diluted foods with meat flavorings.

- **NATURAL FORM:** An emphasis on naturally complexed nutrients – not just isolated synthetics or food fractions.

- **SPECIAL INGREDIENTS:** Whole grains and legumes specially bred to increase nutrient content and decrease anti-nutritional factors – not genetically modified, fractionated flours or meals, stripped of most of their nutritional value.

- **FREE RANGE:** Meats from animals which live and feed in nature as opposed to confined animals fed manipulated diets.

- **FATTY ACID BALANCE:** High in essential fatty acids, including omega 3's for immune, skin, and coat health – not processed, improperly balanced, altered, potentially toxic or destroyed fatty acids.

- **ENZYMES:** As present in all natural foods – no heat-processed food devoid of inherent enzymes resulting in digestive and pancreatic distress.

- **PROBIOTIC CULTURES:** Living microorganism cultures to create intestinal balance and health, plus prebiotic oligosaccharides to promote probiotic growth – not food devoid of living elements creating increased vulnerability to pathogens.

- **VITAMINS AND MINERALS:** In their most bioavailable forms, with pepper extract to increase absorption by as much as 250% – not singular, improperly balanced, poorly bioavailable synthetics.

- **PHYTONUTRIENTS:** An array of antioxidants, phytonutrients, immune stimulants, and metabolic enhancers from fresh plant sources – not disregard for the weight of scientific evidence proving their benefits.

- **FRUIT EXTRACTS:** Certain fruits are powerful natural antioxidants and antimicrobials.

- **AGE NONSPECIFIC:** Highly palatable, naturally balanced for pets at all life-stages – not artificially manipulated to meet arbitrary age parameters.

- **GENTLE:** Easily tolerated by allergic companion animals – not fractionated ingredients, additives, and synthetics often resulting in adverse reactions.

- **SYNERGISTIC:** Designed to be freely rotated for variety and maximum nutrition – not touted as a mythical "100% complete" diet to be fed indefinitely.

- **ADDITIVE-FREE:** Freedom from non-nutritional ingredients – not additives merely to create color, texture, taste, smell, stool consistency, or shelf-life.

- **NATURAL PRESERVATION:** Natural antioxidants; oxygen- and light-barrier packaging; fats and oils purged of oxygen by special processing – not synthetic preservatives and permeable packaging permitting nutrient degradations by oxygen and light.

- **NUTRITION-FIRST PROCESSING:** Specialized processing to protect fragile nutrients – not production only to maximize production rate and profitability.

- **OPTIMAL NUTRITION:** Specifically designed to mimic archetypal diets and hence optimize health – not simply meet minimum regulatory standards to make a minimum "100% complete" claim.

IDEAL PROCESSING METHODS

- **COLD PROCESSING:** The only processing method that does not destroy important raw natural food attributes.

- **WHOLE INGREDIENT STORAGE:** Grains and legumes should not be ground until ready for processing and therefore do not begin degradation before processing. For example, wheat can lose up to 40% of some nutrients within 12 hours of milling.

- **NATURAL INSECT CONTROL:** Stored ingredients enrobed with a special, natural, nontoxic insecticide, which not only suppresses insect infestation, but is a nutrient as well.

- **MOLD AND MYCOTOXIN TESTED AND NEUTRALIZED:** Mycotoxins are an insidious poison potentially present in all dried foods. They should be tested, and special nutrients incorporated that bind and neutralize them if present. [1]

- **EXTRUSION:** Dry, wet, and steam injected extrusion of ingredients maximizes nutritional value. [2]

---

1. *Wysong Health Letter*, "Mycotoxins in History," 1991; 5(10). *Wysong Health Letter*, "Liver Cancer," 1993; 7(5). *Cancer Res*, 1992; 52(2):267-74. *Plant Science*, 2000; 157(2):201-207. *Res Microbiol*, 1996; 147(5):385-91. *Rev Argent Microbiol*, 1979; 11(3):108-13. *Z Ernahrungswiss*, 1976; 15(2):168-76.
2. Mercier C et al, <u>Extrusion Cooking</u>, 1989. Guy R, <u>Extrusion Cooking: Technology and Applications</u>, 2001. *Feed Tech*, 13(8):29. *CRC Crit Rev Food Sci Nutr*, 1978; 11(2):155-215.

Fresh meat and vegetable injection into the extruder, rather than pre-processed, dried, and rendered products simply mixed with grains and then extruded.

Extrusion monitoring to achieve optimal cooking (gelatinization – makes plant starches digestible) of grains, inactivation of anti-nutritional factors, and protection of nutritional value.

Fats and oils micro-bubbled™ with a special atmosphere to purge oxygen, and are stabilized with effective, natural Wysong Oxherphol™ antioxidants.

- **SPROUTING:** The only processing method that actually increases micronutrient levels.*

- **STORAGE:** Fragile ingredients are kept in cold storage or in oxygen-free containers until processed.

- **DRYING:** Performed effectively to reduce moisture to prevent deterioration and maintain nutritional value.

- **ENROBING:** Fragile, heat-sensitive ingredients such as enzymes, essential fatty acids, probiotics, and certain vitamins incorporated after the completion of processing.

- **FRESH BATCHING:** Products not mass-produced and warehoused, but rather made fresh to order as much as possible.

NUTRIENT SPARING PACKAGING

It does little good to go to great pains in creating highly nutritious products, only to have them degrade because of inadequate packaging design. Remember, nutrition is directly proportional to the speed with which a food degrades. Rapid degradation is a sign of good nutrition.

The challenge is, therefore, to use fresh foods that can degrade rapidly, but take safe measures to slow the process. This is difficult and costly, so traditionally producers have taken the easy road – omit fragile

---

* *Crit Rev Food Sci Nutr*, 1980; 13(4):353-85. *Crit Rev Food Sci Nutr*, 1989; 28(5):401-37.

nutrients or use insignificant levels to still permit label claims, embalm them with artificial preservatives and process all semblance to life from them until they are inert food ghosts.

Here are things that should be done:

- Employ the processing methods described above.

- After processing, foods should be immediately packaged if possible and not bulk stored.

- Oxygen should be flushed from packaging and replaced with a non-oxygen atmosphere or vacuum packed.

- Packaging should be both a light- and oxygen-barrier since both can accelerate degradation.

- Small portion packs are preferable to large bulk packages.

- Packaged products should be delivered as fresh as possible and rotated properly at the retail level.

—25—

THE INGREDIENT LABEL GAME

The simplicity of knowing what you are getting when you shop the meat and produce aisles at the grocery store is lost once you move into the center aisles. That's the domain of the processed food industry where everything starts to become nondescript. Who really knows what's in the syrups, gravies, flakes, nuggets, powders, creams and mushes? I mean really. Anyone can say anything on a label. True they are regulated, but no government official watches over what goes into every package. We hope they are honest, but the lure of $ can skew ethical judgment.

But no matter, the food magicians with their bevy of label cosmeticians can convince you that what lies within is "value-added" and far, far better than what you might be able to harvest out of your backyard garden. A lot of money is used to brainwash us about packaged products because that's where the profit lies. The profit is there because producers can deceive you into believing there is something of greater value where it is in fact not and you'll never know. That's not so easy with an apple, a bundle of lettuce or a lamb chop, which are clearly what they are.

Keep this in mind as you choose among packaged pet foods. Actually write a note on the inside of your eyeballs when you move to the pet food aisles. Unlike almost everything else in the grocery sections, which are just intended as components, condiments or recreation (a lot of that) for human menus, pet foods are pushed as "100% complete" meals. It's the mother of all "value-added," cosmetically groomed and embalmed food trinkets.

This is not to say processed foods cannot be made with merit. But the right starting materials must be there in the beginning.

The most important basic ingredient is the motive, credentials and research of the producer.

If the start is a marketeer with dollar signs in the eyes, watch out. So, to begin, know the company and their depth in terms of competency and commitment to health. Anyone can say "science," "natural," "health," "prevention." Find out if they are saying it to woo you or they really mean it. Are they just copying what others have done that seems marketable, or are they true leaders, innovators, researchers, thinkers and educators?

Remember, labels are not designed by accident. They are carefully crafted to hit all your hot buttons and make you feel all warm and fuzzy about what you are feeding your pet.

When I first began developing foods, "natural" was considered quirky, grade of ingredients was hardly addressed, additive dangers were passed over, and emphasizing the health importance of probiotics, enzymes, phytonutrients, antioxidants, omega 3's, freshness, wholeness and highlighting the importance of packaging was like quackery.

Now, after years of research revealing the truths about the critical links between health and nutrition, and exposure of the inferiority of conventional pet foods, things are changing. But I don't believe the weight of scientific evidence is the reason many manufacturers have adopted some of these innovations. It is primarily because the public is becoming aware, more concerned with their own health and now sees the need to put nature back into their lives.

That's a market. Where there is a market, there will be profiteers. Wherever money flows big time (the pet food industry is about $13 billion), there can also be big time chicanery.

I'll get to that in a moment, but first let's review a variety of ingredients which are still used primarily for reasons of low cost, and for which there are better alternatives. These ingredients are seen primarily in the middle and lower end products which are trying to achieve a low price point. However, some use them and still tout the products containing them as premium or even super premium.

Here are a few examples:

BREWER'S YEAST – what is left over from the beer brewing industry. It is the inactive, non-fermentative, cooked yeast fraction with most nutrients spent. A superior choice is whole yeast culture.

WHITE RICE – polished rice with the highly nutritious bran removed. Whole brown rice is superior.

BREWER'S RICE – polished rice sections that have been discarded from the manufacturing of wort of beer, and which may contain pulverized, dried, spent hops. (Fed alone polished rice products can cause the nutritional disease beri beri.) A superior choice is whole brown rice.

WHEAT MIDDLINGS – particles of wheat bran, wheat shorts, wheat germ and wheat flour and other refuse from milling. Although this does contain some protein and fat, the high fiber content which accounts for the majority is composed mostly of the non-nutritious coarse outer hull coverings of the wheat kernel, creating high bulk that dilutes nutritional value. This is a very inexpensive "filler" type ingredient. A superior choice is whole wheat – particularly the ancient Egyptian varieties.

SOYBEAN MILL RUN/SOYBEAN MEAL/SOYBEAN FLOUR – Processed end products of soybeans with many valuable vitamins, minerals, phytonutrients, antioxidants and essential fatty acids lost. A far better choice is whole extruded soybean.

MEATS AND MEAT MEALS – The quality can range all over the board. Fresh meat is of course superior to prerendered meats and meals. Few manufacturers are even capable of this. It's expensive, slow and difficult. Don't be misled by pictures of dressed chicken and T-bone steaks, that's not what you're getting in pet foods. Just look at the price. Dressed chicken and T-bones aren't even the best nutritionally since organs, tendons, cartilage, and even digestive tract combined with muscle meat provide better nutrition.

CORN SYRUP – a refined sugar added for calorie content and palatability. The saccharides present are simple sugars, and are absorbed quickly, not fully metabolized, and therefore add unnecessary body fat and increase susceptibility to a broad range of dental and metabolic diseases.[1] A better choice is to eliminate it.

BEET PULP – the dried residue extracted from the processing of manufactured sugar. It contains pure sucrose, as in common white refined sugar. Sucrose is quickly absorbed into the liver without being fully metabolized, converted to fat, and shunted to fat depots throughout the body. Like corn syrup, this ingredient can increase predisposition to dental and metabolic diseases. The fiber content of beet pulp is used as a filler and as a binder to "artificially" create better-formed stools. Specialized forms of beet pulp containing oligosaccharides that help promote beneficial probiotic growth in the digestive system are a different matter.[2]

FISH MEAL – dried ground tissue of undecomposed whole fish or fish cuttings, with or without extraction of part of the oil. This is not the entire fish, and therefore does not contain many of the fat-soluble vitamins, omega 3 fatty acids, or minerals found in whole fish. Fish meal is very unstable and easily oxidized and must be stabilized with preservatives, but this is rarely done early enough or well enough.

CONDENSED FISH SOLUBLES – obtained from condensing the "stickwater." (The aqueous extract of cooked fish free from the oil; contains aqueous fish cell solutions and water used in processing.) Much of the oil soluble nutrients (some of the most important) of fish have been removed, along with water-soluble vitamins lost through leaching in the water used to cook the fish.

There are many more fully approved – but questionable from a health perspective – ingredients which can be used to divine "100% complete" pet foods. The following list, egregious as it is, comes right from the official AAFCO publication:[3]

- dehydrated garbage
- undried processed animal waste products
- polyethylene roughage replacement (plastic)

1. Atkins RC, Dr. Atkins' New Diet Revolution, 2001. *Am J Clin Nutr*, 1999; 69(4):647-55. *Am J Clin Nutr*, 1999; 69(3):448-54. *Br J Nutr*, 2002; 87(2):131-9. *Equine Vet J*, 2001; 33(6):585-90. *J Nutr*, 1999; 129(7 Suppl):1457S-66S.
2. *Am J Vet Res*, 2001; 62(4):609-15. *J Anim Sci*, 1995; 73(4):1099-109. *J Anim Sci*, 1995; 73(4):1110-22. *Enzyme Microb Technol*, 2001; 28(1):70-80.
3. Association of American Feed Control Officials, 1998 Official Publication.

- hydrolyzed poultry feathers
- hydrolyzed hair
- hydrolyzed leather meal
- poultry hatchery by-product
- meat meal tankage
- peanut hulls
- ground almond shells

Well, those are the easy things to spot. Most of the above ingredients at least look suspicious. But what do you do when you get a food that claims "human grade," "natural," "endorsed by veterinarians," "fresh," "organic," "additive free," "naturally preserved"; or they have every manner of oh-so-healthy ingredients...berries, fish oil, fruits, veggies, sprouts, probiotics, enzymes, natural vitamins, antioxidants, nutraceuticals? Why, their pamphlets and labels would have you think they are inserting a Thanksgiving Day feast in every nugget. It even makes me salivate.

THE NEW WAVE OF PET FOOD BUZZWORDS

"Natural"
"Fresh"
"Whole"
"Organic"
"Herbal"
"Antioxidant"
"Omega-3 Fatty Acids"

WITH A SMIDGIN OF:
"Cures Disease"
"Prevents Disease"
"Stops Aging"
"Reverses Aging"
"Extends Life Indefinitely"
"The Lame Will Walk"
"The Dead Rise"...
Yada Yada

Fig. 48. Words are cheap but they can make for expensive and tantalizing pet foods. Mere polished labels and alluring claims do not make good nutrition. Look deeper into the company before assuming the best.

The health benefits of such ingredients depend upon their form, ratio to other nutrients, and dose. If scientific knowledge is not applied here, not only may the ingredients be ineffective, they could create toxicities. For example, the inclusion of omega 3 fatty acids, if not stabilized properly, could be a source of oxidative chain reactions and free radical cascades. Free radical pathology underlies just about every serious degenerative disease known.*

Unfortunately, such toxic effects are not immediate and thus the consumer will not see a problem until it's too late. They will feed this "natural," "human grade" omega 3 fish oil-containing product contentedly, year after year, confident they are enhancing the health of their pet. After all, the package says so, the company's little marketing brochure says so, and maybe a pet professional or retail outlet says so, too.

How can the poor pet owner possibly sort through the buzzwords and decide among all this bounty of goodness? What about all the beguiling advertising where the food can wear as much makeup as the actors?

Well, sorry to say, you are pretty much on your own here. As you now know, regulators can't save you, the "100% complete" claim can't, advertising can't be trusted, professionals can't and neither can you rely upon embroidered labels and pamphlets embellished with all the wholesome words in the world.

Like so many things in life, it's just not simple. Good things always take time and effort. Do you want something good – like health – for you and your pet? Reason, open your mind (but not so much that your brain falls out), use your intuitive sense, study and learn a little, and be skeptical. That's what this book is all about. If you've gotten this far, you are a good candidate for the health dividends that can come.

I wish I could tell you that all you needed to do was find a food without various nutritional bogeymen or with certain fancy natural

---

* Wysong RL, Lipid Nutrition – Understanding Fats and Oils in Health and Disease, 1990. *Wysong Health Letter*, "Oxidized LDL Antibodies," 1993; 7(5):3-4. *Ann N Y Acad Sci*, 2001; 928:226-35. *EXS*, 1992; 62:411-8. *Science*, 1983; 221(4617):1256-64. *J Toxicol Environ Health*, 1981; 7(1):125-38. *Lancet*, 1992; 339(8798):883-7. *N Engl J Med*, 1992; 326(21):1444. *Science*, 1988; 240:640-2. *Science*, 1988; 240:1302-9. *J Am Oil Chem Soc*, 1976; 53:673. *Arch Biochem Biophys*, 1966; 113:5.

ingredients. If I could, I would have never written this nor spent the last twenty-five years of my life researching the matter.

What has preceded and what follows this chapter will give you more specific and well-rounded direction... and most importantly put you in health's driver's seat. Here are a few more general, but most important, criteria to use to get you started:

1.   How long has the company been in business? Have they truly created anything of unique value in that time or are they merely copying or creating label dressing? It has taken me decades to create the products we have, yet new products come out constantly that for all appearances look similar to ours. Obviously there can be embedded value in products the label will never fully reveal. This can't occur overnight.

2.   Do they have their own manufacturing plant or is their product merely off the shelf from a toll manufacturer dressed up to be something special? Most toll manufacturers are into efficiency and speed of production. That is why many years ago I found I had to build my own plant if I wanted to create truly healthy products.

3.   What is the underlying philosophy, purpose and motive? Is it health, or sales? Do they help you become informed and self-sufficient or do they merely point you to their products?

4.   Who heads the company? Is it someone with skills in health, nutrition and food processing, or merely an entrepreneur? Health is serious business and health is what nutrition is all about. Just having someone on the payroll with credentials is not reliable if the person having the final say is basically a businessperson.

5.   What does their literature demonstrate? Is it depth of knowledge, or mere marketing? In this regard, search their materials to see if they have references to the scientific literature. If it is not clear they are current in the science, what chance is there that their products will be properly grounded in science? Remember, nature is not different from science; they are one and the same.

If nutrition is a serious health issue, which all pet food manufacturers seem to agree on, then serious science and competency should be brought to the table. Should you trust a surgeon who was never schooled, or a drug made by someone with no training in chemistry or pharmacology? So why trust pet foods made by marketers with no significant training or skills in science, medicine or nutrition?

If pet foods were being presented as just one of many food options, that's one thing. Then it really would not matter much, since variety would cover nutritional sins. But that's not the case. Pet foods are intended to be fed exclusively, and – what's more – grandiose claims of health benefits are made. Pet food companies lay claim to a serious health issue, but usually bring no credible credentials to the table. It's like unschooled people being doctors with no license.

You then must decide if what you're getting is smoke and no fire, or a big hat and no cattle. Check the credentials.

I know this creates no easy formula for deciding, since it will require a little probing and judgment, but the comfort of knowing you are not just another pawn in a profiteer's cap is worth the trouble.

—26—

RECIPES FOR A HEALTHIER PET

gain, let me preface this section by reminding you that the best recipes contain, at least in some proportion, foods which your pet accepts in a raw state. Seek organic products, which would be most pure and uncontaminated by pesticides, herbicides, GMO's (genetically modified organisms) or other additives.

Although designed with simplicity in mind, some of the recipes below may call for ingredients with which you are unfamiliar. Some are exclusive Wysong products, so you may need to request further information.

These recipes are offered as suggestions to get you accustomed to experimenting with and varying your pet's meals. They are only a few of dozens possible. Since animals are quite forgiving by nature, and will almost always give you another chance, feel free to experiment and try many different things.

If cleanliness of the meat you wish to use is in question, rinse it well, and disinfect with Citrox™. Vegetables which are not organic should also be cleaned with Frugie Wash™ and rinsed well prior to use.

The following recipe amounts may need to be adjusted based on the size and/or activity level of your pet. As a guide you may use the recommended feeding amounts per cup as described on Wysong dry food packages.

Uneaten portions should be mixed with Oxherphol™ antioxidant and stored in the freezer for long-term, or in the refrigerator for 2-3 days.

SUPER NUTRITION GROCERY LIST

FROM THE STORE (organic if possible):

✓ Meats – chicken, beef, lamb, turkey
- Cheaper cuts with gristle are fine
- Ask butcher for trimmings and bone dust from saw blades
- Variety of organs
- Giblets

✓ Bones –
- Beef knuckle bones (dogs)
- Chicken wings, necks, tails (cats, kittens, puppies)

✓ Veggies – anything you would eat raw
- Finely chop or puree
- Fresh frozen, if fresh are unavailable

✓ Nuts – raw almonds, pecans, walnuts, cashews
- Pecans, almonds and walnuts should be soaked for about twelve hours and brown tannin water rinsed away
- Finely chop or puree

✓ Fruits – anything you would eat raw
- Ask produce manager for overripe or bruised fruit. Clean, remove too-far-gone fruits. What stores throw away will amaze you and help you save money.
- Finely chop or puree

✓ Sprouting Grains and Seeds –
- Ready-made sprouts
- Or learn how to do it yourself (see <u>The Wysong Book Store Catalog</u>, page 255)

✓ Dairy –
- See if you can find a farmer who will sell you raw milk. Make yogurt from it.
- Active culture, whole milk cottage cheese or plain yogurt
- Raw milk cheeses
- Regular cheeses, especially cheddar, mountain jack and Swiss, which are excellent for dental health

FROM WYSONG (request literature for further information):

(Again, let me remind you that you need not use any commercial product, including ours, to create optimal health. Prey, carrion, the farmer's slop bucket and table scraps fed with care, were all fine prior to the advent of the processed food industry. The merits of natural foods are as obvious as the merits of a mother's breast over canned formulas. At the same time, however, I know, in our modern hectic world, convenience and prepackage are important to most people and are here to stay. Wysong products are simply my sincere attempt to make such products conform to good science and get as close to the real thing as possible. Judge them with the same scrutiny I ask you to use throughout this book.)

✓ Any of the many different Wysong Dry Diets – Vary without regard for the name.

✓ Any of the many different Wysong Canned Diets – Vary without regard for the name.

✓ Any of the frozen raw Tundra™ Diets

✓ Archetype™ dry raw Diets

✓ Canine Biscuits™ and Cat Treats™ – Dry snacks with nutrition.

✓ Real Bones™ – A specially prepared non-heat-processed chew bone made from meat, cartilage, marrow and bone.

✓ Biotic™ dry sprinkle-on supplement – Use with any processed food to add life: enzymes, probiotics, vitamins, minerals.

✓ PDG™ supplement – Use to increase protein and nutrient-density. Very palatable. Especially useful in illness.

✓ Call of the Wild™ – Use to balance raw meat meals.

✓ E.F.A.™ – Use to increase essential fatty acids, especially health-giving omega 3's.

✓ Whole Food Concentrate™ – A complete spectrum of vitamins and minerals. Every nutrient known in a blend of all natural vegetable foods.

✓ Peanut Butter Plus™ – Organic peanut butter with Whole Soy™, essential fatty acids and minerals. A great treat and wonderful way to hide pills.

✓ Whole Soy™ – Not a soy by-product, but the whole bean processed to release all the special nutritional benefits of soy.

✓ Natural Honey™ – Raw and enzyme-rich. A great occasional treat and dressing.

✓ Cheezyme™ – Sprinkle-on dry cheese, probiotic and enzyme condiment.

✓ Food C™ – Vitamin C from foods, not synthetics.

✓ Spectrox™ – Powerful antioxidants from nature.

✓ Oxherphol™ – Natural antioxidant to preserve home-prepared meals.

✓ Citrox™ – Natural antibacterial rinse to help prevent food-borne pathogens on food.

✓ WellSpring™ – Add to purified water as an antioxidant, electron-donor and antiacidotic.

✓ Whole Salt™ and Garlic Whole Salt™ – Mineral-rich salts.

✓ Dentatreat™ – Natural cheese active dental preventive.

✓ Mother's Milk™ – Colostrum, probiotic, enzyme-rich milk substitute.

✓ Super Flour™ – Whole organic grains, antioxidants, probiotics and natural minerals.

✓ Herbed Extra Virgin Olive Oil™ – High in healthful omega 9 oils and herbal antioxidants.

SAMPLE MEALS

Just a few of myriad possibilities using the preceding. Remember, variety is the key.

ROUTINELY:

> Add WellSpring™ to water.
> Use Biotic™, Pet Inoculant™ and E.F.A.™ if using any processed or cooked food.
> Use Call of the Wild™, Pet Inoculant™ and E.F.A.™ with raw meats and organs.
> Use Oxherphol™ for any home-cooked or raw meal containing oils or fats.
> Use Citrox™ to clean raw foods.

DAY 1:　　Fresh meat of choice

DAY 2:　　Wysong Archetype™
　　　　　　　Wysong Canned Diet of choice

DAY 3:　　Meat of choice (vary from
　　　　　　　　Day 1)
　　　　　　　Organs of choice

DAY 4:　　Dry Wysong Diet of choice

DAY 5:　　Wysong Canned Diet (vary from Day 2)
　　　　　　　Raw soaked nuts
　　　　　　　Fruits or veggies
　　　　　　　Garlic Whole Salt™

DAY 6:　　Archetype™
　　　　　　　Sprouts
　　　　　　　Wysong Canned Diet of choice

DAY 7:　　Wysong Frozen Diet of choice
　　　　　　　Wysong Dry Diet of choice

DAY 8:　　Fast – water only

DAY 9:　　Bones only, fresh or Wysong frozen

DAY 10:　　In a hurry? Wysong Dry or Canned only

DAY 11: Table scraps

DAY 12: Cottage cheese
Archetype™
Honey
Berries
Whole Soy™

DAY 13: Wysong Dry Diet of choice
Peanut Butter Plus™

DAY 14: Wysong Frozen Diet of choice
Meat of choice
Whole Food Concentrate™

DAY 15: Fruits
Veggies
Food C™

DAY 16: Wysong Canned Diet of choice
Archetype™
PDG™

DAY 17: Fast
Bones only

DAY 18: Organs
Wysong Dry Diet of choice

DAY 19: Poached or steamed fish
Spectrox™

DAY 20: Tripe
Bone dust

DAY 21: Wysong Frozen Diet of choice
Veggies
Whole Food Concentrate™

DAY 22: Yogurt
Mother's Milk™
Fruit

DAY 23:   Wysong Canned Diet of choice
               Raw Eggs

DAY 24 ON: Repeat above, or be creative

TREATS

Raw bones and Real Bone™ are the ideal snacks. But if you prefer the biscuit type treats, here are some nutritionally enhanced delicious recipes.

PEANUT BUTTER PLUS™ VEGETARIAN DOG BISCUITS

  3 cups Wysong Super Flour™
  1 egg (organic if possible)
  ¼ cup Wysong Peanut Butter Plus™
  ½-1 cup water (best if enhanced with Wysong WellSpring™)
  Wysong Oxherphol™ Natural Antioxidant Preservative –
     Oil (4 drops) or Powder (1¼ tsp.)

Heat oven to 300° F. Blend Super Flour with egg and Peanut Butter Plus, and add water and Oxherphol while mixing, until a stiff but workable dough is formed. Dust surface and dough with flour, roll to about ⅛ inch thickness and use cookie cutter of choice, or use a knife to cut into rectangular shapes. Place close together on greased (organic butter or olive oil works well) cookie sheet (they do not rise or spread). Bake 45-60 minutes. Make sure they are quite hard. Put in an open bowl overnight to finish hardening.

ALL MEAT™ TREATS

  Approximately 2 cups of Wysong Super Flour
  1 or 2 small eggs (organic if possible)
  1 large (14 oz.) can of Wysong All Meat ™ Diets (any variety)
    or crushed Archetype™
  ½ cup milk
  ¼ tsp. Wysong Whole Salt™ or Garlic Whole Salt™
  1 Tbsp. of Wysong Herbed Extra Virgin Olive Oil™
  1 Tbsp. of yogurt
  Wysong Oxherphol Natural Antioxidant Preservative –
    Oil (4 drops) or Powder (1¼ tsp.)

Wysong Cheezyme™ (optional - see directions)
Wysong Dentatreat™ (optional - see directions)

Mix all ingredients. Spoon mixture onto a greased (organic butter or olive oil works well) cookie sheet so that each cookie dollop is the size of a half dollar. Bake at 300° F until they are hard. Dust with Wysong Cheezyme and Dentatreat after they have cooled. Store in refrigerator.

CHEESE TREATS
3 cups Wysong Super Flour
1 tsp. Wysong Garlic Whole Salt
½ cup Wysong Herbed Extra Virgin Olive Oil
1 cup shredded cheese (organic if possible)
1 egg beaten
1 cup milk
Wysong Oxherphol Natural Antioxidant Preservative –
   Oil (4 drops) or Powder (1 tsp.)
Wysong Cheezyme (optional - see directions)
Wysong Dentatreat (optional - see directions)

Mix all ingredients. Dust surface and dough with flour, roll to about ½ inch thickness and use cookie cutter of choice, or use a knife to cut into rectangular shapes. Place close together on greased (organic butter or olive oil works well) cookie sheet (they do not rise or spread). Bake 25 minutes at 350° F. Cool on a rack. Dust with Wysong Cheezyme and Dentatreat after they have cooled. Store in refrigerator.

SECTION III

QUESTIONS AND FALLACIES

*If Everyone Believes It,
It Probably Ain't So*

SECTION III

—27—

PUTTING SOME "OLD WIVES' TALES" TO REST AND ANSWERING YOUR QUESTIONS

1. **Doesn't raw meat abound in trichinosis and parasites which can infect humans or animals? I've always heard that raw meat should be avoided.** Even though raw meat is the natural diet, fish, rabbit and pork may all need to undergo cooking to destroy parasites such as trichinosis and tapeworm. These three meats should be used least frequently in the choice of meats for your pets, but are very good occasional supplemental foods. It can be argued that an animal in proper health may not succumb to parasites.* They may enter the body but will be defeated by the body's natural defense mechanisms, defense mechanisms which are brought to their most perfect state by raw foods. The benefits of raw ingredients far exceed their dangers.

2. **If a puppy or kitten needs such different nutrition from an adult, and adult animal nutrition is so very different from the older pet's nutritional requirements, can't I do a great deal of damage supplementing foods at home?** Age is one of the most confusing factors in pet feeding. The "life-stage" basis for feeding animals serves to justify marketing approaches, not sound nutritional logic. In the wild, the young's dietary choices do not differ from those of the very old. As puppies are weaned, for example, they are fed the regurgitated diet of the adult mother. And older animals don't suddenly find new food sources previously undiscovered. The key to optimal

---

* Pottenger FM, <u>Pottenger's Cats: A Study in Nutrition</u>, 1983. *J Exp Med*, 1986; 163(5):1113-31. *J Parasitol*, 1980; 66(3):413-9. *J Immunol*, 1998; 160(7):3453-61.

health is natural food variety, not so-called scientifically designed life-stage manufactured diets.

3. **I've heard raw egg whites are dangerous. Is this true?** This may be true if egg whites are fed in great excess, or as the sole food. The avidin in raw egg white could cause a biotin vitamin deficiency. However, no wild animal would ever have an all-egg or almost all-egg diet, nor would they eat only the white. So, this is not a valid concern. Biotin lost by feeding raw egg white is in fact replaced with the biotin in the yolk of the whole egg.* This is an excellent example of why wholeness is superior to food fractions. Whole raw eggs are an excellent part of your pet's menu.

4. **There are such strong warnings about feeding cats dog food and vice versa. Should I be worried when they eat out of each other's bowls?** There is little if any substantial difference between dog and cat foods. The same ingredients are used in each. Any danger is removed by following the principle of variety, and never singularly feeding day in and day out any commercial food, regardless of its label claims.

5. **My dog is overweight and nothing seems to make a difference. Should I feed a "light" brand or one high in fiber?** The modern plague of obesity in pets and people is a result of modern sedentary living and processed carbohydrate based foods. To solve the problem, these causes must be addressed. Lack of fiber is not the cause of obesity, neither is lack of "light" (low meat and fat) food. Follow the Optimal Health Program™ (see pages 195-208) with a special emphasis on the All-Meat Canned Diets™, frozen Tundra™ and Archetype™ Diets. Supplement with fresh meats and organs as well. Don't worry about the fat, worry about the carbohydrate. That is what screws up metabolism and results in increased depot fat.

Your pet is designed to burn fat for fuel. When you feed carbohydrates, the body preferentially uses them for fuel and spares the fat. The result, increased body fat.

---

* *Indian J Exp Biol*, 1993; 31(2):151-5. *Br J Nutr*, 1967; 21(4):801-9.

Secondly, consider that in the wild your pet would spend most of its waking time in the interesting, challenging, and physically demanding pursuit of food. Now your pet has to do nothing in order to eat. See the problem?

Find fun active things to do with your pet. That's healthy for you both and builds the wonderful bond. If you need help on what to do to keep your pet active, talk to local trainers, pet stores and read books on the subject.

Additionally, do the obvious regarding amount of food fed. Inactivity deserves little food, particularly if you are feeding the nutrient dense foods suggested above. Yes, there may be begging, but that is more a symptom of boredom than anything.

Keep your pet active, feed right in kind and amount, and the weight will normalize safely and healthily.

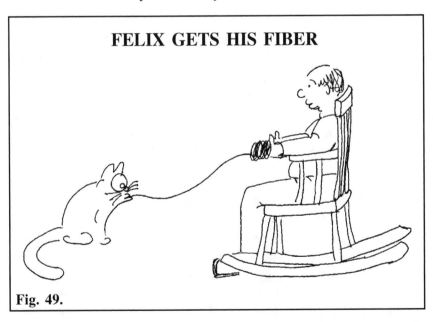

FELIX GETS HIS FIBER

Fig. 49.

6. **Whenever I give home-prepared foods, I get varying degrees of firmness in stools. Shouldn't stools be firm and hard? Are looser stools a sign of something wrong?** Ingredients are put into commercial pet foods specifically to produce smaller, harder stools. This is for the convenience of the pet owner. It has no correlation to nutritional soundness. Looser stools would be seen in the wild

setting. Adjusting from one diet to another is often accompanied by stool changes. Thirty days or more may be required in some cases to reach an equilibrium. Supplementing with Biotic™ Supplement, Pet Inoculant™ or live, active-culture yogurt should help to keep the digestive tract balanced.

7. **Does eating raw meats bring out a "killer instinct" in dogs and cats, making them do things they normally would not, such as kill farm chickens?** The better the diet, the more healthy the neurological system and behavior.* The way pets are raised and trained when young, and the way they are treated throughout their lives determines how they will behave. Making sure your pet is well fed, knows his property boundaries, is properly trained, and is not hungry from even subtle deficiencies caused by exclusively feeding packaged products are all critical to a well-adjusted, content and happy pet.

8. **Sometimes my pet stops eating completely. Is this normal?** Dogs and cats in the wild on natural diets do fast once in a while, sometimes once or twice a week, as part of a natural cycle. Also, in the wild, food just may not be found for a day or two. All creatures, including humans, are designed to fast. Although sometimes alarming to the pet owner, a day or two of fasting promotes healing (notice that a first step in recovery from illness is loss of appetite), and gives the digestive system needed rest.

9. **What is the recommendation on bones for dogs? None? Raw? Cooked? Only large bones? Only small bones? Almost everyone I ask has a different opinion!** Look to nature for guidance. First of all, in the wild bones would never be cooked. Only raw bones would be part of the wild diet. Cooked bones should not be fed because they can splinter into sharp fragments and be too easily consumed in excess. If raised with regular access to raw bones, pets will rarely overconsume, which can happen when an animal deprived of its natural diet by being fed only from bags and cans is

---

* *Wysong Health Letter*, "Vitamin B$_6$ in Mother and Infant Behavior," 1990; 4(6). *Int J Vitam Nutr Res*, 2002; 72(2):77-84. *Urology*, 2002; 59(4 Suppl 1):4-8. *J Nutr*, 1997; 127(1):184-93. *Nutr Neurosci*, 2002; 5(1):43-52. *Health Psychol*, 2000; 19(4):393-8. *J Paediatr Child Health*, 1997; 33(3):190-4. *Am J Dis Child*, 1955; 90:344-8. *Am J Clin Nutr*, 1990; 51:6. *J Nutr*, 1981; 111:848-57.

suddenly offered a bucket of real food – bones. Large beef knuckle bones are difficult for an animal to get into trouble with and they can provide nutritional benefits, healthier teeth and gums, and relieve boredom. Raw chicken necks, wings and tails are excellent supplements for cats, and for puppies and kittens to wean on. When first introducing bones, just make sure your pet does not overconsume, since this can cause constipation. To begin, you may wish to offer the bone two or three times a day for short intervals only. After a while, assuming you are converting to a more healthful all-around diet, your pet will regulate its bone consumption.

10. What about food poisoning? Can't my pet get Salmonellosis or other food-borne illness if the foods are not cooked thoroughly? Yes, this is possible, particularly since the overuse of antibiotics has created resistant strains of pathogenic organisms. Food should be cleaned thoroughly not only to help remove possible pathogens, but to remove pesticides. Disinfecting with Citrox™ in lieu of cooking is the choice many have made. Others choose to lightly cook by baking, stir frying, broiling or boiling. In this case, being sure to not overcook will help preserve some of the nutritional advantages of the raw product. Selecting fresh products and cleaning well removes most danger. Also maintaining a healthy digestive tract through supplementation with probiotics such as found in Biotic™ supplements (Call of the Wild™, F-Biotic™ or C-Biotic™), Pet Inoculant™ or live active yogurt helps to combat harmful pathogens.* The advantages of an all-raw diet far outweigh the disadvantages – in fact the increased health resulting can protect against the disadvantages. Concerns should also be allayed by remembering that in the wild animals regularly consume scavenged, filthy, rotten, decaying meals with no ill effects.

11. If I prepare foods at home, how can I be sure my pet is receiving the proper balance? The natural diet is naturally balanced. An animal in the wild does not make sure it eats from the "four food groups" daily, yet it thrives if enough of its natural food is present. Of course, in the home setting you are making the choices rather than

---

* *Wysong Health Letter*, "Competitive Exclusion for Control of Infection," 1999; 13(9):1-3. Wysong RL, "Biotic™ Means Life," 2002. Wysong RL, "Rationale for Probiotic Supplements," 2002. *Nature*, 1973; 241:210-211. *Aust Vet J*, 1977; 53:82-8. *J Am Vet Med Assoc*, 1998:1744-174. *J Food Prot*, 1981; 44:909-913. *Poult Sci*, 1995; 74:1093-1101. *J Clin Microbiol*, 1998; 36:641-647.

your pet, so variety is required. Follow the suggestions we have presented in this book, and balance should be no problem. Additionally, mixing home prepared foods with the prepackaged Wysong foods and supplements helps insure balance.

12. **I notice that pet foods have all of those vitamins and minerals in them. Do I need to get a vitamin/mineral supplement for my home-prepared meals and supplements?** Again, if we look to the model in the wild, the answer becomes obvious. Supplementation of modern pet foods is done only because many of the nutrients are destroyed, altered or stripped from the product during processing – or were never in the inferior starting ingredients. If you are able to feed high quality fresh and whole products, and combine these with health-quality packaged diets or supplements, there should be no additional need for vitamin/mineral supplementation.

13. **Where is the best place to buy meats and produce? Is what is available at the supermarket fine?** Much of the food available in today's supermarket is intensively farmed. This means it has been grown with high yield as the primary goal rather than nutrition and safety. Thus, some products, even though they may look wholesome, may be very low in nutrients and contaminated by pesticides, herbicides and food-borne pathogens. Other than growing your own, there is no sure way to know the quality of the food you eat. Short of this there are other options: buying from organic producers, finding local farmers who will sell to you and can give you a specific food history, and making sure food bought from the grocer is cleaned thoroughly, are the best alternatives. In any event, raw grocery foods are far superior to processed foods which often use the inferior by-products of these same grocery foods. The choice is yours. Buy the factory waste from the human food industry, packaged prettily with outrageous claims of "completeness," or buy the real thing.

14. **Does my large breed puppy need a special food?** In the past few years, several pet food manufacturers have launched special "large breed" puppy formulas designed to prevent developmental bone disease such as osteodystrophy and osteochondroses. There are two known causes for these diseases, genetic predisposition and over-feeding/over-supplementing by pet owners. Manufacturers noticed

that osteodystrophy and osteochondroses could be prevented by controlling calcium-phosphorous ratios and calorie consumption.

Over-supplementation with calcium has long been a problem for the pet feeding public. By feeding isolated nutrients, such as calcium, it is indeed possible to throw ratios and balances off, resulting in bone disease.[1] It is also true that by limiting caloric intake that disease may decrease. This is nothing new and nothing unique to large breed dog feeding. Overeating any food can result in disease.

In spite of audacious claims to the contrary, no one knows what perfect nutrition is. "Large breed" foods are known to contain rice flour, dried beet pulp, grain sorghum, and dried eggs to control caloric intake. How did the large ancestors of today's dogs manage without these ingredients, or how do the huge great cats, such as lions or tigers, manage to grow without caloric restriction?

Cycling through the various Wysong Diets, and providing fresh whole food, provides the important variety needed for large breed puppies. Each diet is formulated a little differently, which offers your pet an increasing opportunity to receive a broader spectrum of nutrients, and decreases the potential for developing allergies or sensitivities to any particular ingredient. By feeding with a more natural-food-based program, the chances of overeating are less. There are no shortcuts or magic processed food formulas when trying to reach optimal health.

15. **Should domesticated dogs eat the same thing as wolves?** Ideally, yes. The nutritional requirements of wild dogs are no different than that of their domesticated counterparts. They are genetically identical in both genotype and phenotype.[2] Feeding dogs pet foods does not change them genetically. This is Lamarckism (inheritance of acquired characteristics) and has been disproven for over one hundred years. Wolves and other wild canines fed processed dog foods

1. *Vet Rec*, 2000; 147(23):652-60. *J Int Med Res*, 1999; 27(1):1-14. *J Nutr*, 1986; 116(6):1018-27. *J Nutr*, 1989; 119(12 Suppl):1846-51. *Mech Ageing Dev*, 2001; 122(9):963-83. *J Am Coll Nutr*, 1997; 16(5):397-403. *Adv Exp Med Biol*, 1992; 322:73-81. *Mech Ageing Dev*, 2001; 122(14):1511-9. *Mech Ageing Dev*, 2001; 122(7):595-615. *J Am Geriatr Soc*, 1999; 47(7):896-903.
2. Lange KL, "Wolf to Woof – The Evolution of Dogs," *National Geographic*, Jan 2002. Fogle B, <u>The New Encyclopedia of the Dog</u>. 2000. *American Scientist*, July/August 1994;336-347. Olsen SL, <u>Origins of the Domestic Dog</u>, 1985. Sheldon JW, <u>Wild Dogs: The Natural History of the Nondomestic Canidae</u>, 1992. Thurston ME, <u>The Lost History of the Canine Race</u>, 1996.

will survive, though poorly, just like modern domesticated canines survive – poorly – plagued with all of the degenerative diseases common to their human counterparts eating processed foods.

If domesticated dogs were turned loose to consume their natural prey diet, they would survive just like the wolf and dingo do – all, incidentally, eating the identical food. Sufficient time has not elapsed to make domesticated creatures genetically dependent upon specifically tailored processed recipes. Modern commercial foods have only been widely used for about the past 50 years. In that short time creatures genetically tuned to wild prey have not suddenly converted their genetics to the hammer mill, extruder, oven and retorter. All life from the beginning of time has been sustained by eating the fresh raw natural foods from the natural environment.

This is the reason that the Wysong Optimal Health Program (see pages 195-208) teaches people how to feed fresh raw foods and appropriately supplement when feeding processed commercial diets.

16. **Must pet foods be tested on laboratory animals to prove their safety?** Even though there is no invasive, toxic, or disease-inducing experimental abuse in feeding trials, there is nonetheless a cruelty in keeping animals in a caged environment for such tests.

Additionally, the tests do not prove what they are intended to: "100% completeness." Feeding trials are performed on caged animals and are short-term (generally 26 weeks at most). Such tests deny that nutrition can have effects beyond the few weeks used in a feeding trial. Undetected nutrient imbalance in youth has, for example, been shown to affect both animal and human, adult and all age susceptibility to many chronic degenerative diseases, and even impact the health of future generations.* A feeding trial does not measure this.

Further, results from a laboratory-bred puppy raised on concrete in stainless steel cages, placed under fluorescent lights, breathing conditioned air does not necessarily correlate to real animals in homes and back yards.

---

* *Wysong Health Letter*, "Don't Let Apparently Youthful Health Fool You," 7(12):6. Price W, <u>Nutrition and Physical Degeneration</u>, 1982. Pottenger FM, <u>Pottenger's Cats: A Study in Nutrition</u>, 1983. *J Am Coll Cardiol*, 1993; 22(2): 459-67. *J Am Med Assoc*, 1999; 281:727-35.

Further, such tests are found to be ineffective. In a recent issue of the *Journal of the American Veterinary Medical Association*, Dr. David Dzanis of the FDA Center for Veterinary Medicine stated, "The formulation method does not account for palatability or availability of nutrients. Yet a feeding trial can miss some chronic deficiencies or toxicities." Dr. Rogers of the University of California stated, "Some foods that pass the feeding trial still won't support animals over the long term...The maintenance protocol lasts only 6 months, the effects of an excess might not cause a problem for several years."[1]

In short, feeding trials in no way assure animal owners that optimal health will be maintained if the tested products are fed exclusively over a lifetime. The best "feeding trials" are with at-home, well-loved companion animals.[2]

---

1. *Wysong Health Letter,* "Nutritionists Seeing the Light," 1997; 11(11):3. *J Am Vet Med Assoc*, 1993:1400.
2. *Wysong Health Letter,* "A Letter from Dr. Wysong Regarding Animal Testing," 1997; 11(11):1:

Dear Friend:

There are very few animal or human experiments that are really necessary. But, I must admit that early on we were guilty of some of this nonsense. We did a few animal-feeding studies under pressure by customers (not to excuse my own naiveté) to create the kind of "scientific data" they were used to looking at, or were told by others to look for. We stopped jumping through these hoops when I could not justify holding animals in cages, regardless of how nicely we treated them, to prove what was already obvious to any thinking person. I'm sure sales are lost because we are not performing AAFCO (American Association of Feed Control Officials) laboratory feeding trials to brag "100% complete and balanced perfect nutrition" malarkey.

Nonsense to create sales is not right. I sleep better at night knowing that no animal is caged in a laboratory somewhere (to prove what is obvious to any "thinking person") for our profit. There are some things that simply need no proof.

Laboratory proofs are just assurances and corroboration of what is already evident. Common sense tells us what is required for optimal health. What would you think if I told you that the only way we could know what lions, bears, ants, elephants, rhinoceroses, hyenas, robins, or eagles should eat would be to cage several of each, and then perform long, complicated, placebo-controlled, double-blind, crossover, scientific feeding studies? You would say, "What? I already know what they should eat. It's what they're already eating."

We don't need some food scientist or nutritionist to tell us how many milligrams of vitamin B_6, international units of vitamin E, or grams of protein, creatures need. They obviously get what they need by eating it raw, whole, natural food. The simplicity of this is so overwhelming it is essentially passed over by the entire food industry and scientific community. What does your pet need to eat? The answer: What it would eat if it were released into the wild. What should you eat? What you would eat if you were released into the wild. Granted, today's humans and companion animals cannot be released into the wild, but that does not mean we should not model our diets to retain as much of the character of the archetypal pattern as it is possible to achieve.

17. Aren't pet foods without corn, soy or wheat less likely to cause toxicity?

Permit me to begin this by repeating a very important nutritional principle: Anything can be toxic in sufficient quantity. Or, put another way, the dose makes the poison. Even elements absolutely essential to life, such as oxygen and water, can kill if taken in high enough dosages.[1]

With this preliminary understanding, one can then properly evaluate the continuing emergence of claims about how a substance or an ingredient is toxic. The edge is taken off claims that "soy is toxic," "corn is toxic," "alfalfa is toxic," and so forth, if the critical element of dosage is considered.

If the ingredients that might be used in a pet food are dismantled, literally thousands of different chemicals can be found. If any one of these chemicals is isolated and fed at high doses to almost any creature, toxicity is going to result. Remember, dose makes the poison.

There has been a debate raging about how natural toxins in natural foods – such as carototoxin in carrots, steroids and estrogens in ginseng, carcinogenic hydrazines in mushrooms, solanine and trichlothecene in potatoes and canavanine in alfalfa – are more toxic than herbicides and pesticides.[2] This argument is fueled by pesticide and herbicide manufacturers justifying and downplaying biocides in our food supply. It does, however, point out that anything can be toxic, even something as wholesome as a carrot.

There has been recent alarm created in the pet food industry by a marketer suggesting that saponins, a class of chemicals found in a variety of plant ingredients such as soy, are dangerous to pets. Sure they are…if isolated and given in sufficient dose or if a high level of soy is fed continually. But, so too is any vitamin, mineral, amino acid, or any other component of a natural food toxic – given in sufficient doses.

---

1. Ottoboni MA, The Dose Makes the Poison, 1984. Heiby WA, The Reverse Effect: How Vitamins and Minerals Can Promote Health and Cause Disease, 1988. Casarett LJ et al, Casarett & Doull's Toxicology: The Basic Science of Poisons, 2001.
2. References often cited include FASEB J, 2001; 15(1):195-203. FASEB J, 1997; 11(13):1041-52. Med Oncol Tumor Pharmacother, 1990; 7(2-3):69-85. Annu Rev Entomol, 1994; 39:489-515. Chambers JE, "Insecticide toxicity and future research needs," 1992; Proceedings 2nd Princess Chulabhorn Science Congress on Environment, Science and Technology.

Saponins, like lectins, phytic acid, and even fiber, are common in plant ingredients and can exert harm if isolated and given in extraordinarily high dosages. But as these ingredients exist within the integrated complex of whole, natural foods at natural low levels, they can exert many beneficial effects. For example, various compounds belonging to the class known as saponins, such as triterpen oligoglycosides, elatosides, escins, and senegasaponins are being studied because of their ability to treat cancer, hypercholesterolemia (In one review of 38 clinical studies over a period of 17 years, involving 730 volunteers, blood lipid profiles [cholesterol, triglycerides, HDL, LDL, etc.] were improved.), diabetes, alcoholism, and inflammatory conditions. Saponins have the ability to slow the digestion of complex carbohydrates such as starch, which tends to moderate blood sugar levels, and even decrease the absorption of alcohol. Through this action it is believed that saponins may actually help prevent, as well as treat, blood sugar abnormalities.[1]

Other concerns related to soy include antinutritional factors such as enzyme inhibitors, hemagglutinins, and phytase. In sufficient dosages these compounds can interfere with digestion, promote blood clotting, and bind minerals. But again, the key is dosage. Properly processed soy (such as by high temperature, short time extrusion), eaten in variety with other nutritious ingredients, produces health rather than disease.

A class of beneficial soy compounds is isoflavones, including genistein, which has estrogenic (female hormone) activity. These phytoestrogens can counteract the carcinogenic effect of environmental estrogenic substances to which we, and our pets, are increasingly exposed.[2] Soy phytoestrogens can inhibit cancer-causing estrogen receptors in breast tissue, testosterone-sensitive prostate cancers, and suppress angiogenesis (blood vessel formation) in tumors.[3]

---

1. *Science News*, December 9 1995; 148. *J Nutr*, 2001; 131(3s):1000S-5S. *J Nutr*, 1995; 125(3 Suppl):581S-588S. *Rocz Panstw Zakl Hig*, 1994; 45(1-2):125-30. *Ceska Slov Farm*, 1995; 44(5):246-51.
2. *Wysong Health Letter*, "Feminization of the World," 1994; 8(3). *Lancet*, 1994:284.
3. *Wysong Health Letter*, "Soy As Therapy," 1999; 13(3). *Arterioscl Thromb Vasc Biol*, 1997; 17:2524-31. *Am J Clin Nutr*, 1997; 65:166-71. *J Agric Food Chem*, 1997; 45:4635-8. *Lancet*, 1997; 350:990-4. *Nutr Cancer*, 1997; 27:31-40. *Proc Natl Acad Sci USA*, 1998; 95:3106-10.

The debate will go on endlessly, with one side arguing dangers, the other benefits. You need not get involved or worry if you are following the *entire* Optimal Health Program. (Not just feeding exclusively one diet day in and day out.) Perfect health is never certain, but you will be doing the best you can for your companion animal. You should be varying the diet, cycling among foods (some have soy, some don't, some corn, some not, some wheat, some not, etc.) and using a variety of fresh, whole foods as well. It is this diet variety that also increases the safety of all foods and changes arguments about the toxicity of any chemical within any one ingredient into non-issues.

18. I saw on the web that vitamin C is toxic to pets. Why is it in some pet foods? The critical point to keep in mind with regard to potential toxicity of any substance is that the dose makes the poison. Even water and oxygen, certainly "essential" nutrients, are toxic at high enough dosages. Vitamin C too can be toxic if overdone. For example, Teare, et. al. used 1200 mg of vitamin C daily (25-50 mg is sufficient for beneficial effects) in dogs to induce toxic results.[1] Massive doses of vitamin C to achieve toxicity are very misleading and irresponsible. People look to scientists for honest, fair, informed, and balanced (not sensationalized) direction. Again, any substance used at extreme levels over a long period of time may cause organ damage, as well as other health problems. If supplemental vitamin C were at harmful levels, all canines in the wild would die, since prey food contains vitamin C at levels even higher than that which is in pet foods.

Dozens of reports in the scientific literature demonstrate that vitamin C, at moderate levels, may benefit species that are able to synthesize it.[2] Further, vitamin C (natural and synthetic) is a water-soluble vitamin, which means that it is not stored in body tissues. Excess vitamin C not used by the body (animal or human) will be excreted via the urinary system.[3] It is one of the safest vitamins known.

1. *Cornell Vet*, 1979; 69(4):384-401.
2. *J Vet Med Sci*, 1998; 60(11):1187-93. *J Cardiovasc Pharmacol*, 2000; 36(6):687-92. *Vet Med Small Anim Clin*, 1968; 63(7):696-8. *Am J Vet Res*, 1986; 47(7):1633-7. *Res Vet Sci*, 2001; 71(1):27-32 *J Appl Physiol*, 1999; 87(5):1595-603. *Semin Vet Med Surg (Small Anim)*, 1997; 12(3):212-22. *Vet Med Small Anim Clin*. 1967; 62(4):345-8.
3. *Proc Natl Acad Sci U S A*, 2001; 98(17):9842-6. *Acta Vitaminol Enzymol*, 1985; 7(1-2):123-30.

Synthetic vitamin C and natural vitamin C are indistinguishable as isolated molecules, and are excreted by the kidneys via the same process, without causing damage. (The dangers of D-stereochemistry is irrelevant since manufacturers produce and sell only the L- form.) Urine pH may temporarily become more acidic if high doses are used. However, urine pH is affected by many substances such as meat protein (a high proportion of a carnivore's diet), which also causes urine acidification. (With this said in defense of synthetic vitamin C, I still opt for the natural food-content form.)

The Optimal Health Program is a "recipe" for life based on the belief that all creatures will experience their best potential when they live as closely as possible to their genetic, archetypal expectation (see pages 195-208). Natural forms of nutrients are different from the synthetic forms because of their complex interrelationships with other beneficial biochemicals.

Natural vitamin C in pet foods is used primarily as an antioxidant and is included at a level that is not harmful and cannot be proven so by any existing evidence. Fat-soluble form vitamin C used as a food antioxidant in home prepared or commercial foods is effective, safe, and very important. It is a preferred substitute for chemical preservatives such as BHT and BHA, which have been proven to cause health problems. The danger from oxidized fats and free-radical pathology is far greater than any conceivable harm from the low levels of vitamin C used to prevent it.*

Arguments that pets don't need vitamin C is pure guesswork, not science. On the contrary, a ubiquitous vitamin such as vitamin C that is increasingly being shown to exact dramatic preventive and therapeutic effects is indeed likely required in spite of an unrealistic and exaggerated "study" that seems to show the contrary.

19. Don't different breeds need different diets? The argument that different breeds have different requirements may be true, but no truer

---

* Wysong RL, <u>Lipid Nutrition – Understanding Fats and Oils in Health and Disease</u>, 1990. Wysong RL, "Rationale for Nutritious Oils," 2002. Wysong RL, "Oxherphol™ Technical Information," 2002.

than that different humans have different requirements and different animals within a breed have different requirements. This concept of biochemical individuality was first described by Dr. Roger Williams (the discoverer of vitamin B_5) decades ago, and used as a strong argument against those who would insist on "standards" for determining the "average" nutritional requirements for everyone.* It does not provide the logical or empirical basis for attempting to specifically set nutrient standards for any group within a population.

I disagree with the reductionistic approach to nutrition and health. It is the approach taken by the majority of the food industry. Nutrition is not reducible to milligrams, IU's and micrograms, but rather is holistic. Reductionism is the basis for the myth of the "100% complete" manufactured diet and is the fundamental cause of today's health woes in humans and companion animals.

Nutrition is individual. Every organism is genetically unique. Further, it is not within the capability of science to determine with exactness what the requirements are for every single creature, much less whole populations, species, breeds, etc. To suggest that anyone can do so is misleading. The same can be said with regard to what is toxic for a particular species, and at what levels.

For example, one could state that collies require 270 IU's of vitamin D per kilogram (are we sure it's not 270.015375948?). What specific collie are we talking about? How big, what age, and what precisely is in the rest of its diet? What is its metabolic rate? What is its specific digestive capacity? How much sun and exercise does it get? What is the source of its water? What is the quality of the air it breathes? What are its social interactions? What specific genetic strengths and weaknesses does it have? Are its foods heated, exposed to oxygen, and light? What are the interactions between the food ingredients when they are heated, etc.?

These considerations are all important, just like "breed," in determining nutrient needs. This logic is just another version of the flawed reasoning of the pet food industry – that nutritionists can create 100%

---

* Williams RJ, <u>Biochemical Individuality: The Basis for the Genetotrophic Concept</u>, 1998. Williams RJ et al, <u>The Biochemistry of B Vitamins</u>, 1998.

perfect foods because they "know" how many IU's of vitamin D, etc. a dog needs. Such fabricated diets based on specific requirements (only valid until the scientific board meets the next time) have caused immeasurable disease and suffering for companion animals.

20. Wouldn't feeding my pet vegetarian foods be more humane? If truth is the objective, the truth is that carnivores' health is best served by feeding meat products. This absolute dependency has been made clear in numerous scientific studies.*

A case in point is the thousands of deaths and untold suffering of cats from taurine (an amino acid) deficiency in commercial cat foods (see Proofs, pages 74-85). These were not vegetarian foods, but were deficient because the meats used were processed, which resulted in the loss of taurine. A vegan diet is essentially totally devoid of taurine. Other examples of carnivorous design include the inability to form vitamin A from plant carotene or niacin from tryptophan, the incapacity to synthesize several urea cycle intermediates or regulate hepatic amino acid catabolic enzymes, and the increased utilization of iron from meat foods. Obvious features such as teeth, hunting instinct, design of the digestive tract and behavior pretty much close the case.

Is it ethically correct to doom captive animals to suffering and death by feeding them a diet they would never naturally eat in the wild, and for which they are not genetically adapted? The choice is to inflict suffering and death if we do not feed our pets as they are genetically programmed, or inflict death on the food required for health.

All life requires the diminishment of other life for survival. A cow kills grass, a cat kills a mouse, a whale eats a fish, an elephant mutilates a tree, an immune cell destroys a bacterial invader, and so forth – throughout all of nature. This is truth, real and unavoidable.

Now then, we may not like the fact that sustenance of life requires the taking of life (I certainly don't), but that does not change the fact. We

---

* Pottenger FM, Pottenger's Cats: A Study in Nutrition, 1983. *Comp Biochem Physiol*, 1996; 114(3):205-9. *J Nutr*, 1985; 115(4):524-31. *Aust Vet J*, 1992; 69(10):249-54. *Annu Rev Nutr*, 1984; 4:521-62. *Am J Vet Res*, 2001; 62(10):1616-23. *Vet Clin North Am Small Anim Pract*, 1991; 21(5):1005-9. *Science*, 234:764-8. *Am Vet Med Assoc*, 1992; 201(2):267-74. *J Am Vet Med Assoc*, 1993; 203(10):1395-400. United States Patent No 5030458, 1991.

can try to avoid this by creating arbitrary definitions, for example, condoning the killing of non-"sentient" creatures and those without a "brain and nervous system." But who gets to decide what "brain," "nervous system," or "sentient" is, and who gets to be lucky and fall under these rubrics? Who decides how to draw lines when in reality there are no clear demarcations among life forms? True, a blade of grass appears clearly different from a cow, but the spectrum of life must be looked at in its entirety. It is one thing to say we "feel" that this or that food is ethically wrong, a purely subjective decision. It is quite another to attempt to justify that choice by creating objective physical distinctions which do not exist.

Quanta, subatomic particles, atoms, molecules, prions, viruses, bacteria, protozoa, plankton, plants, insects, invertebrates, fish, reptiles, amphibians, and mammals are a continuum in form and function. Pain and fear do not suddenly appear with one certain creature along the "simple" to "complex" scale of living creatures, so that we can easily decide what can be killed and eaten without cruelty. Cognizance of and reactions to stimuli (another way of saying fear and pain) exist throughout life in a variety of forms and degrees. If this were scaled from 1 to 100, would a 46 be okay to eat but not a 47, a 12 but not a 13, a 74.965 but not a 74.966?

There are no clear separations except those we artificially impose. The more we learn, the more it becomes impossible to unequivocally classify. Without classification, it is impossible to assign right versus wrong in order to eat based upon physical criteria.

All living creatures show mental characteristics: the ability to react to stimuli, process information, and be self-corrective. A brain and nervous system is just one means. Those who study plants closely conclude that they too have the ability to react to stimuli (sentience?), and although they cannot move, do produce a complex array of chemicals, (more complex than humans, in lieu of mobility) in response to danger and can even communicate this over distance to other plants that likewise respond.* Does anyone really know what goes on in the

---

* *J Chem Ecol*, 2001; 27(11):2233-52. *Science*, 1999; 284(5414):654-7. *Plant Physiol*, 2002; 128(1):271-81. *Curr Opin Plant Biol*, 2002; 5(1):43-8. *Curr Opin Plant Biol*, 1999; 2(1):65-70. *Novartis Found Symp*, 1999; 223:74-109.

PAGE 148

"mind" of a plant? Can we simply conclude they don't have one because they don't have legs?

Whatever criteria we decide upon to establish what is ethical or unethical to eat breaks down on its edges since life is a continuum. All life, all matter – the entire universe – is inextricably interrelated. There are no clear lines other than those we artificially and arbitrarily create.

My heart is with those who seek to listen to their inner voices and treat all of nature with love and respect. My mind, on the other hand, forces me to face the reality that feeding improperly is a clear and avoidable cruelty. Is it any less cruel to make an obligate carnivore such as the cat "go meatless" than to keep a fish, but not in water? The consequence may be delayed for the cat, but is just as sure.

So there is no *PHYSICAL* or *BIOLOGICAL* (not to be confused with morality we create for social order such as banning the taking of another human's life) certainty as to what is or is not ethical to eat. (This ethical dilemma is, however, a luxury of modern supply convenience. Pets turned loose in the wild kill prey. Humans turned loose in the wild likewise find and kill prey or die.) There is, however, certainty about what is or is not healthy to eat. The food a creature is genetically adapted to is the healthy food. If we violate this law, cruelty in the form of disease, suffering and death will result.

It is therefore a choice of whether to, as humanely as possible, take the life of others for the sustenance of our nutritional health, or arbitrarily make choices that will cause disease, suffering, and death to ourselves and the creatures in our care.

21. **Won't a pet food with dry meat meal give more protein than one with fresh meat?** Let's examine the currently popular argument that dried meat meals are superior to fresh meats using the logic of nature as the preeminent principle. It is claimed that if dried meat meal is used in dry pet foods, then more actual meat can be included than if fresh meat were used, which is 70% water. However, meat meal proponents cry foul because fresh meat users can list meat higher on the ingredient list, because ingredient order is by weight. Thus, fresh meat users get to include the 70% water factor as meat. Dried meat prod-

ucts may have more meat, but it will look like less on the label compared to foods using fresh meat. This seems like a reasonable complaint at first glance, but one must also consider the nutrient value of meat meal.

Let's use archetypal genetic context, the logic of nature.

If the number one goal in pet feeding is the weight of meat, why buy dried pet foods at all? Dried manufactured foods (except Archetype™) require starches to form a nugget through extrusion processing. They are thus diluted by grains whether fresh or dried meats are used. Purchasing fresh meats from the grocery store obviously better achieves this high meat goal. It's 100% meat.

However, if dried foods are used because of their convenience, then should the goal be to find the food with the highest amount of meat on a weight basis, or to find a food with the highest quality and most nutrient dense form of meat? As long as basic caloric and protein needs are met – which essentially all commercial foods do – the most important nutritional consideration becomes nutritional quality with the objective of immune system enhancement to slow aging and stave off chronic degenerative diseases.

Put simply, meat meals are inferior to fresh meats. Meals are made through grinding, cooking, and then drying meats into a granular powder. This task is performed by processors, apart from the pet food plant. The meals are then binned, stored, and trucked to the pet food manufacturer. The pet food manufacturer then stores the ingredient in bins until added to the formula. It is then cooked again during pet food processing, dried again and then put into its final package and stored some more.

On the other hand, fresh meats are not precooked and stored, but only cooked once into the final pet food. Do we not intuitively know that a fresh steak would be much better for us than a beef patty made from precooked, powdered meat stored in a package and then cooked again? Freshness is as fundamental to nutrition as gasoline is to an automobile. Science confirms this intuition. Heat, exposure to air and light, and age, are all the enemies of nutritional value. Meat meals bathe in these vitiations. Fats are oxidized creating dangerous free-radicals (not entirely solved by adding preservatives), proteins combine with carbohydrates in Maillard reactions to form toxic end products, nutrients are leached and lost, amino acids are diminished (e.g. arginine, taurine) and converted to D-stereoisomers, rendering them unavailable to the body.*

This only begins the list of destruction processing can do. The trick is to do the least possible, not process twice as occurs with the use of meat meals. There is little merit in arguing that you own a new Mercedes if in reality it has been totaled and then rebuilt from used parts. Using fresh meats in pet foods puts only a small dent in the fender of nutrition, using meat meals puts it in the junkyard. Quality is the key, not quantity. Coincidentally, manufacturers who criticize the use of fresh meat do not have fresh meat processing capabilities. This capability is extremely expensive and very labor intensive. It is not a cost-effective way of just playing games with labels.

22. **If a manufacturer does not believe the "100% complete" myth and recommends variety or supplementing, does this mean its foods are incomplete?** Claiming one food is complete, a perfect fit for any animal, is like saying one pair of pants can fit anyone. Not only are processed foods by definition incomplete, one food could not possibly meet the biochemical individuality of every creature.

This is the reason to vary the diet and add fresh foods and supplements. These recommendations are not made because a food manufactured with this understanding, such as Wysong, is somehow less than others who claim their foods are "100% complete," or because such foods do not stand alone. Such foods can, in fact, be far more than "100% complete" because of continuing efforts to reach the ideal,

---

* Wysong RL, Lipid Nutrition – Understanding Fats and Oils in Health and Disease, 1990. *Wysong Health Letter*, "Nutrient Loss During Processing," 1997; 11(11):1. *Wysong Health Letter*, "Processing," 1989; 3(1). *Wysong Health Letter*, "The Fragility of Vitamins," 1997; 11(10). *Wysong Health Letter*, "Ubiquitous B Vitamin Deficiency," 1997; 11(12). *Wysong Health Letter*, "Dangers in Cooked and Cured Meats," 1994; 8(6). *Wysong Health Letter*, "Glycosylation," 1990; 4(1). *Wysong Health Letter*, "Potato Vitamin Loss," 1992; 6(12). Wysong RL, "Biotic™ Means Life," 2002. *J Am Med Assoc*, 1990; 263(1):35. *Environ Mol Mutagen*, 2002; 39(2-3):112-8. *J Food Sci*, 1992:1136. *Feedtech*, May 1997:39-43. *J Agric Food Chem*, 2002; 50(6):1647-51. *J Toxicol Environ Health*, 1981; 7(1):125-38.

rather than contentedness with regulatory minimums that permit announcing "complete" on a label.

23. Isn't varied feeding and supplementing very expensive? Yes, varying the diet, using supplements, and purchasing fresh foods is more complicated than pouring one food out of a package. But check your refrigerator and cupboard. How many foods and supplements are there for human people? Dozens, probably more than a hundred. Is that complicated? Yes. Would you do it differently if you found a "100% complete" human food? Certainly not. Variety is the spice and essence of good nutritional health. That holds true for the animal people in the family as well.

As for cost, health-first designed products are expensive in ingredients, production, and packaging. Better things simply cost more. But what is received creates considerable added value that is literally free. How do you put a price on health and vitality? What is the value of avoiding acute or lingering illness?

Although it is true that if every supplement and food were used, it may seem that the cost is more than just feeding a brand exclusively. But when nutritious products are used in variety as recommended, and the decreased amount of food necessary is considered (due to the concentrated high quality), and the decreased chance for illness measured, the right choice should be apparent.

24. Should I buy the food that is cheapest if ingredients look the same as the more expensive foods? Companies have for many years promoted what they feel will capture a market. However, they have not taken up the cause of optimal health. Rather, they promote their product with the misguided and dangerous "100% complete" claim. This may beguile a well intentioned pet owner, thinking they have perhaps captured the health advantages at a bargain, but no processed food should be fed exclusively, if health is the objective.

Yes, companies can list enzymes, probiotics, whole grains, essential fatty acids etc., on labels. But is this mere label dressing to woo sales? Apparent imitations of truly healthy products can be made that cost less. They usually cost less because they are less. The manufacturer knows what they are worth and could not survive by charging less than that.

You usually get what you pay for. Healthy and nutritious products are expensive.

In the end, consumers must place a lot of trust and faith in manufacturers. They simply cannot know for sure what is colored by marketing and what is substantive value. Label and literature claims are only that, claims. Labeling reveals only the tip of the iceberg...and that tip can be sculpted to look as attractive as possible. It is the underlying motives of the producer and the foundation upon which products are built that reveal true value or danger.

From such information and comparisons, make your choice of trust.

—28—

21 PET FOOD FALLACIES
(a brief review)

1. **As long as a pet is fed a "100% complete and balanced" pet food, it will not suffer from nutritionally related diseases.**
   FALSE. Science does not have 100% knowledge of anything, much less nutrition. It follows, therefore, that exclusive feeding of such erroneously based diets will likely cause, not prevent, disease (see pages 2-4).

2. **If the ingredient listings on two different pet foods are the same, it means that both pet foods contain the same things.**
   FALSE. Names of ingredients may vary, the same ingredients may vary in quality, and relative levels of ingredients may differ widely even though the ingredient listings may be identical. A food with 30% chicken meat, bone and giblets and 15% whole brown rice can have the same ingredient listing as a food with 20% chicken heads, feet and intestines and 20% refined white rice. Same label, but vastly different nutrition (see pages 25-26).

3. **If the label on a pet food bag reads chicken, beef, lamb, cheese, rice, and so forth, the package contains basically the same foods humans eat.**
   FALSE. The ingredients used in pet foods are usually by-products of the human food industry. Manufacturers mislead consumers by picturing human-type foods in advertisements but then use materials entirely different than in the pictures. For example, dressed grocery store chicken is not the same as pet food ingredient "chicken" which usually is comprised of heads, feet and intestinal tracts. Grocery store steaks and roasts are not the same as the pet food ingredient "beef"

which may consist of almost any part of a cow carcass (see pages 20-24, 28-29).

4. **Feeding pets raw bones is more dangerous than feeding commercial pet foods along with biscuits to clean the pet's teeth.**
   FALSE. Raw bones were eaten by dogs and cats for eons before manufactured grain-based biscuits. Furthermore, animals in the wild do not experience the dental disease that modern companion animals do. Processed biscuits add interesting variety to the diet but do little more for teeth cleaning than do dry pet foods (see pages 36-37, 136-137).

5. **The present dental and gum disease epidemic in pets is not related to the "complete and balanced" pet foods they are eating.**
   FALSE. Biscuits and nuggets may be crunchy, but do not adequately clean an animal's teeth. They can leave a gummy residue which serves as a matrix leading to gum disease and dental caries. Additionally, additives, sweeteners and other refined or artificial ingredients in processed foods can damage teeth in animals just as they do in humans (see pages 36-37).

6. **Table scraps should not be fed because they will upset the "balance" of formulated pet foods, and because they are of inferior quality to packaged pet foods.**
   FALSE. Good table scraps (not human junk food leftovers) are excellent for animals when fed in variety. Most pet foods contain ingredients from the same food families as those found on the human dinner table. Fresh foods from the dinner table have increased freshness and nutrient value over their processed pet food counterparts (see pages 38-42, 137-138).

7. **A pet food that has passed the AAFCO (American Association of Feed Control Officials) feeding trial tests is best as a pet's only food.**
   FALSE. Such feeding trials are only 26 weeks long. Additionally they are performed on caged laboratory animals. Such testing does not

assure animal owners that optimal health will be maintained if these products are fed exclusively over a lifetime. In fact, foods passing such tests have caused serious, even fatal, nutritional diseases. Examples include mycotoxemia, as well as imbalances in zinc, potassium, and taurine. Additionally, there is evidence of degenerative diseases that arise later in life – obesity, periodontitis, cancer, arthritis, autoimmunities, hormone imbalance, organ disease, digestive problems, cataracts, skin disorders, and susceptibility to infection – directly related to feeding processed foods exclusively. Health may be fine during a short-term feeding study or while animals have the vigor of youth, but this apparent nutritional adequacy is deceptive, obscuring the relationship of later life diseases to processed foods (see pages 12-16, 140-141).

8. **If a pet has an allergy, this can be cured by eliminating pet foods that contain the offending ingredient and buying a new special allergy formula pet diet.**
   FALSE. The cause of modern pet food allergy is not a pet food ingredient. The cause is a compromised immune system resulting from a compromised modern life-style, and singularly fed, manufactured diets. Seldom does a pet have an allergy to the singular ingredients for which they test positive, if these ingredients are fed fresh, raw and whole. When pet foods are manufactured, the ingredients are altered and complexed into new forms of chemical combinations for which it is impossible to predict sensitivity. The only way to know if an animal is sensitive or allergic to a food is to feed it (see pages 48-49).

9. **The more digestible a food is, the better that food is.**
   FALSE. To a degree this is true of course, but if percent of digestibility is the key to good nutrition then that would mean that a 100% digestible diet – zero fecal output – would be the best diet of all. This is, of course, absurd. Animals need some bulk and indigestible material for a properly functioning digestive tract. A small, firm, hard stool that is easy for owners to discard does not necessarily equate with good nutrition or health (see pages 11-12).

10. **Pet foods in paper bags can retain their full nutritional value for many months.**

FALSE. Who would like to eat meat, dairy products, cereals and grain products after they had been stored on a shelf for months, or perhaps longer than a year? Yet this is what is suggested by pet food manufacturers who guarantee shelf-lives for many months and even a year. Rocks and cardboard last indefinitely on a shelf – wholesome foods do not. Time is the enemy of good nutritional value. Nutrition is not mortuary science. Freshness should be of utmost importance to animal owners regardless of shelf-life claims (see pages 54-55).

11. **More expensive premium-brand pet foods are better than cheaper brands.**

FALSE. An expensive brand can actually cost less to produce than a more inexpensive brand. Often the price of a food is set based upon marketing and corporate costs rather than actual ingredient value. The high cost of modern day marketing and advertising can result in more marketing in the package than nutrition (see page 27).

THE PREMIUM PET FOOD MYTH

"I'M SURE GLAD I DON'T USE THOSE BAD GENERIC FOODS THAT CAUSE NUTRITIONAL IMBALANCES"

THE TRUTH: PREMIUM PET FOOD HAS CAUSED DISEASE AND DEATH DUE TO IMBALANCES OF TAURINE, CARNITINE, POTASSIUM . . .

Fig. 50.

12. **The majority of the cost of a pet food is related to the quality of ingredients.**

FALSE. The majority of the cost of most commercial products is due to markups, packaging and advertising, not nutritional value (see page 27).

13. Pet food processing does not change the nutritional value of the ingredients listed on the label.

FALSE.   The high heat and pressure used in modern food processing greatly alters, diminishes and can completely destroy or even convert to toxins some important food elements. Pet owners are mistaken if they look at an ingredient listing and picture in their minds fresh foods as they see them in a grocery store (see pages 20-24).

14. Overweight pets need to be put on "Lite" formulas and fiber to lose weight.

FALSE.   Most "Lite" formulas increase fiber content and decrease fats and meats. The cause of obesity in modern pets is not a lack of fiber. The cause is high carbohydrate processed foods, sedentary living, pampering with snacks, and feeding more food than is necessary to sustain the animal's activity (see pages 134-135).

SEE... you're fine. Let's get a snack.

Fig. 51.

15. A high protein food is a better quality food.

FALSE.   A high protein percentage does not speak to the value of protein. If large quantities of low-value protein are consumed, organ stress can occur and damage to the animal's metabolic systems can result. Quality of protein, particularly as available in fresh products, is far more important than quantity (see pages 149-151).

16. Pets require special life-stage diets.

FALSE.   In the wild, animals eat essentially one diet consisting of a variety of raw, natural foods for their entire life. A 10-year-old wolf eats the same foods as a 3-month-old one. Life-stage formulation is a marketing scheme, not a nutritional necessity (see pages 46-47, 133-134).

17. Cats on foods with low ash and magnesium, and high acid, will not develop urinary problems.
FALSE. Cats don't develop FUS because of magnesium and ash. They develop FUS because of the sedentary, homebound life-style imposed upon them and because they are being fed commercial diets that have deviated too far from the natural, fresh, raw foods the animal is adapted to (see page 188).

18. Feeding an animal raw meats, organs and bones is dangerous.
FALSE. There is no evidence to demonstrate that feeding fresh raw foods from the grocery store can cause more harm than feeding processed, embalmed, fractionated, additive-laden, synthetically fortified products from pet food manufacturers. In fact, animals eating raw unprocessed foods survived for eons in good health in the wild, and still do (see pages 36-37, 133, 136-137).

19. Veterinarians are highly schooled in cat and dog nutrition.
FALSE. Most veterinarians take at most one nutrition class in school. Much of the nutritional education they get is propaganda presented to them by commercial pet food interests, both during their school years and while in practice. Veterinarians who are truly skilled in nutrition and preventive health develop such skills on their own (see pages 20-21).

20. Pets today are living longer, healthier lives than before packaged pet foods came along.
FALSE. In fact, animals in the wild with sufficient natural food sources do not have the chronic degenerative diseases that are ravaging modern pet populations being exclusively fed supposedly "complete and balanced" modern processed pet foods (see pages 74-85).

21. If I feed raw meats, I will cause food poisoning.
FALSE. In the wild, the only diet for carnivores is raw meat. They will also eat scavenged, decaying, flyblown food that is teeming with bacteria. Steam cleaned, sterile, processed foods are not a natural diet, regardless of label claims. Although pets today may not have healthy populations of protective intestinal flora (a result in itself of eating

processed sterilized foods) and may have a bout of digestive upset from food-borne pathogens in raw foods (highly unlikely), the alternative of getting serious degenerative disease later in life from sterile processed foods is a far greater risk. Raw foods should be a part of the daily diet of pets to help insure optimal nutrition. Probiotic organisms incorporated into Wysong Diets and supplements help prevent food-borne illness when raw foods are fed (see pages 133, 137).

SECTION IV

DEFENDING THE TRUTH

Errors Unanswered Create Realities That Are Illusions

PREFACE

There is, of course, debate among pet food producers. Each believes, or at least must try to convince consumers to believe, that their product is best.

The marketing and advertising resources of the 13 billion dollar pet food publicity machine can be persuasive. For the average consumer, sorting hype from substance can be very difficult. As a result, most people take the easy road and follow the most impressive glitz, the brands most predominant in the media (money makes this possible, not worth), or lore, myth, rumor and fad.

Most pet food producers (in spite of promotion to the contrary) give secondary attention to nutrition (other than mandated by regulation) and have neither depth of scientific understanding nor logical health design. Primary effort is focused on chasing consumer trends. They follow, not lead.

The "100% complete" myth absolves producers from nutritional innovation. Why do more when you're already perfect? How much more intellectually honest it is to not pretend to have arrived at absolute truth. Nutrition is a process, not an end result. As research and discovery proceed, products should be advanced toward the goal of optimizing health. Products should be better today than they were a year ago, and better a year from now than today.

But most pet foods are essentially the same, and remain the same, whether they are generic, premium, or "natural." Differences are created by deliberate construction of marketing propaganda, not by what is in the package. This is not to say that formulas do not vary (mostly in unimportant ways), only that the philosophic approach to design and processing remains essentially the same.

As I have explained, it is possible for anyone with some capital (no expertise necessary) to contract with any of dozens of pet food manufacturers to make a "new" food to market. "New" may be only the packaging and brand name. Contract manufacturers have many standard formulas they will allow aspiring pet food marketers to use. Then, to make it "different" and "new," it is only necessary to add or remove a little of this or that. *Violá!* A "new" pet food is born. There are now hundreds of companies and thousands of brands, with nothing really new achieved. Processing remains the same, ingredients usually remain the same, and therefore the only truly "new" things that happen are perceptions created by packaging and marketing.

Although the true purpose of industry should be to create useful, high quality products, the advanced ability to deceive or mislead through marketing and advertising techniques makes it possible to convince consumers that quality is high where it is not. Complex products in health care and nutrition are particularly susceptible since the public is not sufficiently informed to cut through to the truth. The temptation for modern enterprises, under tremendous pressure to sweeten the bottom line, is to make it cheaply, convince the public that it is more, and sell it expensively.

You now, however, armed with the philosophic framework discussed in this book, know better. The truth – creatures are designed for their natural in-the-wild foods – acts like a filter to separate true health value from flimflam and potential disease.

The following section will give examples of how pet food marketing can be evaluated using this truth. I have before me the literature and website material from four different producers. They have been chosen because they have either directly or indirectly criticized the health and nutritional approach described in this book, or demonstrate egregiously the points made above. Excuse me for getting a little excited here and there in the responses. Hopefully, you'll see why.

The outrageous claims, falsehoods, exaggerations and incompetence revealed in what follows, and prevalent throughout the industry, put pets in harm's way. All to turn a dollar.

After some 25 years of research into the diet-disease link, I am convinced that food is serious business. Feed wrong, and suffering and death wait. Feed right, and full health potential is possible.

Only the most highly educated and skilled are permitted in the medical community. All to attempt repair for what in large part could have been avoided. If food can prevent and reverse disease, which it can (see fifteen years of the Wysong Health Letter with thousands of scientific references), then why should we not require similarly stringent skills and training for those making foods? In fact, is not preventing cancer even better and more important than the effete and cruel cut, burn and poison "remedies" we make sure doctors are credentialed and skilled at? Is not food the most important medicine of all?

Instead, anyone off the street can make a pet food and position themselves as an expert to the public. All that's needed is some money and meeting the absurd "100% complete and balanced" criteria. A fancy brochure and pretty packaging pretty much dupes the public.

See the problem? See why I might get a little upset when I can see that this incredibly useful tool (food) for preventing and relieving so much pain and suffering, is treated like a mere mundane business opportunity with open license to use every imaginable sales, advertising and marketing gimmick – including outright lies and the pretense of health competency and concern?

You must be able to sort out the pretenders from those who are properly motivated and know what they are doing. This section, plus the principles previously outlined, will help you see how to do that.

—29—

COMPANY A* VS. THE TRUTH

(EXCERPTS FROM VARIOUS COMPANY A ADVERTISEMENTS)

Company A: *"No prescription is more valuable than knowledge."*

Truth Response: There is also nothing more dangerous than a little bit of knowledge presented as if it were authority.

Company A: *"When (Company A) introduced the first natural dog food into the U.S. in 1974, people were surprised that it didn't contain the usual ingredients found in other dog foods. We didn't use soybeans, wheat or corn – the number 1, 2 and 3 allergies of dogs that cause them to chew at the root of the tail or lick their feet... We use amaranth, millet, barley and stone-ground brown rice."*

Truth Response: Company A did not produce the *"first natural dog food."* Just calling something *"natural"* does not make it so. A natural food is the food which matches the genetic expectation of the species. Amaranth, millet, barley and stone-ground brown rice, claimed ingredients in Company A's Product, are not natural foods for dogs or cats.

Food allergies are usually manifest in digestive disturbances, not *"chewing the root of the tail,"* normally a sign of flea allergy dermatitis.

Pet food grains are ground by steel hammer mills, not *"stone"* grinders. *"Stone-ground"* sounds quaint and gentler than using a hammer mill, but the net effect – milled grain – is the same.

---

* Name of company withheld to be kind.

Company A: *"We never use animal fat or poultry fat, which is rancid and may contribute to heart disease and cancer. We use canola oil and flaxseed oil, which are good for the immune system. Our flaxseed oil doesn't contain hexane; a chemical used by other flax oil companies. Our flaxseed oil helps the heart and is used by dogs with cardiomyopathy. Our flaxseed oil helps to reduce the incidence of epileptic seizures."*

Truth Response: Animal fat is the natural fat consumed by carnivores. If Company A does not use it, how can they claim their food is *"natural"*?

All animal fat is not *"rancid."* This would only be true if the fat were not properly stabilized. Highly unsaturated vegetable oils used in Company A's product are much more susceptible to rancidity than animal fat.[1] Flaxseed oil is so unstable it should only be eaten as freshly ground seeds or as a separate supplement in light impervious, nitrogen-flushed glass bottles kept in the freezer. Putting flaxseed oil in pet food paper bags, which are then stored on shelves, is a sure formula for rancidity and free-radical pathology.

Animal fat does not *"contribute"* to heart disease and cancer *per se.* This plays to popular misconceptions and the "low fat," "low cholesterol" fads, but does not reflect current science. There are nutritional factors within animal fat that are even cardioprotective and anticarcinogenic.[2]

Animal fats are *"good for the immune system,"* too. They contain important essential fatty acids, fat-soluble vitamins and other fat-soluble nutrients valuable to carnivores not found in canola and flaxseed oils.

Hexane is not used by most companies in the manufacture of nutritious flaxseed oils. If it is used, it is then removed from the final product in good manufacturing methods.[3] This is an attempt to create a bogeyman where there is none.

---

1. Wysong RL, <u>Lipid Nutrition – Understanding Fats and Oils in Health and Disease</u>, 1990. *Z Lebensm Unters Forsch*, 1995; 200(1):47-51. *J Food Sci*, 1987; 52(3):832. *J Food Sci*, 1988; 53(6):1897. *Science News*, 133(21):332. *Price-Pottenger Nutrition Foundation Health Journal*, Winter 1996:8.
2. Wysong RL, <u>Lipid Nutrition – Understanding Fats and Oils in Health and Disease</u>, 1990. *Proc Natl Acad Sci U S A*, 2001; 98(23):13294-9. *Med Clin (Barc)*, 1998; 110(17):641-5.
3. Companies offering hexane-free flaxseed oil include Wysong Corporation, Reliance Vitamin Company, Inc., NOW Foods, Vitamer Laboratories, Suzanne's Brand, Doctor's A-Z.

Cardiomyopathy in pets has been caused primarily by deficiency of the amino acid taurine, not flaxseed oil (see Proofs, pages 74-85).

Where is the epidemiological proof that the flaxseed oil in Company A's product decreases the *"incidence"* of epilepsy? If the FDA sees this unsubstantiated claim (as well as most others in the ad) they could remove Company A's product from the market.

Company A: *"We never use sunflower oil. Cancer researchers use sunflower oil to induce cancer tumors in rats. Sunflower oil contains no omega 3, essential fatty acids, so necessary for development in unborn and young animals."*

Truth Response: Sunflower oil does contain omega 3 fatty acids. It is also very high in omega 9 fatty acids (olive oil factors), is quite stable and has many health benefits.* Attempting to paint sunflower oil and animal fat as the bad guys, and canola and flaxseed oils as the good guys, is overly simplistic and attempts to convince by creating or playing to ignorant prejudices. There are benefits and dangers to all food ingredients including every one used in Company A's products.

Company A: *"(Company A) never uses chicken. We use fish and lamb. All the Oriental dogs, Arctic dogs and dogs from England, Scotland, Ireland and water dogs were fed fish in their diets and sea vegetation. Our sea vegetation...is always fed with our dog food. It works through the thymus and thyroid glands for the immune system."*

Truth Response: Company A *"never"* uses chicken because *"Oriental,"* *"Arctic,"* *"dogs from England, Scotland, Ireland and water dogs"* ate *"fish and sea vegetation."* How does this constitute a valid reason not to use chicken? Are *"water dogs"* and those from the named countries somehow better than dogs from others (assuming the claim that they only eat fish and seaweed diets is true)?

---

* Food and Agriculture Organization of the United Nations, "Fatty Acid Composition of Rapeseed and Low Erucic Acid (Canola) Oil Compared to Olive Oil, Soybean and Sunflower." *J Anim Sci*, 2001; 79(5):1201-8.

How does Company A's *"sea vegetation... work through the thymus and thyroid glands for the immune system"*? No credible scientific explanation here or documentation, just a claim.

Company A: *"Chickens are about the worst ingredient that could be put into dry dog food. In the 1970's, Dr. Virginia Livingston-Wheeler published her book, "Chicken; Cancer in Every Pet." She stated that cancer is almost 100% transmitted through the DNA and into the eggs. We don't use eggs in our dog food."*

Truth Response: So chicken and eggs cause cancer in every pet. Simple enough. All an owner has to do is feed Company A's product, which has fish and lamb, and there never need be a worry about cancer. This is Nobel Prize stuff.

Company A: *"In the U.S., many poultry farmers put ethoxyquin into the chicken's drinking water. Ethoxyquin is rated as a hazardous chemical by its manufacturer. It is supposed to make the egg yolk a brighter yellow, so you will think you are getting fresh eggs when you're not."*

Truth Response: Ethoxyquin is an antioxidant used to preserve vitamins and prevent fat rancidity, not a drinking water additive. Ethoxyquin is not used to make the yolk *"yellow,"* that is merely a side effect. Ethoxyquin is not considered a hazardous chemical by the manufacturer unless improperly used. It is a food additive.*

Company A: *"In the U.S., many poultry farms put female growth hormones into chicken feed to produce big-breasted chickens for the fast food industry for chicken breast sandwiches. However, doctors are now seeing young boys developing breasts, small sexual organs and low sperm count. Young girls, as young as eight years of age, are experiencing their periods."*

---

* Monsanto Company, St. Louis, MO.

Truth Response: *"Female growth hormones"* are not fed to chickens.[1] Chickens have not been proven to cause breast development in boys and early menses in girls. These are incredible, outrageous and irresponsible claims – all to get you to buy their pet food.

Company A: *"The May 26, 1991 Atlantic Journal-Constitution Magazine warned about eating chicken. The magazine interviewed 84 Federal poultry inspectors in five states in the U.S. 'Every week, they found millions of chickens leaking yellow pus, stained by green feces, and contaminated by harmful bacteria and marred by lung and heart infections and cancerous tumors. These chickens were shipped out for (human) consumption. The inspectors no longer eat chicken.'"*

Truth Response: Lay magazines are not the source of sound science. Horror tales can be told about what is seen in every meat processing plant – including those which process the *"pus,"* *"cancerous,"* and *"feces"*-contaminated carcasses in the lamb and fish for Company A.

Company A: *"Chicken by-products may be beak, feet and feathers. Digest is the full guts of the chicken – including any manure in the chicken when it is slaughtered."*

Truth Response: Good quality chicken by-products do not contain heads, feet and feathers.[1] Are we to believe that Company A's product contains prime fish fillets and racks of lamb? It's a real good bet they use *"by-products"* too. The ad doesn't really get into what they use, just creates a chicken bogeyman, which can only be vanquished by Company A products.

The definition of poultry by-products is "free from fecal matter," according to AAFCO.[2] Company A is either deliberately promoting a falsehood, or ignorant of basic ingredient composition.

Digest may or may not contain the *"full guts."* So what if it did? The natural diet of carnivores is the *"full guts"* of their prey, often the

---

1. USDA Food Safety and Inspection Service, "Focus on: Chicken, Consumer Education and Information," September 2000.
2. Association of American Feed Control Officials, 1998 Official Publication.

preferred first part of the meal.[1] Is Company A really advocating a natural diet or only interested in sensational arguments and hyperbole?

Company A: *"In December 1997, China slaughtered a million and a half chickens. E. coli and Salmonella were found in chickens and ducks there. Some people died. Cooking chicken does not kill these diseases. It only deactivates them for a while. That is why at Thanksgiving, you are told to refrigerate the turkey after it is carved. Room temperature activates these diseases."*

Truth Response: E. coli and Salmonella can be found in any carcass, including fish and lamb. Heat does kill pathogenic organisms.[2]

True, turkeys should be refrigerated. Do fish and lamb not have to be refrigerated?

Company A: *"To help eliminate this perceived or real allergy, (Company A) has replaced the yeast with flax meal."*

Truth Response: Any ingredient, not just yeast, can cause allergy. Removing ingredients because a misinformed public thinks "yeast causes allergy" shows that the producer is following, not leading.

Company A: *"...the risk of cancer is increased by 69% if you use sunflower, safflower, or corn oil. (Company A) never uses these oils in their products. But some other dog food companies do use sunflower."*

Truth Response: Precisely 69%? Sunflower and safflower oil do not cause cancer unless improperly processed, left unstabilized or fed in excess.

Company A: *"No matter what other dog food companies tell you, it is a waste of money to buy dog foods that list probiotics and digestive enzymes on the label. These are killed at*

---

1. Wysong RL, "Rationale for Archetype™," 2002. Tabor RK, <u>The Wild Life of the Domestic Cat</u>. Purves WK et al, <u>Life – The Science Of Biology</u>, 1992. Busch RH, <u>The Wolf Almanac</u>, 1998. Ewer RF, <u>The Carnivores</u>, 1973. *J Wildl Manage*, 1972; 36:3. *J Wildl Manage*, 1980; 44(3):583-602. *J Mammal*, 1977; 4:2. *Aust Wildl Res*, 1983; 10:3. *Aust Wildl Res*, 1983; 10:3.
2. Neidhardt FC, <u>Escherichia Coli and Salmonella: Cellular and Molecular</u>, 1999.

120° and dog foods are cooked at 325°. Also, some companies say they mix the enzymes with oil and spray them on after the temperature drops below 120°. Not possible! The food must be cooled before it is bagged. As the oil cools, the probiotics and enzymes separate from the oils and fall to the floor of the mill."

Truth Response: Probiotics and enzymes are certainly not a waste of money. Abundant research proves this.* It is an absurd claim that probiotics and enzymes mixed with oils *"fall to the floor of the mill"* if cooled. Wysong has successfully enrobed dry foods by this method for years. This producer is, again, either deliberately misleading, or does not know the first thing about food processing.

Company A: *"...(Company A's product) takes 22 days to get into the body. That is the rate of change in cells."*

Truth Response: *"22 days"* to get into the body? Exactly? Where's the evidence for that? What does *"Company A's product," "22 days,"* and *"rate of change in cells"* have to do with anything? Nothing, because there is neither logical nor scientific sense here.

Company A: *"White dogs absorb much ultra-violet light. This drains the immune system. (Company A's product) will help."*

Truth Response: Company A's product helps white dogs prevent immune system drainage from ultraviolet light? Where is the proof? Why has nature created perfectly fit creatures such as white birds, arctic foxes and polar bears that survive just fine without Company A's product?

Company A: *"Dogs are 11% trace minerals and 4% vitamins."*

---

* *Wysong Health Letter,* "Competitive Exclusion for Control of Infection," 1999; 13(9):1-3. *Wysong Companion Animal Health Letter,* "Probiotics for Crohn's and Cancer," 1997(1). Wysong RL, "Biotic™ Means Life," 2002. Wysong RL, "Rationale for Probiotic Supplements," 2002. Wysong RL, "Rationale for Enzyme Supplements," 2002. *J Allergy Clin Immunol,* 2002; 109(1):119-21. *Am J Clin Nutr,* 2001; 74(6):833-9. *Curr Gastroenterol Rep,* 2001; 3(4):343-50. *Am J Clin Nutr,* 2001; 73(6):1147S-1151S. *J Ren Nutr,* 2002;12(2):76-86. *Gut,* 1998; 43:196-202. *Cancer Chemother Pharmacol,* 2001; 47 Suppl:S55-63. Howell E, <u>Enzyme Nutrition</u>, 1986.

Truth Response: There is not a shred of evidence anywhere that *"Dogs are 11% trace minerals and 4% vitamins."* Isn't there a little fat and protein there, too?

Company A: *"As the arsenate passes through, it takes the arsenic out with it. So the arsenic is not absorbed."*

Truth Response: Arsenate is not an antidote for arsenic poisoning. Arsenate is a potent toxin used in pesticides and as a preservative. It also induces cancer. Arsenic, on the other hand, is at low levels beneficial to health.[1]

Company A: *"If you look under a microscope at a molecule of whole blood and a molecule of chlorophyll, there is only one atom difference."*

Truth Response: Whole blood is not a molecule. It is millions of molecules.[2] Don't bother looking for a molecule since such cannot be seen with the naked eye using a microscope. Would you trust someone to draft your will who had not learned the alphabet, a plumber who did not understand the difference between water or electricity, or a surgeon who thought heart removal would cure high blood pressure? Why entrust your pet's health to those who do not know elementary science? And, incidentally, chlorophyll differs from hemoglobin by more that one *"atom."*[2]

Company A: *"The processing of (Company A's product) takes place in Scotland. We no longer get our kelp from Norway since the Chernobyl meltdown. The meltdown caused radiation contamination."*

Truth Response: If Chernobyl contaminated Norway (Is this where Chernobyl is?), what's so clean about Scotland, a close neighbor?

Company A: *"They say they use Vitamin E (tocopherols) as a preservative. But that lasts only 30 days."*

---

1. Morris C, <u>Inorganic Chemistry</u>. 1992.
2. Stryer L, <u>Biochemistry</u>, 1995. Nelson DL et al, <u>Lehninger Principles of Biochemistry, Third Edition</u>, 2000.

Truth Response: Science has proven that vitamin E tocopherols can exert antioxidant effects much longer than *"30 days."* [1]

Company A: *"We can prove there is no ethoxyquin, no BHA, no BHT in our dog food, because we use the vacuum-packed bags."*

Truth Response: Vacuum packaging does not prove the absence of such chemicals. Also, what about Company A's products which are not vacuum packed? Also, what about the fact that ethoxyquin is commonly used in fish meal, an ingredient in Company A's products?

Company A: *"...corn and soybeans were to be fed **only** to food producing animals, but never to companion animals or people."*

Truth Response: Humans and animals have consumed corn and soybeans for thousands of years.

Company A: *"(Company A) is the **only** dog food company that is a member of the Organic Trade Association."*

Truth Response: Anyone can belong to the Organic Trade Association. [2] Why take credit for organic, when Company A's products are not organic?

Company A: *"(Company A)'s dog foods use no chemical preservatives... We use the natural preservative of rosemary in our oils."*

Truth Response: The active components in rosemary are chemical preservatives. [3]

Company A: *"(Company A's product) contains blueberries. It helps with bladder and kidney struvite stones. It acidifies the*

1. *Poult Sci*, 1996; 75(8):1039-46. *J Anim Sci*, 1997; 75(10):2634-40.
2. Organic Trade Association, PO Box 547, Greenfield, MA 01302, (413)774-7511.
3. Wysong RL, "Oxherphol™ Technical Information," 2002. *Int J Food Sci Nutr*, 2000; 51(5):327-39. *Int J Food Microbiol*, 1997; 37(2-3):155-62. *J Agric Food Chem*, 2001; 49(11):5560-5. *J Food Prot*, 2001; 64(9):1412-9. *J Agric Food Chem*, 2000; 48(11):5548-56. *J Food Prot*, 2000; 63(10):1359-68.

stones and helps to prevent FUS in cats or feline Urinary Syndrome or FLUD. It works the same in dogs. These struvite stones/crystals are the result of a too alkalis system. Blueberries are acid. It helps to dissolve the crystals."

Truth Response: There is no evidence that blueberries prevent urinary stone problems in pets. Stones are caused by many factors, not just a *"too alkalis* (sic) *system."* [1]

Company A: *"The chondroiten molecules are so large that they can't be absorbed. The American Association of Feed Controls has never approved these ingredients in pet food."*

Truth Response: *"Chondroiten"* (sic) molecules can in fact be digested and assimilated to benefit joint health.[2] AAFCO approval of ingredients is certainly not the measure of their health benefits. Additionally, Company A has used many ingredients not approved by AAFCO.

1. Wysong RL, "Biotic™ Means Life," 2002. *J Nutr*, 1994; 124(12 Suppl):2643S-2651S. *J Nutr*, 1998; 128(12 Suppl):2753S-2757S. *Vet Clin North Am Small Anim Pract*, 1996; 26(2):169-79. *J Endourol*, 1999; 13(9):659-63. *J Am Anim Hosp Assoc*, 1999; 35(4):297-301. *J Am Vet Med Assoc*, 1995; 207(11):1429-34. *Int Urol Nephrol*, 1994; 26(5):485-95. *J Am Vet Med Assoc*, 1996; 208(4):547-51. *Urol Clin North Am*, 2000; 27(2):287-99.
2. *Wysong Health Letter*, "Chicken Cartilage for Rheumatoid Arthritis," 1994; 8(1). Wysong RL, "Rationale for Contifin™, Glucosamine Complex™ & Arthegic™," 2002. Clouatre D, Glucosamine Sulfate and Chondroitin Sulfate, 1999. *J Am Med Assoc*, 2000; 283(11):1469-75. *Prog Drug Res*, 2000;55:81-

—30—

COMPANY B[1] VS. THE TRUTH

(RESPONSE TO COMPANY B'S WEBSITE CRITIQUE OF WYSONG)

The following is a listing of ingredients claimed not to be in Company B's foods because they are "unfavorable" for health, according to their "research" (unidentified):

Company B: *"Ground Corn...is a common cause of food allergies in pets and is not used in (Company B)'s products."*

Truth Response: Research has shown that corn is not the *"cause"* of allergy, but rather, many allergies result from a compromised immune system due to singular reliance on so-called "100% complete" foods such as Company B's product.[2] Rotating through various foods, some with, some without corn, is the best preventive and "cure" for allergy. Company B also ignores the fact that hybrid, high-lysine, hypoallergenic corn varieties can be used. This also makes their strawman comparisons invalid.

Company B: *"Poultry Fat is a byproduct of meat processing. The origin of the contributing animals is never known; the source can be any fowl (turkey, chicken, geese, buzzard, etc.) and the resulting oil is very low in linoleic acid... (Company B) uses high quality Chicken Fat which has the highest levels of linoleic acid."*

---

1. Name of company withheld to be kind.
2. *Wysong Health Letter*, "Food Allergies," 1998; 12(5):1-2. *Wysong Health Letter*, "Pets Allergic to Everything," 1997; 11(9):3-4. *Allerg Immunol (Paris)*, 2001; 33(9):351-6. *Tierarztl Prax*, 1993; 21(1):53-6. *J Am Vet Med Assoc*, 1991; 198(2):245-50.

Truth Response: Poultry fat is not a *"byproduct."* Company B claims poultry fat is inferior, yet Company B products contain chicken fat (isn't chicken poultry?), which is as much a *"byproduct"* as anyone else's poultry or chicken fat.

Fat from various species of poultry provides a broader spectrum of nutrients than fat from a single species (chicken). Poultry fat does not come from *"buzzards."* Talk about hyperbole and sensationalism!

Animals are not so much deficient in linoleic acid, an omega 6 fatty acid, as they are deficient in omega 3's. Linoleic acid at high levels (as claimed in Company B's product) is proinflammatory, thus promoting the allergic reactions Company B's product is supposed to prevent.* A better choice is high levels of antiinflammatory omega 3's and phytonutrients which help prevent allergic reactions.

Company B: *"Whole ground extruded soybeans are used in some foods as a supplemental protein ingredient. Although the product has been processed to eliminate the 'bloat' often associated with soybeans, this ingredient can still pose a problem for animals allergic to soy."*

Truth Response: Whole extruded soybeans are not used as a protein supplement, but rather because of their high content of omega 3 fatty acids, lecithin, and important phytoestrogens.

Foods with high levels of fresh meat do not need soy for *"supplemental protein."*

True, some animals are allergic to soy (very few), but so too can they be allergic to every one of Company B's ingredients.

Company B: *"Most pet food ingredients contain enough sodium to meet a dog or cat's nutritional needs. The salt in the (Company B) products comes only from the natural ingredients. We do not add salt as a flavor enhancer."*

Truth Response: Salt from ancient geologic sources containing dozens of trace minerals commonly deficient in modern human and animal

---

* Wysong RL, <u>Lipid Nutrition – Understanding Fats and Oils in Health and Disease</u>, 1990.

processed diets is not the same as refined table salt.[1] Such salt is not added to increase sodium levels or flavor as Company B suggests.

Company B: *"Dried Kelp is seaweed from the families Laminariacae and Fucaeae which has been dried. Kelp is added to pet foods primarily as a source of iodine, but it can be very high in salt and potassium. (Company B) does not add kelp or other salty ingredients to any of its foods."*

Truth Response: What purpose does stating Latin names for kelp families serve? Kelp is an excellent natural source of iodine and many other trace minerals.[2] Potassium is universally deficient in modern processed diets.[3] If kelp is high in potassium, that is a reason to include it, not exclude it as Company B suggests.

Company B: *"Yeast Culture is an unnecessary flavoring ingredient, used in inexpensive pet foods in an attempt to compensate for a lack of real food flavors. In addition, yeast is an allergen for some animals."*

Truth Response: Yeast culture is not used as a *"flavoring ingredient,"* but as a rich source of naturally complexed vitamins, active enzymes, mannanoligosaccharides and immune stimulating glucans.[4] Company B does not seem to even know what the ingredient is.

Company B: *"Chicken digest is a palatability enhancer... (Company B)'s products have their own satisfying flavors that come from natural human grade ingredients that are used."*

1. Wysong RL, "Rationale for Whole Salt™," 2002. *Price-Pottenger Nutrition Foundation Health Journal*, 1999; 21(2):574. *J Amer Coll Nutr*, 1987; 6(3):261-70.
2. Lerr WR, Kelp, Dulse, and Other Sea Supplements, 1983. *Z Ernahrungswiss*, 1998; 37(3):288-93. *Arch Latinoam Nutr*, 1998; 48(3):260-4. *Nippon Eiseigaku Zasshi*, 1990; 45(3):795-800.
3. *J Am Vet Med Assoc*, 1987; 191:1563-8. *Clin Chem*, 1987; 33(4):518-23. *J Am Vet Med Assoc*, 1989; 194(11):1604-8. *S Afr Med J*, 1982; 61(24):929-30.
4. Dickenson JR et al, The Metabolism and Molecular Physiology of Saccharomyces Cerevisiae, 1998. *Am J Clin Nutr*, 1999; 70(2):208-12. *Biosci Biotechnol Biochem*, 2001; 65(4):837-841. *J Biol Chem*, 2000; 275(40):30987-95. *J Dairy Sci*, 1998; 81(5):1353-7. *Poult Sci*, 2000; 79(2):205-11.

Truth Response: Digest is a food that has been broken down (digested) by enzymes. The process predigests complex proteins, rendering them more digestible and palatable. High quality digests are extraordinarily nutrient dense and very expensive.[1]

Company B: *"Chicken Meal is considered to be the single best source of protein in commercial pet foods. (Company B) uses high quality, low ash chicken meal extensively. This ingredient is very digestible, very palatable, and very expensive."*

Truth Response: Most high quality foods use low ash poultry meal, so this is not a unique Company B feature. Chicken meal is not the best source of protein. The best source of protein is whole fresh chicken minus the feathers, not just rendered (cooked twice) chicken meal, meat and skin as in Company B's product. Egg, incidentally, is the most complete form of protein, not chicken meal.[2]

Company B: *"(Company B) uses table-quality cottage cheese, straight from its retail container. The cottage cheese has only trace amounts of lactose and because of its limited inclusion in the formula, the ultimate amount of lactose in the finished product is insignificant and would not be in sufficient supply to cause an intolerance problem."*

Truth Response: Are we to understand that someone hand scoops cottage cheese out of retail containers into Company B products? Extruded foods, such as Company B's product, are produced at many tons per hour. Company B does not explain how such retail package hand scooping is compatible with production rates at several tons per hour. What does *"straight from its retail container"* have to do with good nutrition? If it is used at *"insignificant"* levels, say one *"retail container"* per ton, what's the point other than label dressing?

---

1. Association of American Feed Control Officials, <u>1998 Official Publication</u>.
2. Food and Agricultural Organization of the United Nations, Joint FAO/WHO Expert Group on Protein Requirements "FAO Nut meeting," Rep Series No 37, W.H.O. TRS 301, 1965. McCance et al, <u>The Composition of Foods</u>, 2001. Sim JS et al, <u>Egg Nutrition and Biotechnology</u>, 1999. Burley RW et al, <u>The Avian Egg: Chemistry and Biology</u>, 1989.

Company B: *"(Company B) uses only high quality lamb meat from New Zealand, not the lamb by-products found in some other pet foods."*

Truth Response: Are we to believe Company B adds lamb chops and racks of lamb to their products at a retail price of approximately $10.00 or more per pound? How could this be when Company B foods cost about $1.00 per pound retail, and half that at wholesale? Company B needs to describe exactly what the special *"high quality"* lamb product is to explain this conundrum.

Company B: *"The chicken (Company B) uses is not only human grade, but also tested to be free of hormones, antibiotics and pesticides, as well as chemical preservatives such as BHA, BHT and ethoxyquin... (Company B) uses only fresh, whole fruits and vegetables, like you would buy at the grocery store, in our foods."*

Truth Response: Human grade can mean by-products from human grade processing. These are the same *"human grade"* ingredients virtually all other manufacturers use. If Company B means their ingredients are human grade right from the grocery store, then it must be explained how they can process, package, and ship their products for far less cost than the price of these ingredients, and why most of their ingredients are not found in the grocery store. (Incidentally, as of this printing, the phrase "human grade" has not even been approved by pet food regulators.[1-2])

Company B: *"Glucosamine, together with Chondroitin Sulfate, is believed to stimulate the rebuilding of the cartilage matrix and to play a role in the fight against osteoarthritis."*

Truth Response: Properly formulated foods using fresh meat, tendon, cartilage and bone contain natural sources of proteoglycans and all classes of collagen, providing excellent building block nutrition for joints and all connective tissues. If Company B is using isolated or synthetic glucosamines and chondroitin, then their products are illegal since these are unapproved ingredients at this time.[2]

---

1. *Petfood Industry*, March 2002:79.
2. Association of American Feed Control Officials, <u>1998 Official Publication</u>.

Company B: *"Natural Flavors are minimally processed flavor ingredients that do not contain synthetic or artificial components. (Company B) uses only quality Chicken broth as a Natural Flavor in (Company B's product). This is much like a reduced broth you would use in making your own gravy to intensify the flavor of the food naturally. A proprietary blend of herbs and spices is used as a Natural Flavor in (Company B) products."*

Truth Response: If Company B's product is made of such outstanding ingredients, why must it be spiked with *"flavor ingredients"*? Company B criticizes other manufacturers for using flavorings, so why do they use them? Why wouldn't hand-dipped cottage cheese, buzzard-free fat and human levels of vitamins be sufficient?

Company B: *"Sodium Ascorbate is a non-acidic form of Vitamin C. Vitamin C cannot be stored by the body, so it must be replaced every day. Sodium Ascorbate has a neutral (non-acid) pH, making it safer for sensitive stomachs."*

Truth Response: Company B is using human nutrition guidelines erroneously for feeding cats and dogs. For humans, vitamin C is an essential vitamin. For cats and dogs, it is not, since they are capable of synthesizing it. If Company B does not understand this fundamental principle, why should consumers trust their expertise in making a "100% complete and balanced" food? (This is not to suggest vitamin C could not benefit cats and dogs under certain circumstances, but this is not because cats and dogs require human vitamin levels as Company B argues.)

Company B: *"Apples provide important 'protector' nutrients, as well as plenty of carbohydrates and fiber — essential for your pet's good health. (Company B) uses fresh, whole Washington apples, right out of the box, like you would find in the produce section at your local market... Carrots provide flavor and important nutrients, including 'protector' antioxidants. (Company B) uses only fresh, whole fruits and vegetables, fit for human consumption. (Company B)'s* *carrots are not pre-processed, so they retain the healthy qualities of the foods you serve at your own table."*

Truth Response: These ingredients are evidently included to appeal to human food folklore, such as "an apple a day…" and "carrots for the eyes." Although cats and dogs may benefit some from occasional fruits and vegetables – a practice recommended using the real fresh, whole form – once these ingredients have gone through processing they are diminished nutritionally and are certainly not required for *"carbohydrates and fiber."*

Company B: *"Whole Steamed Potatoes are freshly-cooked Idaho and russet potatoes."*

Truth Response: In actual fact, all extruded ingredients in Company B's product are *"steamed"* just like what occurs with all other extruded pet foods. Company B needs to explain what exactly the merits of *"Idaho"* and *"russet"* *"steamed"* potatoes are.

Company B has selected a few features to try to frame an attack against Wysong on their website, but neglects many important features.

For example, the Wysong feeding program is characterized by:
- High digestibility
- Easily tolerated by allergic companion animals
- High in natural chondroitin, glucosamine and collagen for joint and connective tissue health
- Active enzymes
- Probiotic cultures and probiotic-enhancing artichoke and garlic oligosaccharides (prebiotics)
- Chelated and naturally complexed minerals and 74 trace mineral natural sea salt
- Natural pepper extract, which enhances vitamin and mineral utilization by as much as 250%
- Fruit extracts for antioxidant and antimicrobial activity
- Most bioavailable forms of vitamins

- Specific design to optimize health – not simply meet regulatory standards

- Nutrient dense to optimize health – not least-cost, nutrient-depleted food fractions

- Specialized processing to protect fragile nutrients – not production only to maximize profitability

- An emphasis on naturally complexed nutrients – not just isolated synthetics

- Fresh, non-processed living food ingredients – not food devoid of all living elements

- Freedom from non-nutritional ingredients – not additives merely to create color, texture, taste, smell, stool consistency or shelf-life

- Fresh meats, whole ingredients – not just pre-rendered by-products and grain fractions

- Nutrient preservation with natural antioxidants (Oxherphol™), Nutri-Pak™ oxygen- and light-barrier packaging, and fats and oils purged with oxygen – not synthetic preservatives in permeable paper and plastic packaging with contents easily spoiled by oxygen and light (see pages 64-67).

These features are far more important, if health is the objective, than *"straight from its retail container," "table quality," "steamed," "human vitamins," "food groups," "human grade,"* and...last but not least, *"buzzard"*-free.

—31—

COMPANY C* VS. THE TRUTH

(RESPONSE TO MATERIAL [CHART AND FOOTNOTES] CIRCULATED AT A NATIONAL VETERINARY CONVENTION BY COMPANY C)

Company C: *The chart states that Wysong Maintenance™ contains ground whole corn as the first and primary ingredient.*

Truth Response: This is incorrect. The first ingredient is chicken, which is the entire chicken minus the feathers. All other foods that they list, including Product C, contain yellow corn as the primary ingredient. Dogs are not herbivores. They are carnivores. It is universally understood that meat products are superior to ground yellow corn for the canine. Meat products can be seven to ten times more costly per pound than ground yellow corn.

Company C: *States that Wysong products are not in compliance with AAFCO regulations.*

Truth Response: States require AAFCO compliance in order for a product to be sold. Wysong products are registered in every state in the country by registrars who do whatever is necessary to maintain compliance (even though we disagree with much of it). Company C does not indicate how the Wysong label is not in compliance; they simply make the unsupported claim that it is not.

---

* Name of company withheld to be kind.

Company C: *States their product contains Ester-C.*

Truth Response: This is a mineral polyascorbate, a calcium chelate of ascorbic acid. It is a synthetic compound, derived from synthetic ascorbic acid. How does this support the Company C claim to *"natural"*?

Company C: *Implies their ingredient listing is better than Wysong.*

Truth Response: Of the first four ingredients in this comparison, the second and fourth entries in Company C's product are rendered meat products, while the first ingredient in Wysong Maintenance is chicken (fresh, whole).

All seven of the first Wysong ingredients (Chicken, Ground Corn, Ground Wheat, Ground Brown Rice, Ground Oat Groats, Poultry Fat, and Ground Extruded Whole Soybeans) are substantial, high quality, highly expensive, whole food ingredients. Of the first seven ingredients in Company C's product (Ground Yellow Corn, Poultry Meal, Ground Whole Wheat, Meat Meal, Animal Fat, Oatmeal, Beet Pulp, Dried Kelp), three are questionable in value as primary ingredients: animal fat, beet pulp, and dried kelp. Fat is of course necessary, but it is an empty calorie source. Beet pulp is simply a by-product fiber source and dried kelp must be in the diet at very low levels as an herbal mineral source.

Company C: *Animal fat is listed as being preserved with Vitamin E (D-alpha tocopherol) and Vitamin C.*

Truth Response: D-alpha tocopherol is a poor food antioxidant.* It is readily degraded by heat and, although a good *in vivo* antioxidant, it is not the preferred natural food antioxidant. A better choice is Oxherphol™, which consists predominantly of the delta and gamma epimers of vitamin E, which are proven to be highly effective food antioxidants. Company C also states that they use vitamin C to preserve fat. Vitamin C is not soluble in fat, therefore, how can it preserve fat? In order to solubilize vitamin C in fat, if this is what the company is doing, they must use agents such as propylene glycol, but this is not listed on the label, and is not a

---

* Wysong RL, "Oxherphol™ Technical Information," 2002. *Chem Phys Lipids*, 1984; 35(3):185-98. *J Agric Food Chem*, 2000; 48(8):3130-40. *J Agric Food Chem*, 2001; 49(4):1724-9. *Nahrung*, 2000; 44(6):431-3.

natural food ingredient. If they are using other means to accomplish this, it is not explained. Therefore, one must wonder how effectively the fats are stabilized. If they are not stabilized, the foods have the potential of generating peroxide free radicals, which are far more dangerous than if synthetic preservatives were used.

Company C: *Recommends considerably less food per pound of body weight than any other manufacturer.*

Truth Response: From a logical standpoint it appears that these comparisons must certainly be in error since Company C is using corn and other less expensive, low nutrient ingredients as primary ingredients. In their first ingredients they have wheat, fat, and beet pulp. It would be difficult to believe that it would require 25 to 50% less of Company C's product to maintain the same dog as one being fed a food where the first three ingredients are high quality meat and whole food sources.

Company C: *Does not add copper to their products because of its potential harm. They reason that copper occurs naturally in grains, meat, and salt, and therefore is not necessary as a supplement.*

Truth Response: By the same reasoning, no vitamin or mineral would be required to be added or fortified into pet foods since all nutrients occur naturally in all natural foodstuffs. They do not allow for the alteration, complexing, and losses that occur inevitably as a result of all processing. Although it would be best to not have to add any fortification to a food, it is not apparent from what Company C has done to their food that they have removed the possibility of deficiency of this nutrient as a result of either formulation or processing. Certain genetic predispositions to concentrating liver copper occur in a percentage of some breeds such as Bedlington Terriers and West Highland White Terriers, but this accounts for an extremely small fraction of pets and does not justify alteration of pet foods designed for all breeds. On the other hand, there are other breeds, such as the Malamute, which can have a predisposition to copper deficiency.* Copper participates in dozens of critical enzyme functions and the risk of deficiency exceeds the risk of excess.

---

* *J Am Vet Med Assoc*, 1988; 192(1):52-56; 190(6):654; *Companion Anim Prac*, 2(7):3.

Company C: *Purports that dairy products, including dried whey, which is used in dry Wysong Maintenance, may contribute to diarrhea or loose stools due to lactose (milk sugar) intolerance.*

Truth Response: We have seen no proof to associate loose stool to whey. Whey and other dairy products are used effectively in many pet foods without complication. A Company C brochure states *"Our formula includes fresh milled grains, quality beef, fish and poultry, dairy products…"* since they previously stated that dairy products cause diarrhea, why are they criticizing others who use dairy products?

Company C: *Claims that poultry fat cannot be preserved.*

Truth Response: Poultry fat can be preserved effectively with Oxherphol™. In tests against synthetics, Oxherphol™ proved as or more effective in maintaining poultry fat against oxidative degradation.[1]

Company C: *Claims that the only mineral chelates allowed by AAFCO in pet foods are those used in (Company C) products.*

Truth Response: This is incorrect, since the ultimate mineral chelate is that which is part of natural ingredients themselves. In documented studies using mineral complexes derived from yeast culture, which is an approved AAFCO ingredient, minerals have been shown to be absorbed and retained much better than those from either synthetic chelates, such as Albion's, or inorganic mineral sources.[2] If Albion is the only chelate allowed, why is Company C using Inter-Cal Ester-C™, which is also a chelate? Does this mean the Company C's label is not approved by AAFCO?

Company C: *States that rice bran is high in fat and must be stabilized, and if the fat is removed, it is removed with the use of solvents, making it "unnatural."*

---

1. Wysong RL, "Oxherphol™ Technical Information," 2002. *Food Tech*, 1982; 6:1-6.
2. Southgate DAT et al, <u>Nutrient Availability: Chemical and Biological Aspects</u>, 1989. *Proceeding on Mineral Elements*, 1981:615-621. *Nutrition Reports International*, 1987; 36(3). *Nutritional Reports International*, 1985; 32(1).

Truth Response: The fact that rice bran contains fat and must be stabilized is irrelevant. The main danger is not the fat, but the inherent lipases, which can degrade fats. These enzymes are inactivated with heat.[1]

Company C: *Claims their foods contain "heat stabilized vitamin and chelated mineral supplements."*

Truth Response: Natural vitamins and minerals are by nature heat sensitive.

Company C: *"We're extremely generous with linoleic acid, a super smooth blend of animal and vegetable fats essential for healthy, shiny coats."*

Truth Response: It is not clear what *"super smooth"* means. It is also not clear that high levels of linoleic are what pets at present need, since all pet foods that are grain-based likely contain a surplus of this omega 6 fatty acid. The predominance of omega 6 fatty acids in the diet is believed to result in tipping the scales toward increased arachidonic acid cascade metabolism, which can result in a wide range of inflammatory and immune disorders.[1-2]

Company C: *Claims their older dog formulas use high quality proteins in small amounts so that the kidneys are not "overworked."*

Truth Response: There is no evidence that older dogs cannot utilize high amounts of high quality protein. In a controlled clinical study, older dogs even with one kidney removed experienced no difference in kidney function whether on 18% or 34% protein.[3] Once the kidneys are compromised, then perhaps lower levels of protein are important. This is not the same as saying high levels of high quality protein, which is common in the natural carnivore, predisposes them to kidney disease. They produce no evidence to prove their claim.

---

1. Wysong RL, Lipid Nutrition – Understanding Fats and Oils in Health and Disease, 1990.
2. *Metabolism*, 2002; 51(3):327-33. *Am J Clin Nutr*, 2002; 75(1):119-25. *Metabolism*, 1998; 47(5):566-72. *Metabolism*, 2000; 49(8):1006-13. *Nutrition*, 2001; 17(7-8):669-73. *Eur J Gastroenterol Hepatol*, 2001; 13(2):93-5. *Nutrition*, 2002; 18(3):235-40.
3. *Am J Vet Res*, 1994; 55(9):1282-90.

Company C: *In their feline formula, they tout "low ash, low magnesium."*

Truth Response: This follows the marketing thrust of other companies. It is not ash and magnesium that are the singular causes of urinary stones (FUS/FLUD) in cats. The ability of a diet to generate an acid urine is the primary consideration in this disease, if it is diet induced. Additionally, FUS/FLUD is a multifaceted condition that can have an etiology ranging beyond dietary considerations.*

To evaluate the true merit of any food, many criteria must be used, including:

What is the philosophic objective of the product? Company C states that they wish to scientifically design pet foods using natural ingredients. This is commendable, but what do they mean by science? What do they mean by natural? "Science" tells us that there are no differences between natural and synthetic nutrients. "Science" also tells us that a manufacturer can claim their food is "100% complete" if it simply meets NRC minimums. Since minimums have only been set for fewer than half of the known essential nutrients, is "science" the best criteria? We do not suggest that science cannot or should not be used; it is just a question of what is the "science" being used? This is not stated in Company C literature. The word is merely name-dropped.

Using "natural ingredients" provides wide latitude by their definition. Company C uses synthetic mineral chelates, synthetic vitamins, food fractions, and inferior by-products. The better question is: Does the food approach, as closely as possible, the diet of a carnivore in the wild?

Once the philosophic objectives are clearly stated by a producer, it is important for them to outline exactly how they have been consistent with their objectives. In other words, what specific actions, innovations, and

---

* Wysong RL, "Biotic™ Means Life," 2002. *J Nutr*, 1994; 124(12 Suppl):2643S-2651S. *J Nutr*, 1998; 128(12 Suppl):2753S-2757S. *Vet Clin North Am Small Anim Pract*, 1996; 26(2):169-79. *J Endourol*, 1999; 13(9):659-63. *J Am Anim Hosp Assoc*, 1999; 35(4):297-301. *J Am Vet Med Assoc*, 1995; 207(11):1429-34. *Int Urol Nephrol*, 1994; 26(5):485-95. *J Am Vet Med Assoc*, 1996; 208(4):547-51. *Urol Clin North Am*, 2000; 27(2):287-99.

creations have they made that set their products apart from others and makes them consistent with their stated objectives? In examining Company C's literature, no significant health innovation in the formulation, ingredient selection, or processing is revealed.

It is important to be able to examine literature and documentation from a producer that demonstrates their level of competence. Literature I have been presented with from this company, as sent to us from customers, provides no scientific documentation, but plenty of incorrect comparisons, contradictions, and unsubstantiated claims.

—32—

COMPANY D[1] VS. THE TRUTH

This producer advocates breed-specific formulations to match each breed with the perfect, "100% complete" diet it uniquely requires. Examples of breed-specific, nutritionally-related disorders include zinc-responsive dermatitis in huskies and malamutes, vitamin A-responsive dermatitis in cocker spaniels, lethal acrodermatitis in bull terriers from zinc and/or copper, copper storage disease in Bedlington terriers, and skeletal abnormalities in large breeds fed free-choice high caloric density foods, to list a few. The argument that different breeds may have different requirements may be true, but no more true than that different humans have different requirements and different animals within a breed have different requirements. This is biochemical individuality and was first described by Dr. Roger Williams (the discoverer of vitamin B_5) decades ago, and used as a strong argument against those who would rely on "standards" for determining "average" nutritional requirements for everyone.[2] There is not a logical or empirical basis for specifically setting nutrient standards for any group within a population.

Nutrition is individual. Every organism is genetically unique. Further, science cannot determine with exactness what the requirements are for every single creature, much less whole populations, species, breeds, etc. The same can be said with regard to what is or is not toxic for what species (breed), and at what levels.

For example, one could state that collies require 270 IU's of vitamin D per kilogram. What specific collie are we talking about? Again we must ask: how big, what age, and what precisely is in the rest of its diet? What is its metabolic rate? What is its digestive capacity? How much sun

---

1. Name of company withheld to be kind.
2. Williams RJ, <u>Biochemical Individuality: The Basis for the Genetotrophic Concept</u>, 1998. Williams RJ et al, <u>The Biochemistry of B Vitamins</u>, 1998.

and exercise does it get? What is the source of its water? What is the quality of the air it breathes? What are its social interactions? What specific genetic strengths and weaknesses does it have? Are its foods heated, exposed to oxygen and light? What about the interactions between the food ingredients when they are heated?

These considerations are all important, just like "breed," in determining nutrient needs. Breed-specific logic is just another version of the flawed reasoning of the pet food industry – that nutritionists can create 100% perfect foods because they "know" how many IU's of vitamin D (etc.) an animal needs. Such fabricated diets based on scientific requirements (only valid until the scientific board meets the next time) have caused immeasurable disease and suffering for companion animals.

The following is a response to letters directly to Wysong from Company D:

Company D: *Any pet food containing vitamin C is guilty of making their food toxic. Pet food manufacturers use a synthetic coal tar derivative of vitamin C which is different molecularly from natural vitamin C. Synthetic vitamin C is in the D (toxic) form. Synthetic vitamin C is closer to ascorbyl palmitate.*

Truth Response: Vitamin C is not a synthetic *"coal tar derivative."* Ascorbic acid (vitamin C) is synthesized from sugars such as dextrose. If basic biochemistry is not understood, why should animal owners believe infallibility when it comes to creating food recipes for them?

Natural vitamin C is different from the synthetic form not because it is a *"coal tar derivative,"* as you assert, but because of its complex interrelationships with other biochemicals. Synthetic vitamin C is not molecularly *"different"* than the molecule of isolated natural vitamin C. They are biochemically indistinguishable.[1]

The stereochemistry of vitamin C (whether it is D- or L- form) is not relevant, since manufacturers produce and sell only the L-form.[2]

---

1. Stryer L, Biochemistry, 1995. Nelson DL et al, Lehninger Principles of Biochemistry, Third Edition, 2000. Tolbert et al, Ascorbic Acid: Chemistry, Metabolism, and Uses, 1982. Davies MB, Vitamin C: Its Chemistry and Biochemistry, 1991. Haworth WN, "The Structure of Carbohydrates and of Vitamin C," 1937; Nobel Lecture.
2. F Hoffman-La Roche Ltd, "Roche Vitamins: Vitamin C in Human Nutrition," 2000.

Synthesized ascorbic acid is not *"closer"* to ascorbyl palmitate than the molecular configuration of natural ascorbic acid.

Vitamin C used as a food antioxidant in home prepared or commercial foods (provided it is made fat-soluble as in ascorbyl palmitate) is effective, safe and very important.[1] The danger from oxidized fats and free-radical pathology is far greater than any conceivable harm from the low levels of C used to prevent it.

Company D: *You must make each diet for each breed different because, for example, some animals can synthesize cobalt in their liver while others can't. Thus, some breeds don't require cobalt.*

Truth Response: No creature can *"synthesize"* elements such as cobalt. Cobalt is an atom in the periodic table and as such does not change (except perhaps in nuclear physics experiments), nor is it synthesized. There is not even a direct requirement for cobalt in animals. Microorganisms produce cobamides (including vitamin B_{12}) from cobalt but this is not a "synthesis" of cobalt. The cobalt atom is somewhat unique in that it can exist in biological milieu in three oxidation states due to its unpaired electron in the 3dx2 orbital, but this does not represent synthesis.[2] If you are serious about this assertion you are advocating alchemy and transmutation, which are as scientifically valid as a flat Earth.

Company D: *Because research has proven vitamin C is toxic, it is ludicrous for you to have it in your foods.*

Truth Response: *"Ludicrous"* does not rationally dismiss the fact that dose does make the poison whether or not the poison acts instantly or over long term.[3] This concept is the foundation cornerstone to the entire field of modern toxicology. You have no evidence that low levels of vitamin C to protect important nutritional fatty acids from oxidation, are anything but beneficial over the long or short term. The one study you cited in

1. Wysong RL, "Oxherphol™ Technical Information," 2002. *Food Addit Contam*, 1989; 6(2):201-7. *J Food Prot*, 1999; 62(6):619-24. *J Am Oil Chem Soc*, 1974; 51(7):321-5. *J Agric Food Chem*, 1999; 47(9):3541-5. *Int J Vitam Nutr Res Suppl*, 1985; 27:307-33.
2. Ebbing DD et al, General Chemistry, 1998. *Annu Rev Microbiol*, 1996; 50:137-81.
3. Ottoboni MA, The Dose Makes the Poison, 1984. Casarett LJ et al, Casarett & Doull's Toxicology: The Basic Science of Poisons, 2001.

your last letter where researchers gave massive doses of vitamin C to dogs and putatively had negative reactions, is an abuse of the scientific literature since in real life nobody would give such amounts to their animal.*

Company D: *As proof that different breeds have different requirements, it is proven that some breeds require only certain amounts of copper. Collies, for example, require 270 IU of vitamin D. Your foods do not show this certain and correct knowledge.*

Truth Response: IU's of vitamin D or mgs of copper in collies and Bedlington terriers misses the point. Your statement, for example, *"collies require 270 IU of Vitamin D per kilogram"* (Are we sure its not 270.015375948 IU's?) , demonstrates that your position is no different than the rest of the pet food industry which believes scientists can create 100% perfect foods because they "know" how many IU's of vitamin D a dog needs. You have fallen victim to the myth of the 100% manufactured diet and so will pet owners who follow your lead. Such fabricated diets based on specific requirements (only valid until the scientific board meets the next time) have caused immeasurable disease and suffering for companion animals. We have obvious logical differences in nutritional paradigms. All of the various "breed-specific" arguments are reducible to one thesis: You think you know exactly what each breed of dog requires in terms of IU's, micrograms and milligrams. We think you don't. On the face of it, your assertion is absurd since any thinking person knows that certainty such as you impute to yourself cannot be justified because – as explained in the previous letter – science is constantly evolving and not at an end point in any discipline. Since your foundation thesis is erroneous, all of the reductionistic specifics based upon it about which breed requires which exact dosage of certain nutrients are invalid.

It is apparent from these few examples (volumes could be written) that truth does not prevail in the pet food marketplace. Marketing, propaganda, sensationalism, absurdity and myth displace common sense.

---

* *Cornell Vet*, 1979; 69(4):384-401.

APPENDIX A

THE OPTIMAL HEALTH PROGRAM

*There Is Such A Thing As Body Ethic
Maintaining Health Is A Moral Responsibility*

PREFACE

The following material outlines an all-inclusive prevention and therapy guide using the principles outlined in this book.

These guidelines demonstrate how the concepts I have discussed can be put into practice and how I have used them in product development.

I do this not to hawk products, but to demonstrate the simplicity of the key to health and how nature can be used to address most any health problem.

FOR PREVENTION AND HEALTH OPTIMIZATION, FOLLOW THESE STEPS:

~FOR PREVENTION~

1. Follow the suggestions at the pyramid base every day.

2. Cycle through the various dry, canned and frozen foods without regard for their names.

3. Supplement with various E.F.A.'s™ alternated, Biotics™ and Pet Inoculant™.

4. Feed fresh, raw foods supplemented with Call of the Wild™.

~DURING ILLNESS~

1. Follow steps #1-4 listed above diligently.

2. Give Immulyn™ daily for immune enhancement.

3. Use PDG™ and Archetype™ for concentrated nourishment if appetite is suppressed.

4. Offer pure water enhanced with WellSpring™.

5. Use the Nutrient Support Formula (NSF) specific for the organ system under stress.

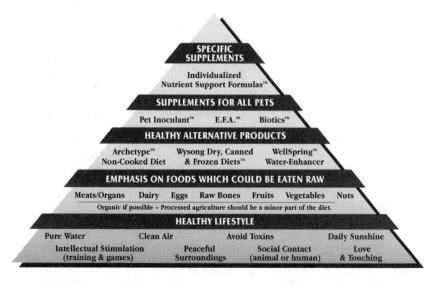

Fig. 52.

DOING THE BEST YOU CAN

Food choices are not a matter of right or wrong, black or white – they are shades of grey. By understanding what is the ideal and what is not, however, intelligent decisions can be made which at least take us ever closer to the healthiest ideal. Try to make choices as near the top of the arrow as possible.

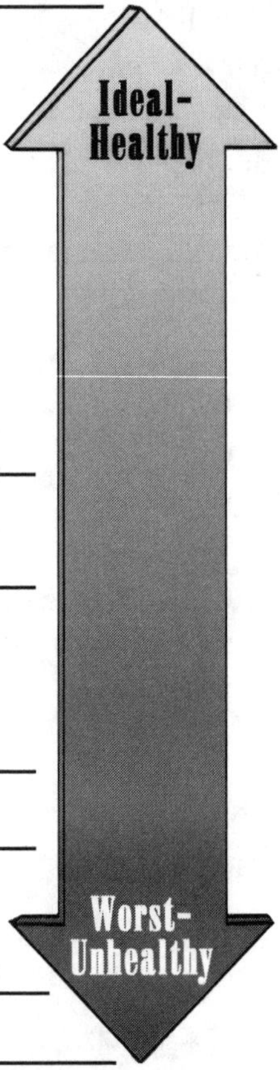

A. Hunted, raw prey (not practical) ——————————

B. Fresh raw meats, organs & bones, minor fresh vegetables & fruits (organic best)[1] + Supplements: ——————————

    • Call of the Wild™ (Vitamin/ Mineral/Enzymes/Probiotics)

    • Pet Inoculant™ (Concentrated Probiotics)

    • E.F.A.™, Marine Lipids™, E.F.A.™ with fish oil[2] alternated (Essential Fatty Acids)

C. As in B, but Archetype™ and Tundra™ non-cooked diets used ——————————

D. As in B, plus Biotics™, but fresh products are cooked or "table scraps" used ——————————

E. Wysong Dry and Canned Diets[3] (best) or premium (next best) or generic (next best) + Supplements (including Biotics™) and fresh raw foods as in B ——————————

F. As in E, but adding fresh cooked foods ——————————

G. As in E, minus fresh, raw or cooked foods——————————

H. Dry and/or canned foods alone ——————————

K. No food ——————————

Ideal–Healthy

Worst–Unhealthy

1. Fed in proportions found in would-be prey: Approximately 62% meat, 11% organs, 2% bone, 25% vegetable.
2. Follow label directions for both Pet Inoculant and E.F.A. Use daily particularly if disease or stress is present.
3. Wysong Diets are formulated, processed and packaged to be as close to the natural diet as possible. A "premium" food is usually high fat and protein, with meat products listed among the first ingredients. A "generic" food is a very low cost, by-product and grain fraction-based diet with meats as minor ingredients. Neither cost nor advertising can be trusted to determine value. A "premium" may be a "generic" nutritionally. Carefully study the ingredients, company philosophy, and results from your pet.

Fig. 53.

PREVENTION/THERAPY GUIDE

How to use the guide: Find the condition on the list. If not there, find the organ system affected (page 204). Then use the key (pages 205-208) to find which products are designed to help. Underlined numbers are for humans only, parenthetical are for animals only, regular-type are for both. Be sure to follow the total Optimal Health Program™ for best results.

DISEASE/ CONDITION	NUTRITIONAL THERAPY (key on pages 205-208)
Addison's Disease	1, (36), (38), (47), (51), (52), 21, 23, 33
Adenoiditis	1, 2, 21, 26, 33
Allergy	1, (36), (38), (45), (47), (51), (52), 2, 21, 33
Amenorrhea	1, 6, 22, 3, 4, 11, 18, 33
Anemia	1, (34), (41), (45), (47), (50), (51), (52), 2, 11, 33
Anorexia	1, (34), (41), (45), (47), (50), (51), (52), 2, 11, 33
Anxiety	1, (36), (38), (45), (47), (51), (52), (55), (56), (57), 2, 31, 33
Arthritis	1, (36), (38), (47), (51), (52), 2, 13, 17, 19, 33
Asthma	1, 30, (36), (38), (47), (51), (52), 2, 21, 33
Atherosclerosis	1, 2, 4, 15, 33
Athletic Stress	1, (34), (42), (45), (47), (50), (51), (52), 10, 11, 17, 12 (M), 18 (F), 33
Bronchitis	1, 30, (36), (38), (45), (47), (51), (52), 2, 33
Bursitis	1, (36), (38), (47), (51), (52), 2, 13, 17, 19, 33
Cachexia	1, (34), (41), (45), (47), (50), (51), (52), 10, 11, 33
Cancer	1, (35), (36), (42), (45), (47), (50), (51), (52), 10, 21, 27, appropriate NSF, 33
Candidiasis	1, (36), (38), (45), (47), (51), (52), 16, 26, 33

DISEASE/ CONDITION	NUTRITIONAL THERAPY (key on pages 205-208)
Cataract	1, (37), (43), (47), (51), (52), 2, 25, 33
Celiac Disease	1, (36), (38), (47), (50), (51), (52), 7, 27, 28, 33
Chicken Pox	1, 2, 7, 16, 21, 26, 33
Chronic Fatigue	1, 10, 14, 32, 33
Colitis	1, (36), (42), (45), (47), (50), (51), (52), 7, 16, 33
Conjunctivitis	1, (36), (38), (45), (47), (50), (51), (52), 2, 21, 25, 26, 33
Constipation	1, (36), (38), (45), (47), (50), (51), (52), 4, 16, 28, 33
Copper Disorder	1, (38), (47), (50), (51), (52), 33
Crohn's Disease	1, (36), (38), (45), (47), (50), (51), (52), 4, 7, 16, 33
Cushing's Disease	1, (35), (36), (42), (45), (47), (50), (51), (52), 12, 18, 33
Depression	1, (35), (36), (45), (47), (50), (51), (52), (55), (56), (57), 24, 32, 33
Diabetes	1, (34), (41), (45), (47), (50), (51), (52), 14, 16, 27, 33
Diarrhea	1, (36), (38), (45), (47), (50), (51), (52), 7, 16, 21, 26, 27, 33
Diverticulosis	1, (36), (42), (45), (47), (50), (51), (52), 7, 16, 33
Dysmenorrhea	1, 6, 22, (37), (40), (43), (47), (50), (51), (52), 4, 12, 18, 31, 33
Eclampsia	1, 5, (34), (42), (45), (47), (50), (51), (52), 4, 11, 14, 17, 33
Edema	1, (37), (43), (47), (50), (51), (52), 15, 23, 33
Emphysema	1, 30, (36), (38), (45), (47), (50), (51), (52), 2, 21, 26, 33
Epilepsy	1, (35), (42), (45), (47), (50), (51), (52), 24, 31, 33

DISEASE/ CONDITION	NUTRITIONAL THERAPY (key on pages 205-208)
Fatigue	1, (34), (41), (45), (47), (50), (51), (52), 10, 14, 24, 32, 33
Fever	1, (34), (41), (45), (47), (50), (51), (52), 2, 21, 26, 33
Fibromyalgia	1, (35), (36), (42), (45), (47), (50), (51), (52), 13, 17, 19, 32, 33
Gallbladder	1, (40), (45), (47), (50), (51), (52), 16, 20, 33
Gastritis	1, (36), (38), (45), (47), (50), (51), (52), 16, 28, 33
Glaucoma	1, (36), (38), (47), (50), (51), (52), 2, 25, 33
Gout	1, (40), (49), (50), (51), (52), 2, 4, 13, 33
Headache	1, 24, 32, 33
Hemorrhoids	1, 4, 16, 33
Hyperlipidemia	1, (37), (43), (47), (50), (51), (52), 2, 16, 33
Hypertension	1, (37), (43), (47), (50), (51), (52), 2, 15, 23, 33
Hyperthyroidism	1, (35), (42), (47), (50), (51), (52), 12, 18, 33
Hypertrophic Osteodystrophy	1, (36), (38), (47), (50), (51), (52), 4, 13, 17, 19, 33
Hypoglycemia	1, (37), (43), (47), (50), (51), (52), 14, 16, 27, 33
Hypothyroidism	1, (36), (38), (42), (47), (50), (51), (52), 9, 12, 18, 33
Impotence	1, 5, (34), (42), (45), (47), (50), (51), (52), 11, 12, 29, 33
Incontinence	1, (34), (42), (45), (47), (50), (51), (52), 12, 18, 23, 33
Indigestion	1, (45), (47), (50), (51), (52), 16, 28, 33
Infectious Disease	1, (34), (42), (45), (47), (50), (51), (52), 2, 7, 21, 26, 33

DISEASE/ CONDITION	NUTRITIONAL THERAPY (key on pages 205-208)
Influenza	1, 30, 2, 7, 21, 26, 33
Insomnia	1, 6, (45), (47), (50), (51), (52), 31, 33
Irritable Bowel	1, (36), (38), (45), (47), (50), (51), (52), 4, 7, 16, 21, 27, 33
Jaundice	1, (45), (47), (50), (51), (52), 2, 20, 33
Kidney Disease	1, (36), (37), (43), (47), (50), (51), (52), 2, 7, 23, 33
Lactation	1, 5, 6, (34), (42), (45), (47), (50), (51), (52), 4, 11, 14, 17, 33
Laryngitis	1, 30, (34), (42), (45), (47), (50), (51), (52), 2, 4, 21, 26, 33
Lupus Erythematosus	1, (38), (45), (47), (50), (51), (52), 2, 4, 21, 27, 33
Lymphangiectasia	1, (37), (42), (47), (50), (51), (52), 4, 20, 23, 33
Macular Degeneration	1, (46), (47), (50), (51), (52), 2, 17, 25, 33
Measles	1, 30, (34), (42), (45), (47), (50), (51), (52), 2, 7, 21, 26, 33
Memory Loss	1, 5, (45), (46), (47), (50), (51), (52), 4, 24, 32, 33
Menopause	1, 6, 22, (37), (43), (47), (50), (51), (52), 3, 4, 18, 33
Mononucleosis	1, 5, 2, 21, 24, 26, 32, 33
Motion Sickness	1, (45), (47), (50), (51), (52), 20, 28, 33
Multiple Sclerosis	1, 4, 21, 24, 27, 32, 33
Mumps	1, 5, 2, 7, 21, 26, 31, 33
Narcolepsy	1, (45), (47), (50), (51), (52), 24, 32, 33
Nausea	1, (36), (38), (45), (47), (50), (51), (52), 20, 28, 33

DISEASE/ CONDITION	NUTRITIONAL THERAPY (key on pages 205-208)
Obesity	1, (37), (42), (45), (47), (50), (51), (52), 4, 14, 32, 33
Osteoporosis	1, 5, 6, 13, 17, 18, 19, 33
Pancreatitis	1, (36), (42), (45), (47), (50), (51), (52), 27, 33
Parasitism	1, (34), (42), (45), (47), (50), (51), (52), 7, 16, 21, 26, 33
Peritonitis	1, (36), (38), (45), (47), (50), (51), (52), 21, 23, 33
Pharyngitis	1, 30, (34), (42), (45), (47), (50), (51), (52), 2, 7, 21, 26, 33
Pregnancy	1, 5, 6, (34), (42), (45), (47), (50), (51), (52), 4, 11, 14, 17, 33
Premenstrual Syndrome	1, 6, 22, 4, 18, 20, 33
Respiratory Infections	1, 30, (34), (42), (45), (47), (50), (51), (52), 2, 7, 21, 26, 33
Sinusitis	1, 30, (34), (42), (45), (47), (50), (51), (52), 2, 7, 21, 26, 33
Stroke	1, (45), (46), (47), (50), (51), (52), 4, 15, 24, 33
Tonsillitis	1, (34), (42), (45), (47), (50), (51), (52), 2, 7, 21, 26, 33
Ulcers	1, (36), (38), (47), (50), (51), (52),16, 28, 33
Urine Crystals: Oxalate, Urate	1, (37), (40), (43), (49), (50), (51), (52), 23, 33
Urine Crystals: Struvite, FUS	1, (34), (44), (45), (48), (50), (51), (52), 23
Urinary Tract Infection	1, (34), (42), (45), (47), (50), (51), (52) , 2, 7, 21, 23, 26, 33
Vaginitis	1, (34), (42), (45), (47), (50), (51), (52), 2, 7, 21, 26, 33
Varicose Veins	1, (37), (40), (43), (47), (50), (51), (52), 2, 15, 17, 33
Vomiting	1, (36), (38), (45), (47), (50), (51), (52), 16, 28, 33

ORGAN/ SYSTEM	NUTRITIONAL THERAPY (key on pages 205-208)
Autoimmune	1, (36), (38), (45), (47), (51), (52), 4, 21, 33
Dental	1, (37), (40), (43), (47), (50), (51), (52), (54), (55), (56), (57), 2, Probiodent, 17, 19, 33
Dermatological	1, (36), (38), (45), (47), (50), (51), (52), 4, 17, 19, 33
Digestive	1, (36), (42), (45), (47), (50), (51), (52), 16, 28, 33
Ear	1, (36), (38), (45), (47), (50), (51), (52), 2, 4, 21, 26, 33
Eye	1, (35), (36), (42), (45), (47), (50), (51), (52), 25, 33
Heart	1, 5, 6, (37), (43), (47), (50), (51), (52) , 2, 4, 15, 33
Liver	1, (36), (42), (45), (47), (50), (51), (52), 7, 20, 21, 26, 33
Musculoskeletal	1, 6, (34), (42), (45), (47), (50), (51), (52), 13, 17, 19, 33
Neurological	1, (47), (50), (51), (52), 24, 31, 32, 33
Pancreas	1, 5, (36), (42), (45), (47), (50), (51), (52), 27, 33
Prostate	1, 5, (34), (41), (45), (47), (50), (51), (52), 2, 3, 4, 12, 29, 33
Spleen	1, (36), (37), (43), (47), (50), (51), (52), 20, 23, 33
Thyroid	1, (36), (38), (47), (50), (51), (52), 33

PRODUCT KEY

(See page 252 for literature detailing the scientific basis for these items.)

FOUNDATION FORMULAS
OPTIMAL™ ~ multiple vitamins and minerals
ORGAMIN™ ~ major minerals at optimal levels
CHELAMIN™ ~ over 74 trace minerals naturally complexed
NSF SPECTRUM™ ~ a blend of active elements from among all of the Nutrient Support Formulas™
WHOLE FOOD CONCENTRATE™ ~ a blend of 23 fresh, raw, natural food ingredients, providing an entire spectrum of nutrients
SALAD™ ~ a concentrated blend of cruciferous vegetables supplying important phytonutrients and sulforaphanes
SPECTROX™ ~ a spectrum of antioxidants at optimal levels
FOOD A•C•E™ ~ antioxidant vitamins A, C and E, plus others derived only from food
FOOD C™ ~ antioxidant vitamin C derived only from food
MEGA C™ ~ potent vitamin C formula
E.F.A.™ ~ a blend of oils rich in omega-3, 6 and 9 fatty acids
MARINE LIPIDS™ ~ high omega-3 fatty acids derived from cold-water fish
FRESH SQUEEZED FLAX SEEDS™ ~ high omega-3 flaxseed oil and whole seed pulp
PROBIOSYN™ ~ a spectrum of probiotic cultures, probiotic-enhancing oligosaccharides and active food enzymes

FOUNDATION FORMULA KEY

1 =	All Wysong Foundation Formulas
2 =	#1 plus increase Antioxidant dosages (*SPECTROX*™, *FOOD A•C•E*™, *FOOD C*™, *MEGA C*™)
3 =	#1 plus increase *SALAD*™ dosage (concentrated cruciferous vegetables)
4 =	#1 plus increase Essential Fatty Acids dosage (*E.F.A.*™, *MARINE LIPIDS*™, *FLAX SEEDS*™)
5 =	#1 plus increase Vitamin dosages (*OPTIMAL*™)
6 =	#1 plus increase Mineral dosages (*ORGAMIN*™, *CHELAMIN*™)
7 =	#1 plus increase Probiotic/Enzyme dosages (*PROBIOSYN*™)
8 =	#1 plus increase *NSF SPECTRUM*™ dosage
9 =	#1 plus increase *WHOLE FOOD CONCENTRATE*™ dosage
10 =	Increase all dosages

NUTRIENT SUPPORT FORMULA KEY

11 =	*ANAPLEX*™ (muscle growth & energy metabolism)
12 =	*ANDROLOG*™ (healthy male reproductive system)
13 =	*ARTHEGIC*™ (moderation of connective tissue inflammation)
14 =	*CARBOPRIN*™ (sugar & carbohydrate metabolism)
15 =	*CARVASOL*™ (healthy vascular system & heart muscle)
16 =	*COLEX*™ (healthy intestinal tract)
17 =	*CONTIFIN*™ (healthy connective tissues)
18 =	*ESTROLOG*™ (healthy female reproductive system)
19 =	*GLUCOSAMINE Complex*™ (healthy joints)
20 =	*HEPTICENE*™ (healthy liver & gallbladder)
21 =	*IMMULYN*™ (healthy immune system)

NUTRIENT SUPPORT FORMULA KEY (continued)

22 =	*MENSTRUPHEN*™ (healthy female reproductive cycles)
23 =	*NEPHUROL*™ (healthy kidneys & bladder)
24 =	*NEURIDONE*™ (healthy nervous system)
25 =	*OPTHID*™ (healthy eyes)
26 =	*PANCIDRIM*™ (antibacterial nutrients)
27 =	*PANZYME*™ (healthy pancreas)
28 =	*PEPZHAC*™ (healthy stomach & gastric mucosa)
29 =	*PROSTASE*™ (healthy prostate)
30 =	*RESPITONE*™ (healthy respiratory system)
31 =	*SOMNIQUIL*™ (sleep & relaxation)
32 =	*VIVREIS*™ (alertness & elevated mood)
33 =	*WELLSPRING*™ (alkaline ionized water rejuvenator)

COMPANION ANIMAL DIET KEY

Alternate the following #34-#44 Diets with Archetype™ and Tundra™ Diets as a first choice, but other Wysong Diets rotated will also be of benefit.

34 =	*GROWTH*™ *DRY OR CANNED*
35 =	*MAINTENANCE*™ *DRY OR CANNED*
36 =	*SYNORGON*™ *DRY*
37 =	*SENIOR*™ *DRY OR CANNED*
38 =	*ANERGEN*™ *DRY OR CANNED*
39 =	*BIODYNAMIC*™ *DRY*
40 =	*VEGAN*™ *DRY*
41 =	*NURTURE*™ *DRY*

	COMPANION ANIMAL DIET KEY (continued)
42 =	*VITALITY™ DRY OR CANNED*
43 =	*GERIATRX™ DRY OR CANNED*
44 =	*URETIC™ DRY*
45 =	*ALL MEAT™ CANNED* varieties combined with CALL OF THE WILD™ alternated with *TUNDRA™ FROZEN* and *ARCHETYPE™ DRY*.
46 =	Any Diet rotated with others.
	COMPANION ANIMAL SUPPLEMENT KEY
47 =	*BIOTIC™* (enhances & augments the nutritional value of processed pet foods)
48 =	*BIOTIC pH-™* (generates & maintains an acidic urine pH)
49 =	*BIOTIC pH+™* (generates & maintains an alkaline urine pH)
50 =	*PDG™* (provides archetypal nourishment to debilitated or convalescing animals)
51 =	*PET INOCULANT™* (concentrated probiotic cultures & immunoglobulins)
52 =	*E.F.A.™, E.F.A. WITH FISH OIL™, MARINE LIPIDS™ and FRESH SQUEEZED FLAX SEEDS™ alternated* (unaltered essential fatty acids, including omega-3's)
53 =	*CALL OF THE WILD™* (balances all-meat meals)
54 =	*DENTATREAT™* (natural cheese dental preventive)
	COMPANION ANIMAL TREAT KEY
55 =	*REAL BONES™* (non-heat-processed dried bone chew)
56 =	*CANINE BISCUITS™*
57 =	*CAT TREATS™*

APPENDIX B

THE TRUTH WORKS
TESTIMONIALS

An Argument Never Defeats Experience

PREFACE

Direct personal experience is about the best proof we can ever have of anything in life. It may not convince another (nor should it necessarily, it may be a lie, delusion, illusion or mistake), but personally it's about as compelling as things can get. Although this form of evidence is pooh-poohed by the scientific community (and pretty much should be in terms of rigid proof), it must be taken seriously by the individual experiencing the event, and certainly taken notice of by others when the weight of testimony becomes overwhelming.

Thus, I present here some of the unsolicited letters we have received by those who have used the principles outlined in this book. It's rather long, but not without cause. For not only is it clear that these people are honest folk convinced of their experiences, but the sheer volume of testimony should get the attention of anyone, even regulators who insist natural feeding nutrition has nothing to do with health.

It will be apparent from some of the comments that not everyone follows all of my advice. (Actually I learned this sobering lesson long ago from my wife and kids.) People by and large merely want to switch from one brand to another, and thus not change the underlying habit of one food in a bowl day after day. Nevertheless, you will see the dramatic results that can come from even this revision. If folks would follow my whole advice by varying the foods, supplementing and fresh food entrées (see pages 195-208), the results would be even more dramatic, and most importantly, long lasting. Take heed.

VETERINARY KUDOS

VETERINARIAN, ALABAMA: "I thought it sounded too good to be true. After over two years of clinical evaluation, I am convinced that Wysong Diets are head and shoulders above any pet food on the market. And when my clients can notice an improvement in their pets after feeding the food for a few weeks, it makes me feel extra good to know that I have provided a quality service by simply recommending good nutrition."

VETERINARIAN, CALIFORNIA: "One particular case stands out in my mind: A former client's 11-year-old Springer Spaniel (which was lethargic, obese, and had dermatitis and kidney problems) was put on Wysong Diets. Just a few weeks ago I saw her in my former practice and didn't even recognize her dog – he bounced out the door. I noticed his body condition and hair coat. I couldn't believe it was the same dog. She feeds her dog Senior™ and it looks and acts like a young dog. The owner is very happy, to say the least. The dog has only been on Wysong Diets for 5 months!"

VETERINARIAN, GEORGIA: "Wysong Diets produce such rapid and impressive results. Things such as brighter eyes, improved hair coat, weight gain (or loss, depending on the patient's general condition) and more energy are readily observed – and all of this on 25-30% less food. These observations have convinced me that (Wysong Diets) is what a pet should eat, and that quality food is indeed our best medicine."

VETERINARIAN, ILLINOIS: "We contacted all clients who were using (bleep)* or (bleep)* and had them change to Wysong Diets. All cases are doing very well. One woman came to our office to purchase (bleep)*. Another veterinarian had sent her to our hospital because he was out of the (bleep)* which he had recommended she try for her older dog with chronic diarrhea. The (bleep)* wasn't working very well so our technician convinced her to try Wysong Senior™. She called our technician back three days later to report that after trying about 5 different diets, it was Wysong Diets that did the job. She felt Wysong Diets saved her dog's life."

VETERINARIAN, KANSAS: "...It looked good, but I thought nothing is as good as they say it is. So I waited for the inevitable letdown. However, I have been

---

* A super premium food, the identity of which we withhold to protect the guilty. To be fair, any pet can have a health problem eating any food (including ours) since pets are bound to be eating something when they become ill. But you can be sure that pets on properly designed diets as part of the Optimal Health Program (see pages 195-208) will have the best possible health.

in Wysong Diets for 1-1/2 years, and that letdown has never come. The product has been as good as Dr. Wysong had said it was. I have seen spectacular results in skin problems, lactating dogs who were skinny and sick when they whelped, in cats and dogs with digestive problems, and in my own Doberman who had grown sluggish in her old age... The food is without a doubt the best food on the market today. The hardest part is convincing a world which is bombarded by advertising and jaded to any new product's claims."

VETERINARIAN, MAINE: "These diets convert strangers to friends within days oftentimes. Wysong Diets have probably been the most uplifting and challenging thing that has hit my practice in years. It is a new lease on life for the pet, its owner, and its doctor."

VETERINARIAN, OHIO: "I have not only replaced all my 'prescription' diets with Wysong Diets but also find myself now selling more maintenance diets to provide health instead of waiting to cure problems. My most dramatic case was a Lhasa Apso which had been bald for over a year. She had been treated by 3 veterinarians including a leading clinician in Columbus, Ohio and a very well known clinician from Ohio State University. Excellent results were achieved by adjusting thyroid dose and Wysong Diets!"

VETERINARIAN, PENNSYLVANIA: "After practicing veterinary medicine for 25 years, I have never been as excited about a product as I have been with Wysong Diets. The clinical results that I have seen in many animals have been unbelievable. Probably the most dramatic results that I've seen have been in skin disease and hair coat. The health and general well-being of the animal has been quite noticeable. This has greatly increased rapport with our clients. I challenge any other food to produce the consistent results that we have seen in the treatment of skin disease, etc. Any veterinarian that has not tried Wysong Diets in their clinic is missing out on a lot of personal reward."

VETERINARIAN, TENNESSEE: "Having been raised on a dairy farm and working in a predominately large animal practice that stressed nutrition taught me early in my veterinary career that nutrition is extremely important to good health and top performance...when I received information, I became very interested. I became convinced beyond a doubt that the palatability and performance were even better than I had anticipated. Two years have elapsed and my clients and I continue to be amazed at how much better their pets act, feel, and look on the Wysong Diets. My professional reputation is very important to me. I have no reservations about recommending the Wysong Diets to my clients because I know by suggesting them that I am practicing better preventative medicine and enhancing the health of my patients."

VETERINARIAN, TENNESSEE: "It's impossible to discuss Wysong Diets without discussing client comments or testimonials. One that comes to mind is a breeder who raises Shih Tzus. She said, 'I have been raising dogs of all breeds for 20 years, from California to Tennessee, and have used all brands of pet food

---

* A super premium food, the identity of which we withhold to protect the guilty. To be fair, any pet can have a health problem eating any food (including ours) since pets are bound to be eating something when they become ill. But you can be sure that pets on properly designed diets as part of the Optimal Health Program (see pages 195-208) will have the best possible health.

including (bleep)*, (bleep)*, (bleep)*, and (bleep)*, and have never seen better puppies. Stools are fewer and smell less, which is important because my puppies are raised in the house with the family. Lactating bitches have likewise done better with less hair loss and fewer puppy losses on Wysong.' I didn't even know she was feeding Wysong Diets. It turns out that she was buying a box for each new puppy owner – even shipping UPS out of state in areas where it is not available. Personally I believe that the most exciting comment I received at my two hospitals is 'I can't believe how much better he acts – he must feel better.' I have especially noted this in senior dogs. Another comment is 'His teeth sure are better now.' It is exciting offering such nutritious products from which I have actually seen results – not just heard about them."

VETERINARIAN, TENNESSEE: "We had one case of a user of Wysong with 15 pups fed mother's milk only and mother and all 15 puppies were in superb condition and absolutely no supplements were given."

VETERINARIAN, TEXAS: "We have not had any problems converting our clientele to Wysong Diets. We have seen all positive results."

VETERINARIAN, TEXAS: "Never before have I heard so many positive testimonials from my clients concerning pet foods. I've heard everything from the fact that the cat's litter box no longer has that awful odor, to comments that their dogs had the most beautiful hair coats ever seen."

VETERINARIAN, WASHINGTON: "During my 18 months of experience selling and feeding Wysong Diets, I have observed the following: (1) Excellent hair coats, (2) Firming of body fat, (3) Reduction in pain and arthritic symptoms, especially in older dogs, (4) Reduced food intake (40-60%), (5) Excellent palatability. It is the best food that I have ever handled."

VETERINARIAN, WASHINGTON: "We get comment after comment on how they like the improved hair coats, less scratching, less gas, less stool, and increased vitality of their pets. Feline Vitality™ Diet has proven to be an excellent maintenance food for cats of all ages and in helping to prevent urolithiasis."

VETERINARIAN, WISCONSIN: "We have used Wysong Diets since June 1985, and I must say I was somewhat skeptical at first. We are now using Wysong Diets on all ages of animals and have a long enough experience with it to see the benefits. Our clients are beginning to tell us how well their animals are doing, especially in their hair coat, weight, and general well being. Thank you. It has greatly helped us provide a superior food for our patients."

VETERINARIAN, WISCONSIN: "Our clients' comments certainly eliminate any doubts... in the short time that we have been working with the food, we have been impressed on several occasions with the effect it has had on some of our patients with dermatologic, enteric, or urinary problems."

VETERINARIAN, WISCONSIN: "There is only one word to describe it: Fantastic! Even though we have been working with Wysong Diets for only a few months,

---

* A super premium food, the identity of which we withhold to protect the guilty. To be fair, any pet can have a health problem eating any food (including ours) since pets are bound to be eating something when they become ill. But you can be sure that pets on properly designed diets as part of the Optimal Health Program (see pages 195-208) will have the best possible health.

it is fantastic the changes I have seen in the skin and hair coat of my patients on this product. When puppies and kittens are presented for their first inoculations, I automatically put them on Wysong Diets; When they return in three weeks for their boosters, it is very satisfying to both the client and me to see the changes: nice slick coats, pink healthy skin (no dandruff!), and increased energy and vitality in those little guys...Fantastic!"

VETERINARIAN, WYOMING: "In my practice we have never sold a large amount of diets because we never could see any difference between the so-called special diets and (bleep)*. I am so glad your products came along. The results speak for themselves. I could go on for hours telling about them. The best thing is you really feel proud using them in your clinic. I would like for you to tell anyone to call me anytime and I would be pleased to discuss case after case with them. The results they may not believe, for there have been times I'm not sure I have. The products are truly amazing."

VETERINARY CLINIC: "Using the Wysong Diets, we've seen excellent results with skin problems, allergies and digestive, pancreatic and liver disease."

PET PROFESSIONAL KUDOS

BRITISH COLUMBIA, CANADA: "I have been using your products for quite some time now, and my four English Bulldogs are doing really well. By using your food and following your advice they have not developed any of the Bulldog ill health characteristics."

BREEDER, CALIFORNIA: "As breeders, we are constantly being told the majority of our health problems are genetic in origin. Some may be, but I am convinced the majority are due to feeding processed foods for generation after generation. I am extremely pleased to learn of Wysong and have encouraged breeders, through my 'Watchword' column, to study the Wysong Philosophy and use the Wysong products for their dogs and themselves. I have been using the Maintenance™ in my feed trials with wonderful results and can highly recommend it to my puppy buyers. I am very glad to see Dr. Wysong has addressed the need for incorporating raw whole 'living' foods back into the diet, and the C-Biotic™ helps to cover any nutritional gaps in a diet too. I have seen these foods do remarkable things for dogs on a maintenance and prevention level. I recommend the Wysong products without hesitation."

CALIFORNIA: "Our pups, fed Wysong, looked so much healthier they sold for more than past litters. And their mother, on Wysong, looked so good you wouldn't even know she was nursing."

ANIMAL SHELTER, FLORIDA: "Thanks a million for the food. The cats love it and they are thriving on it."

---

* A super premium food, the identity of which we withhold to protect the guilty. To be fair, any pet can have a health problem eating any food (including ours) since pets are bound to be eating something when they become ill. But you can be sure that pets on properly designed diets as part of the Optimal Health Program (see pages 195-208) will have the best possible health.

MAINE: "Just a short note to say your products have helped many animals that we rescue and those of our customers. Our FLV positive cat, Kelvin, is especially grateful for his Immulyn™. That supplement, holistic treatments, and lots of love have caused him to thrive with full-blown AIDS for two years. Pretty good for a cat who was given 6 weeks to live! Thanks again!"

GROOMER, MASSACHUSETTS: "My 10-year-old English Springer has been on Wysong for about 6 years. She is healthy and very active. I am a professional dog groomer and feel I have a well developed sense of a dog's health and well being and drive 18 miles to buy Wysong food for my dog and cat."

BREEDER, MICHIGAN: "I've had my Bulldogs on Wysong and I've never been happier with their health, coats, and general appearance. Even my 'Corky' with allergies is doing better. I've recently had my first litter of puppies since switching to Wysong and I can't begin to tell you the difference in these pups from my other litters. They have been very healthy and vigorous since birth. I've always lost a puppy in each litter, but this time we had 5 and they are all doing beautifully. I was totally amazed at their shiny, thick, beautiful coats on the day they were born. Obviously, I credit Wysong for these beautiful healthy pups."

BREEDER, MISSOURI: "Since we sell show puppies to people all over the country we recommend Wysong...you could not pay me to feed my dogs anything else. Their health and well being is my top concern and my future."

ANIMAL SHELTER, NORTH CAROLINA: "The shelter is currently feeding five different brands of pet foods. Caretakers say that when all five brands are available to the animals, they immediately go to the Wysong first."

ANIMAL SHELTER, NORTH CAROLINA: "What's more, the health of many of the animals has improved markedly since introducing Wysong. One dog, in particular, was so ill that it was to be put to sleep. After two weeks on Wysong, however, it's been reported the dog has rallied and is doing great."

BREEDER, OHIO: "After being a long time user of (bleep)*, we saw that our Doberman show bitch was losing coat luster as well as condition. After having her fully evaluated by a vet, we started searching for a new food. We actually went to buy (bleep)*, but came across Wysong instead. We LOVE IT! She loves it and her improvement is drastic. She is a red and while showing her, she was noted as being darkest red Dobe in the ring. Her overall condition has improved tremendously! We are so pleased with your product and look forward to recommending it to our puppy buyers."

ANIMAL SHELTER, WASHINGTON: "When a new dog comes in and has a choice between the food it came with and Wysong...it dives into the Wysong."

ANIMAL SHELTER, WASHINGTON: "Also, I ordered Anergen™ and 2 dogs with food allergy were not scratching in 2 days! One had long-term deep-seated skin problems. He is old. His eyes had puffy black skin surrounding them. His belly was all black skin. Within a week his belly is turning pink. He used to

---

* A super premium food, the identity of which we withhold to protect the guilty. To be fair, any pet can have a health problem eating any food (including ours) since pets are bound to be eating something when they become ill. But you can be sure that pets on properly designed diets as part of the Optimal Health Program (see pages 195-208) will have the best possible health.

shriek all the time. Now he is calmer and only shrieks when he gets over excited. The other young dog evidently had a mild allergy. We couldn't find the problem at first. His skin was blushed pink but not red. He didn't scratch. The other dogs always nibbled on him. He did not have any parasites, like fleas, lice, etc. When we saw the old dog get better so fast we put the young dog on Anergen and in 2 days…his skin is white. The dogs don't nibble on his skin. Also, we had a lot of stool eaters. That activity has disappeared…"

KENNEL, WASHINGTON: "The food has really turned out nice pups, more muscle and better bone with less fat. We produce 3 or 4 litters a year of Labs and Golden Retrievers. All of our pups have passed their O.F.A. thanks to you."

BREEDER, INTERNET: "I am a long time user/dealer of your products. I have Newfoundland dogs, the landseer variety and the black with white markings. I would like to say this, the landseers owned by many people are dirty, hard to keep white and all around for showing, much more work than mine. The white couldn't be whiter, shinier and cleaner. The black is black, shiny and free flowing. Many complain that the landseer is too much work, when I find them easier than even the blacks to clean up. My dogs are eager to be cover dogs for Wysong."

KENNEL, INTERNET: "My small kennel of Yorkies has never been healthier. Having tried the majority of 'pseudo-natural' foods, I discovered your products and went straight to Anergen™. Their coats are growing, their blueness of coat is returning, and they are very healthy and happy. Some of the brands I had tried made them very aggressive; their coats became brittle, and the itching, oh the itching. (Bleep)* was the worst. I mix a little water with the Anergen, add some spinach or other ground veggies, add the E.F.A.™ and the meals are complete. I have since started my three old cats on the Geriatrx™; they are 14, 12, and 11 years. Yes, the Wysong is a bit more costly, but knowing each bag is fresh and the ingredients are what you say they are (I truly believe you!). Using your products in my kennel is the best thing I have ever done for my dogs. Thank you again for providing such a life enhancing line."

SUPERB HEALTH, DISEASE PREVENTION AND REVERSAL

CALIFORNIA: "Thanks so much for your wonderful high-quality, superior products for my dogs and cats. My pets' eyes, coats, and overall health have never been better. All your products are simply phenomenal! Thanks so much."

CALIFORNIA: "With confidence I feed only Wysong. The results have been tremendous and visibly noticeable. I just purchased her second twenty pounds of food and already three changes have occurred. First of all her coat is much softer and is so shiny I wondered if something wasn't wrong. Really! Second, she doesn't have as much intestinal upset anymore. Before switching her to

---

* A super premium food, the identity of which we withhold to protect the guilty. To be fair, any pet can have a health problem eating any food (including ours) since pets are bound to be eating something when they become ill. But you can be sure that pets on properly designed diets as part of the Optimal Health Program (see pages 195-208) will have the best possible health.

Wysong she had a lot of gas and burped up frequently after eating. They have almost completely disappeared. I would have to say those symptoms have been reduced 95%. Incredible! Third, I've noticed she has more energy in the mornings. Shadow is 1½ years old and at about 13 months of age she slowly stopped bringing me her toys to play with her and slept longer. In the past few weeks she gets up earlier and with her tail wagging she's ready to play and full of energy. This may sound a little exaggerated only after a month on your Wysong food but it is the truth! I know my dog very well and any little change in her, for good or bad, I notice right away. I have never written to a company to tell them how great their product is, but I am so pleased with yours I just had to send my thanks and compliments. Thanks again! Keep up the great work."

GEORGIA: "I have been feeding your diets to my dog since I got him at 7 weeks old (approximately one year). I have also followed your recommendation regarding supplementation with fresh foods. He has thrived!..."

KENTUCKY: "I'm a complete paraplegic and I have just received my first service dog. I have switched him to Wysong. I can't believe the difference."

MICHIGAN: "I have a tiny Yorkie, 11 months old, that has been force fed, had severe hypoglycemic problems, and was destined to be put to sleep every vet said. Baffled why he would not eat, I tried every dog food. I came across Wysong Anergen™. He eats it and our problems are solved. He loves your Archetype™ also. He is a great advertisement for Wysong."

NEW YORK: "We have been giving our Basset Hound Wysong since she was a puppy. Emily has a gorgeous coat and is quite lean. She loves it! My husband and I will never give Emily anything but Wysong."

WASHINGTON: "I was recently introduced to your product by a veterinarian that I took my Siamese cat to. It has been a little over a month since we made the switch, and I am very pleased with the results; their coats are shiny and thick, and my male who lost a lot of weight while sick gained it all back and looks wonderful. The ingredients of Wysong are incredible... My cats are eating better than I am now and it isn't costing me more."

WISCONSIN: "Our Golden Retriever LOVES his Wysong food and we get many compliments for how good he looks! Thanks to you people!"

INTERNET: "I have switched all 6 of my animals over to your food based on a friend's recommendation. I can already tell that my 5 cats and dog are doing very well on the food. Their coats are beautiful, they eat with gusto and some minor things like weepy eyes are starting to get better. I am very happy."

INTERNET: "I have 2 dogs. Until last summer, I fed them regular grocery store food. Then, my little dog, Peanut, became infected with ehrlichiosis. The disease took her sight and almost took her life. As a result, I began feeding Wysong. I really believe that this made a huge difference in Peanut's recovery. No one expected her to survive, but she surprised everybody. She is still blind (and doing remarkably well), and her blood work has stabilized. Both dogs seem to have more energy, and their fur is absolutely gorgeous. Thank you."

INTERNET: "I think your product is terrific! I have tried to get my veterinarian to try carrying the Wysong. Wysong has helped my ailing cat, and my little 3 lb.

dog too. They are solid, and not fat, and they love the food. I get the supplements and use them too, when needed. You guys are fantastic!"

INTERNET: "I would like to take this time to thank you for your product. My Rotti has been eating your food since 8 weeks, and is in perfect health and shape."

INTERNET: "I'm a huge Wysong fan. My Golden who passed away a year ago did wonderful with your products. Thank you for the extended life we were able to have with him as well as the improved quality of life. We are now owned by 2 pups, a Golden Retriever and a Border Collie mix. Unfortunately our Border Collie mix was born with megaesophagus and didn't have long to live. I firmly believe that Wysong saved his life and he is now over 1-year-old and an amazing dog. He of course will always have this problem, but with supplements, Wysong Diets and extra love and care we hope to have him a long time. You wouldn't think he was ill by looking at him. His coat is shiny and beautiful, his eyes are bright and his energy and love of life is fantastic."

INTERNET: "My regular vet told me the dog was going down the tube, he was only 3 years old, but in very bad shape, thin, losing hair, and terrible skin. I put him on Wysong and within 2 months I had him over to a neighbor's asking, 'Do you think this is hair growing in?' Fievel lived 7 more years."

BETTER HEALTH ON LESS FOOD AND MONEY

CANADA: "Someone suggested to me that Wysong was expensive, but in reality it's about a dollar a day for each dog, and if I can't afford that for my animals I certainly shouldn't have gotten them in the first place. I don't know many children (in my income bracket) that live on a dollar's worth of food a day. Thanks for caring about animals."

INTERNET: "I have boasted about your pet food to complete strangers as they were trying to buy other brands. My dogs (3) and my cats (7) have never been healthier. My veterinarian stated that I have the healthiest animals. They are well fed and their coats are beautiful. They eat a lot less food than other brands and they weigh in quite well at the vet. You have the absolute best product available to the public…Please continue to do the fine job you are currently doing with the quality of your products. When I open the sealed packages of food, they smell good enough to eat!!!"

LESS VETERINARY CARE

CALIFORNIA: "I have used Wysong Products for almost 10 years. My AKC Cocker will be 11 years old and your products are so healthy she has never been to the vet! I love Wysong!"

NEW MEXICO: "I am an avid fan of Wysong products for my animals. I have saved tremendous amounts of money on vet bills, besides having good looking pets who are healthier and happier than most."

TEXAS: "Animals fed Wysong Diets for 3 months or longer actually do not require veterinary care as frequently as animals on other diets."

TEXAS: "Dear Dr. Wysong: I hardly know where to begin but I've been meaning to let you know I am thrilled with your products. I have 2 gorgeous Shelties who are now thriving I know because of your food and supplements. Wasn't the case last year... the girls caught something from another animal...Both of mine came down ill and it cost me over $3,000.00 to save their lives.... particularly Sheba, the eldest who at 13 years old was desperately ill. She was treated at Texas A&M Vet School...At her weakest point her ALKP was nearly 4000. Last summer was pure hell for me emotionally and financially as I'm not wealthy by any means. I'm disabled and living on Social Security Disability...but I will do anything for my girls because I love them that much...after all I can't put a price on what they give me in return. After returning from A&M...I made calls to your company.... Both of my girls are on your food and have been over 1 year now...Hepticene™ and Immulyn™. We also gave her C-Biotic™ and a few other of your products. She slowly improved.... Roughly 8-9 months after nearly dying and taking these supplements of yours, her tests were all normal! In fact, her ALKP recently was like 361, I believe. I know it was your products that healed her and continue to make her thrive. She is nearly 15 now, is gorgeous, healthy, active, etc. My other Sheltie Hillary is also on your food and thrives...I've had no vet bills for illnesses from either of them since they got over their sickness last summer. Sheba is still on Hepticene and Immulyn several times a week, but not as often as before. I can't begin to thank you enough for saving the lives of the 2 most precious and meaningful beings in my life. I know you saved them because nothing A&M did seemed to help much. Sheba's improvement began at home with your food and supplements...Thank you for your time and for allowing me to still have my 2 precious babies."

DRAMATIC RESULTS IN PUPPIES AND KITTENS

CALIFORNIA: "I have tried many premium dog foods – never have we seen such dramatic results in our canine kids in such a short time (6 weeks)! The overall healthy appearance, that attitude change with our 'recluse,' the itchy skin problem is gone, need I say more?! I have recommended (HIGHLY) Wysong Diets and C-Biotic™ to several people and will continue to do so."

CALIFORNIA: "My roommate and I swear by your dry cat formulas. About two months ago we adopted 2 kittens that were born wild on the levee near us. We feed them Wysong plus homemade foods. They are the ultimate picture of health. Their coats don't just shine, they glisten!"

GEORGIA: "I am currently feeding your Canine Growth™ formula to my two Australian Shepherd puppies. It is wonderful! I raised the elder dog on (bleep)* which seemed fine at the time. After switching, I noticed (bleep's)* limitations. Their coats are outstanding, their energy levels are high and they have little-to-

---

* A super premium food, the identity of which we withhold to protect the guilty. To be fair, any pet can have a health problem eating any food (including ours) since pets are bound to be eating something when they become ill. But you can be sure that pets on properly designed diets as part of the Optimal Health Program (see pages 195-208) will have the best possible health.

no body/ear/breath odor. I wanted to thank you for producing such an outstanding, environmentally/ecologically sound food."

ONTARIO, CANADA: "Our pet Pomeranian puppy, Poncie, absolutely thrives on Wysong pet food. It was our veterinarian who first referred us to Wysong and I can say that this was the best thing that has ever happened to me as a lifelong pet owner! Thank you for your kindness and once again please accept my deep appreciation for your invaluable products and your innovative methods of animal health care."

TEXAS: "Your food was recommended to us by our vet. Our Golden Retriever really loves your food. We can see a difference in him already. Not only is the food high quality, but it actually looks good and smells good."

INTERNET: "I had to write to tell you about how your Wysong feline food has helped our kitten. Oscar was found in the woods with the rest of his littermates already dead. He was tiny, and a real fighter, and it was love at first sight for me. Unfortunately, we have found out that he had severe malnutrition and parasites internally, and they suspect a genetic disorder in which his body is not developing properly. Well he has gained 5 ounces and is active and talkative and I think it has to do with your wonderful food. He is eating it and loving it, and I cannot thank the makers of Wysong enough. It is really a testament to what the right food can do. We may not see Oscar live a long life, but the life he will have has been greatly improved by Wysong food. Thank you!"

INTERNET: "I have fed my Himalayan cat Wysong exclusively for the past three months. He loves it and is big and strong and very active."

SHOW CHAMPIONS

CALIFORNIA: "Enclosed is a picture of what I believe may be your first 'Boxer' Champion. He's a magnificent animal, a true testament to your fine food."

BREEDER, ILLINOIS: "Some of the other breeders suggested it to me for improving coats and appetites. I am very happy to say it has been amazing. My coats are doing wonderful, there's such an improvement I can't believe it myself. I've finished three of them this year and I do believe it's because of the texture change. I had one girl that lost all of her coat due to allergies and scratching, and have been trying to grow a new coat since last October. She finished with a full coat. I also had one of my boys that had stomach problems all last year and changing food has stopped his intestinal problems completely. I wanted you to know how pleased I am with your products and plan to try some of your other line."

ILLINOIS: "Ever since we have been using your canine diet (feline too!), the health, vigor, coats, and attitudes of our dogs have been absolutely amazing. Every dog we have raised on it, the last four and a half years have not only been easy to finish their championships, but multiple specialty, group winning, and nationally ranked in the top ten during their campaigns as well. I have never been so happy with a product as we are yours! The balance is right-on for their nutritional needs for general health, and it has the correct mixture of fatty acids and other wonderful things that make their luxurious double coats magnificent to work with – week after week for the show ring. Hips, elbows, stifles, and thyroid tests on all our dogs are currently normal, we believe in large part due to your products. Thank you for such wonderful products!"

BREEDER, TEXAS: "Thank you for the good food. My bitch had skin problems, so I switched her to your food. I then sent her to the American Boxer Club Specialty. She won Winners Bitch, Best of Winners and Best of Opposite."

BREEDER, INTERNET: "I am extremely pleased with your food. I am a breeder and professional handler. I specialize in terriers and many times we have difficulties with skin and coat, especially with Westies. In December, I changed my champion male Westie to your food on recommendation. At that time, I was having trouble getting good thick coat and it was extremely slow growing. Also, I noticed that his hair was getting drier and coming out much too easy. I have to admit that when I switched his food over to Synorgon™ and Archetype™ I was not expecting much of a difference till about three months (that seems to be the time I have found most foods to show up and it is also about the time for a cycle of development of their coats). I was pleasantly surprised to see a change starting in about a month. I now have my 3 house Scottie's on it and weaned my most recent litter with Growth™ and Archetype™ (they are now 7 weeks old)."

BREEDER, INTERNET: "Arthur is a '4' generation 'WYSONG WESTIE.' In Canada, he got his Canadian Championship in 2 shows winning 'Best Puppy In Show.' In the U.S., in the two shows he has been in, he has won 'Best in Puppy Sweepstakes,' and 'Reserve Winners Dog' at the Westhighland White Terrier Club of Greater Washington and 'Best Puppy,' also 'Best in Puppy Sweepstakes' at the W.H.W.T.C. of America Roving Specialty, and his class. All of this at 10½ months of age. I know without Wysong he would not be here today."

BREEDER, INTERNET: "My German Shepherd has the nicest, shiniest coat, and is VERY healthy. He's made his first champion point at 13 months, due in large part to his healthy appearance from eating Wysong. He LOVES it!"

PETS PREFER HEALTHY FOODS

CALIFORNIA: "I'm happy to report that when I get home from work each day, she can hardly wait until I feed her...she almost climbs up my side as I prepare the food! Thanks for making such a great product! My Scottie will be fed Wysong dog food from now on."

MAINE: "Speaking of Archetype™, it is hard to express how excited I am about this new product. I find it interesting that as other food companies are just beginning to add probiotics, human grade ingredients etc. that you are already making the next generation of pet food. It sure gives me a great deal of satisfaction knowing that Wysong leads in this new innovation. Watching my cats eat the Archetype for the first time I was surprised to see that they eat it the same way that they eat mice that they have caught. They chunk it down; it was surprising to me to see this. Now, every night at 6:00, they jump up on the counter where they are fed and meow non-stop until I give them some Archetype. Not only do the cats really like this diet, but my dogs like it as well. The first night after feeding Becky, my 7-year-old Gordon Setter, I left the open Archetype on the counter. After leaving the room for a few seconds and then coming back, Becky was on the counter with her front feet tearing the Archetype bag to get more."

MICHIGAN: "We have a Bouvier who loves Wysong. Thanks for making such a terrific product!"

TEXAS: "My sweet old black lab loves Wysong Senior™ and even throws up any other brand of pet food."

WASHINGTON: "Wysong makes the finest pet food available (and one of my cats certainly agrees because she refuses to eat anything else)..."

INTERNET: "I am so pleased I had to take time to write! Our Wile E has been in our lives for about 5 years now. In that time we haven't been able to get her to eat dry food and we didn't buy cheap brands. I then started making her food, and that was a big hit with her. She would pick out the Wysong dry. Yeah, I know, she's spoiled. However, she takes such good care of me and watches out for me in my times of need. That time is more often now due to a brain injury I received last June. Anyway, she loves the Wysong Maintenance™! We don't have to mix it with anything! She chows it down. She scratches less, she looks better, she is a happy girl and that makes us very happy."

INTERNET: "I just learned about Archetype™...They love this food. I gave them each 1 chunk on their food and they went nuts."

INTERNET: "I just wanted to drop you a letter to let you know our experience of receiving your dog food yesterday. Buddy, our dog, loves it. He was all over the box and when I got it open, I could hardly get one of the bags open, and when I did he gobbled down the food before I could put it in his bowl with the homemade food that I make! Now this is a dog that really does not care to eat. He now does! Today his stool was excellent – very important, and he begged for Wysong when I was getting his breakfast ready. That was a first. At dinner this evening, he ate your food before he ate the dog food I make, which was in the same bowl. Very impressive. You have a good product. I am sold."

INTERNET: "I thought you might enjoy hearing about a dog's experience with Wysong. I work for a counseling agency that is funded by our local United Way. Each October, as part of our United Way fundraising, we have a 'Dog's Day Afternoon,' where an employee can contribute a fee and bring their dog to work for the day. During this year's Dog Day Afternoon, a co-worker asked me what I feed my dog because she looks so very healthy and bright. I told her I feed her Wysong and the next day brought her a generous sample for her dog to try as well as my catalogue and literature for her family to read. Several days later my co-worker told me she had been mixing a small amount of Wysong with her dog's food (a popular 'health' brand which shall remain nameless) and her dog had begun to pick out the Wysong pellets and eat only those. She also told me her dog actually gets excited and looks forward to mealtime now. While her dog was not really a picky eater, she was never as excited about eating as she is now. She told me, 'It looks like we will be buying Wysong now.' I always knew the difference Wysong has made for my dog. It is good to see those same results with another's pet. Thanks for making such a quality product and being so concerned about the health of our pets."

INTERNET: "I thought you'd like to know that when I switched to Wysong, I was a bit frustrated. I was told to always make a food switch gradually. Well, it was quite a challenge. I put a bit of the little Wysong nuggets in with their regular (bleep)*, planning to increase the amount of Wysong weekly. My 'little darlings' picked through the food only eating the Wysong."

INTERNET: "Just wanted to let you know that my dog loves your food. I have been so pleased. He goes over to his bowl and licks it the next day even! He has been on several foods and after that initial excitement about a new food, he could barely care, leaving eating dinner until late at night. Now he asks for your food and eats right away or within the hour. Also, I'm not sure if this has anything to do with it, but it seems the stains by his eyes are getting better. No kidding. Just wanted to say thank you very much!"

INTERNET: "My canines are overwhelmed by your food. I am so excited to see them enjoy it – I wish I would have known about your food 8½ years ago."

INTERNET: "My dog and cats love your Archetype™."

INTERNET: "My fussy, allergy-plagued dog LOVED it! I put a small scoop of Wysong with her regular vet-diet food. She usually ignored her dry food until after she had her canned food. Not any longer. She gave the dry food a good, long sniff, took a mouthful of her dry food, spit it out onto the floor and picked out and ate all of the Wysong! When I went back later to pick up her dishes, the Wysong was gone, but most of the vet-diet food was left."

INTERNET: "We are so excited!!! I just ran through the house telling Cubby that he's going to have his treats. (They were temporarily discontinued.) Yay!!! Thank you so much for listening to us all."

MUCH BETTER THAN OTHER DIETS

CALIFORNIA: "All of my dogs were raised on Wysong. Even when they were little. It is the best food I have ever found for pets."

CALIFORNIA: "While it is not my habit to write testimonials for products I use, I felt in this instance compelled to do so because Wysong dog food has made such a marked improvement in my dog's health. I have a 13-year-old Australian Shepherd, who has been one of my best pals for all of his 13 years. A while ago he developed urinary incontinence, a problem for which his veterinarian has been treating him. (He also developed signs of old age and I am right there along with him!) A side effect of the current treatment he is receiving is increased thirst. If I withheld water from him, he experienced loud, labored panting. No one was getting any sleep (since he sleeps in my bedroom) and he seemed to be suffering. I cannot count the number of foods I have tried, all of which have failed, until I found Wysong. After only a few days of feeding him Wysong dog food for older dogs, his thirst diminished, his vitality picked up and he became playful and more interested in life again. After a period of time, I ran out of Wysong and had to make an emergency purchase of another food until I could procure more Wysong. Within a matter of three days we were back to the same

---

* A super premium food, the identity of which we withhold to protect the guilty. To be fair, any pet can have a health problem eating any food (including ours) since pets are bound to be eating something when they become ill. But you can be sure that pets on properly designed diets as part of the Optimal Health Program (see pages 195-208) will have the best possible health.

thirst/panting problems. Sydney's enthusiasm diminished and I could tell he just didn't feel well. The change in his health was immediate and dramatic. In spite of the fact that I had a whole bag of food remaining, I made an emergency call to you for more Wysong. I know that Sydney does not have much longer to live given his age, but I am confident that his quality of life is greatly enhanced by Wysong dog food and that Wysong dog food will add time to his life. I am truly grateful for this product and will use it for all dogs I shall own forever."

FLORIDA: "I had to drop you a line to thank you for this product. The pet shop I go to introduced you to me. I went in to purchase (bleep)* which I had been using for years. I started giving the animals Wysong and I'm hooked on it, why? It's all natural, no BHA or BHT's. The animals seem to thrive on it."

FLORIDA: "I would like to extend my sincerest CONGRATULATIONS to your company for producing and marketing, a truly exceptional pet food. I have tried them all and never have I been as pleased with a product until I was introduced to yours. My 'Golden' is ten years young and, as is the case with many of his breed, he is intermittently bothered with skin inflammation and allergies. I was determined to locate a superior food for him and I truly feel that I have done so with your line of products. It not only satisfies 'Charley's' appetite, but mine as well as a VERY FINICKY consumer. I am so overwhelmingly positive regarding your company and its products that I would also like to inquire about the possibility of acquiring a Distributorship if available."

FLORIDA: "My cats function at optimum health with Wysong Geriatrx™. It's the greatest cat food on the market, believe me, I've tried them all. Helen Girlie and Cappy are both eleven years old and in perfect health because of your food. Thanks so much for developing such a fine food for my friends!"

FLORIDA: "Wysong is the best animal food on the market today in the USA. Thank you."

MASSACHUSETTS: "I wish to express my satisfaction regarding the Wysong Synorgon™ dog food. I have 2 retired male greyhounds who are currently in the process of changing to this kibble. I have spent hours considering many different types of dog food (all premium) and I have chosen Synorgon."

NEW YORK: "My twin 5-year-old boys received twin Rat Terriers from Santa. Two weeks ago one puppy was on the verge of starvation. I became alarmed but finally realized the puppy would rather die than have to eat (bleep)*. I inquired as to what was the best possible alternative and was directed to you. The 'smarter' puppy has finally caught up to the weight of his brother. I am really impressed and wonder if this food could be fed to my twin boys – just kidding."

NEW YORK: "The Wysong Diets are far and away the highest quality diets that I have seen on the market."

ONTARIO, CANADA: "I am very satisfied feeding Wysong food. It is the best I have ever used. I have 6 dogs to feed and they are doing great."

---

* A super premium food, the identity of which we withhold to protect the guilty. To be fair, any pet can have a health problem eating any food (including ours) since pets are bound to be eating something when they become ill. But you can be sure that pets on properly designed diets as part of the Optimal Health Program (see pages 195-208) will have the best possible health.

ONTARIO, CANADA: "I have used almost any and every conceivable cat food (dry & canned) product, natural based and otherwise, and I must say that your products are superlative. I wouldn't even consider feeding anything else. I have a total of 15 cats and with kittens arriving on a regular basis, they thrive on your food. I tell everyone and anyone who has pets about your food and hand out brochures."

PENNSYLVANIA: "I own a 75 lb. black Doberman. I usually feed her (bleep)* or (bleep)*. Just recently my sister who lives outside of Troy, New York introduced me to your Wysong food (Maintenance™). Cleopatra just loves your food and so do I. Her coat has never looked as shiny and I am also impressed with your specs."

TENNESSEE: "We have fed our dog Wysong for 4 years with wonderful results. We have had many comments on his shiny, smooth, dandruff free coat. He has tried other dog foods a couple of times, but we have brought him back to Wysong to stay. Other foods have given him bad breath (both ends), dull fur, dandruff, and a lack of appetite. He loves Wysong and so do we."

TEXAS: "Just wanted to drop you guys a quick line to tell you about how thrilled I am with your products. I feed both dry and canned Wysong to my dog and 2 cats. They absolutely love Wysong, particularly compared to the (bleep)* that I used to feed them just one year ago. I've noticed that their coats are much softer and shinier. I tell everyone I come across about the benefits and joys of feeding Wysong. I've turned many a person into a Wysong believer. In fact, after feeding Wysong to my pets, I became so into and passionate about my three animals that I decided to work full-time in the adoption office for our local animal shelter. The job is very hard (and sometimes frustrating and depressing), but also very rewarding. And, every chance I get, I counsel new adopters on the importance of feeding Wysong to their new pet. I believe this is important. I know that I am not alone because many of my co-workers also feed their pets Wysong and attempt to get more people to try it. I believe many people feed their pets inferior pet foods because either they simply do not know any better, have no motivation to seek out better alternatives, or because it's easier to buy whatever is on their local supermarket's shelves (which usually is not Wysong). Wysong is extremely healthy and beneficial to a pet. Keep up the good work!"

WISCONSIN: "I have tried several different dog foods, Wysong by far is the best food I have ever seen. My dogs really like your food. I have finally put some weight on them while feeding them less food. Thank you for making a good – no great dog food."

INTERNET: "I fed my old dog Wysong Maintenance™ his entire life and he lived a long and healthy life. I now have a 2½-year-old German Shepherd mix who I got from the local shelter when she was 3 months old. A well-intentioned vet convinced me to switch to (bleep)*. Suddenly, everyone we knew who hadn't seen her in a while exclaimed how 'chunky' she'd gotten...Lately, actually for

---

* A super premium food, the identity of which we withhold to protect the guilty. To be fair, any pet can have a health problem eating any food (including ours) since pets are bound to be eating something when they become ill. But you can be sure that pets on properly designed diets as part of the Optimal Health Program (see pages 195-208) will have the best possible health.

months now, she seems to be very itchy and her skin is sensitive. When I flea comb her, I noticed a white chalky streak down the center of her spine that seems to get worse the more I comb her. I decided to do the 'comparison' thing they have on the (bleep)* website and compare to Wysong…Then I went to the Wysong website, and I am once again convinced that Wysong is the way to go. My other dog never had any skin or digestive problems, never had any weight problems, and I don't know why I ever listened to others and switched my German Shepherd to (bleep)*. I am back for good this time."

INTERNET: "I have had both of my Yorkies on your dog food for the past year. I just wanted to let you know just how well they have been doing. Thank you very much for creating such a wonderful product. Your product is far superior to all other products that are on the market."

INTERNET: "I have tried all the natural foods. My dog Amy would almost not eat (bleep)* dog food. She also did not like (bleep)*. She likes yours."

INTERNET: "Just wanted to let you know that my dog loves your products and does real well. I tried a number of natural brands, but stick with Wysong."

INTERNET: "My cats have never been happier! I have four little terrors, ages 6, 5, 4 and 1 year! They are all beautiful, healthy animals... Yet I hadn't seen my eldest cat play since her first litter was born. She is now acting like the kitten she was when we got her!! I will never again purchase another brand!! They used to be (bleep)* kitties, then when they were older, (bleep)*... Your food makes those products look like 'generic-brand Kat Food!!' Thank you for bringing our happy kitty back to us!"

INTERNET: "Our kitty was getting very overweight and was not very energetic as early as 6 months old. We fed him (bleep)* first and went to a lite formula when he got chubby. I then ordered a bag of your Wysong and just couldn't believe the difference. He has more wakeful hours than before, is more playful and kitten-like than he has been for most of his past 18 months. His shape has improved and he looks terrific. He's only been on your food for a few weeks now. I keep marveling over the difference in his healthy shape and his activity level. Thanks so much for making terrific pet foods!"

INTERNET: "We have two Golden Retriever littermates. A male and a female. I switched them over to Wysong after learning how much better your dog food was. They are doing much better on Wysong."

EXCELLENT PREVENTION AND HEALTH FOR CATS

CALIFORNIA: "I have nothing but praise for your cat food. I began getting the Feline Uretic™ when my cat Moses started having problems urinating after a bout of bronchitis. My three cats, Moe, Dorcus, and Peter were new cats!

---

* A super premium food, the identity of which we withhold to protect the guilty. To be fair, any pet can have a health problem eating any food (including ours) since pets are bound to be eating something when they become ill. But you can be sure that pets on properly designed diets as part of the Optimal Health Program (see pages 195-208) will have the best possible health.

Especially Moe, who doesn't like canned food. He was climbing up fences he could never before! He stabilized at an energetic 12 lbs. (He is my Big Orange Cat.) When I moved to La Mesa, in Southern California, I found I had to special order the Uretic™ (and by the case). For me this includes two buses and a fifteen-minute walk, plus $32-35 a pop. After a few times I went generic. Moe gained his old weight back and now has dandruff. Of my new cats Cassia (2-3 years old) got irritable bowel on the generic and Jeremiah (1-2) had teeth so bad from her diet (generic) that a tooth was abscessed. For one month before the doctor's visit I had them on Wysong. Moe got better and so did Cassia. October on generic and all is not well. Wysong is on special order – two cases."

COLORADO: "I want to thank you. My poor cat's immune system just didn't seem to be able to get strong until my vet suggested your food."

GEORGIA: "Just wanted to sing your company's praises for the wonderful pet food you've developed. Wish you could see my cats, see the difference in their appearance and temperaments since I've had them on both the canned and dry foods. They also get the sprinkle on supplements, and I add raw meats, vegetables, and fruits to their diet on a regular basis. All 10 of my cats radiate health and vitality, and incidents of sickness, etc., have dropped considerably since they've been on the Wysong Diets."

IOWA: "In case you didn't know it, you have a miracle product! My wife and I got our first cat 17 years ago. Regardless of the type of food we have given her she has consistently had diarrhea, and frequently has just not eaten. The result is that she has lived her life as a very thin, weak cat. Trips to different vets had not helped, none could provide a solution. We were finally to the place where she was so weak we were planning to have her put to sleep. Our vet suggested we try your Feline Vitality™ product. After years of misery, Sydney eats like a pig! No more diarrhea, she's gaining weight, and she looks a long way from death's door...Since cats can't talk, I hope this says it for her. THANK YOU!"

NEW YORK: "Bandit was in less than healthy condition. Our vet put her on your Feline Vitality™ dry cat food...I have owned cats all my life, and I have never seen a healthier looking or feeling cat! Bandit's fur is sleek, shiny, and soft! Her teeth are bright white and her eyes are bright and alert. Every person Bandit sees says the same thing! We all know it's her diet!"

TEXAS: "Thank you for making such a wonderful pet food available to those of us who love our animal friends. I always get compliments about how great all nine of my cats look. Which only proves you are what you eat!"

WASHINGTON: "As the owner of 2 cats & 1 dog, I have enjoyed the benefits of your fantastic product for 6 years now. My cats are living proof as to its success!"

WASHINGTON: "Ever since my cat was a kitten she has been a 'Wysong Cat.' My cat is still a Wysong Cat and always will be. Her veterinarian claims that the balanced nutrition of Wysong helped her become a healthy cat from the thin sickly kitten she was when I first got her. I know he's right."

INTERNET: "I had to write. I have been using Wysong for approximately 1 month and my cats have never been happier! I hadn't seen my eldest cat play since her first litter was born. She is now acting like the kitten she was when we got her!! I will never again purchase another brand!!"

INTERNET: "I recently started using your F-Biotic™ and am totally amazed with the results! I will be using it from now on and will probably start using some of your other supplements."

INTERNET: "I recently switched my 3 cats to your chicken and turkey canned products. I will never go back to the 'other brands!' My cats are happier, look better (fur and eyes), and just enjoy your product! I am very, very happy with your product. Keep up the good work!"

INTERNET: "My cats love your products. Two bags later, their glossy coats and bright eyes say it all. Thank you for caring as much as I do."

INTERNET: "I have used Vitality™ cat food for several months now and it is obviously a top-quality product – my cat has gone from a scruffy scrawny sickly animal (fed on supermarket pet food) to a magnificent filled-out cat with shiny fluffy fur such as I haven't seen on her in many years. I believe the improvement in her health is entirely due to the change in her diet, because that has been the only major change in her lifestyle lately. THANK YOU!"

INTERNET: "I've been a Wysong enthusiast for years and have fed your wet and dry food to my cats exclusively. Thanks very much for providing our non-human friends with such excellent nourishment."

INTERNET: "Susie and Tiger both look like totally different cats! Very lush coats, attitudes MUCH improved, and they were 'good cats' to begin! Now Suz hops up on my lap for a cuddle, and gives me the evil eye when it's time to go... and she is a LAPFULL! Probably gained 3-4 pounds since I first contacted you. Thanks again for being a big part in saving her life!"

INTERNET: "We didn't think there was much difference in cat foods, but after changing Gimpy to Wysong Vitality™, her coat is shinier, her eyes are brighter and her energy levels are up."

MAKES THE OLD YOUNG AGAIN

CALIFORNIA: "My dog is 14 years old and is thriving on it. She is like a puppy, bounding over hedges, running about, etc. It isn't often that one sees 14-year-old Dalmatians with such good health."

CALIFORNIA: "Thank You! You saved Hank's life. Hank is the most wonderful 13-year-old Lab you can imagine, but six months ago he reached a point where he could not digest *anything*. He gagged and threw up and his poor stomach would rumble and complain and GAS – whew! Because I love this dog so much I was determined there was something out there he could eat and one of those miracles – I found Wysong and he began to thrive. He can digest it with no symptoms. He now can run and hike and acts like a youngster again. Also, his arthritis has disappeared and he can run and jump in the pickup again. Amazing stuff. I should be a representative I've referred so many people to your products!"

CANADA: "I have a 4-year-old Cocker who has had four homes in as many years, and a 14-year-old Border Collie/Cocker who came to me this past year from an elderly man who had died. My dogs' homeopathic vet suggested to me I should be giving them Wysong. I took a chance and bought a bag of Wysong Maintenance™ and both dogs ate it immediately. I have found the perfect diet for my old dog now. He gobbles this up. I have noticed that the old dog is now running and playing and smiling a whole lot more than he used to. Also, the fact that both dogs can now finish their dinner in one sitting is a nice change."

CANADA: "This is in regard to my 17-year-old cat, Mocha. She has had some vomiting and diarrhea with resulting weight loss over the past few months. Her digestion is now back to normal. She has a voracious appetite. We are feeding her 4 small meals a day with PDG™ in it. I want you to know that all her blood work came back absolutely normal! No evidence of kidney or liver abnormalities. The vet was amazed that a 17-year-old cat would show this! I owe all this to feeding her Wysong products and supplements over the last 6 years with raw, fresh food also... Our cats are healthy and never require medical care!"

COLORADO: "I just recently learned about your products from a friend who had them recommended by her vet for her elderly and ailing dog. After only a few weeks of eating Wysong canine foods exclusively, her appearance, stamina, and overall health have taken a dramatic turn for the better! I immediately switched to Wysong products for my own dog. He likes your pet foods more than any he has eaten in the past. Plus, with Wysong's effects on my friend's dog, I am convinced that my dog will live a healthier life."

MASSACHUSETTS: "I AM TOTALLY AMAZED!! My 12-year-old cat has been on Vitality™ only 5 days and I can't believe the change! The difference in her coat and she is playful! I used to give her (bleep)*."

MICHIGAN: "I have been feeding Wysong Senior™ for over two years to my now 14½-year-old Golden Retriever and for a year to my 8-year-old Golden. I put my old dog on the food after he was neutered due to testicular cancer, and I firmly believe that the ingredients in Wysong have helped him become the vivacious, spirited geriatric dog that he is. He suffered what we believe to be a stroke this past winter, and probably because of his otherwise good health he recovered fully... Thanks for making such a great food for my dogs. I won't ever feed anything else!"

NEVADA: "I purchased the Wysong dog food several months ago. What a remarkable change in my 16-year-old mix breed terrier. Off and on I've had to give her other dog foods since then, and always she begins to decline when I run out of Wysong. With other dog foods she can barely place one step over another; after a couple of weeks on Wysong she's running and pulling tight ahead of me and walking me instead of the other way around. She has less trouble going up and down stairs. Thank you. I've bragged about your product

---

* A super premium food, the identity of which we withhold to protect the guilty. To be fair, any pet can have a health problem eating any food (including ours) since pets are bound to be eating something when they become ill. But you can be sure that pets on properly designed diets as part of the Optimal Health Program (see pages 195-208) will have the best possible health.

to my friends but they doubt my dog is 16 years old in the first place, or believe it's just my imagination. But my husband and I are convinced."

OHIO: "When my dog was eating your food she looked and acted a lot healthier. By the way, she is a 13-year-old Doberman and she loved your food! She has a thyroid condition, requiring expensive medication, which causes bare spots on her haunches. When she was eating your food these spots went away and as soon as I stopped feeding her Wysong they returned."

INTERNET: "I have a pup that is half wolf and half German Shepherd. The only dog food she eats is Wysong (puppy and Vegan™). Since I started buying Wysong for her, I decided to feed my older dog the Maintenance™ dog food. Her health and energy has improved drastically! My two dogs and I thank you for your wonderful product..."

INTERNET: "Thank you for your products. I have a very elderly cat who was going downhill steadily... I've been supplementing her and also syringe feeding her for almost 2 years. She's strong willed and her spirit is not ready to give out as much as her body. I have had her on the Wysong Geriatrx™ about 8 weeks, and amazingly enough, came across Archetype™ at my local generic pet supply store. I bought all 4 packages they had. I make a gruel to fill the syringe – a mixture of Geriatrx and Archetype. Since the Archetype, about 3 weeks now, her strength amazingly improved."

INTERNET: "We started our other Standard Poodle, a 5-year-old male, on Wysong, switching from (bleep)* several months ago, as well as our two 15-year-old cats. We've been very pleased with Wysong. We've really noticed a difference in the cats. One cat also used to vomit a couple of times a week, and this seems to have stopped since beginning Wysong. Hairball medicine and hairball cat food did not seem to help. Our Poodle has a good level of energy and always eats his food, whereas before he frequently didn't eat, and we had a problem with him vomiting in the early morning every now and then."

INTERNET: "We have an Irish Setter who will be 18 years old... We have been feeding her Wysong for the last 5 or 6 years and she loves it. Before, she was such a picky eater, we were sure that this has helped her live so long."

BETTER BEHAVIOR AND CONTENTMENT

CALIFORNIA: "Our cats have shinier coats and are more alert and playful since starting them on your foods."

DELAWARE: "I can tell you my dogs have an air of contentment they never had on other foods. Dogs that were destroying things no longer destroy, etc."

ONTARIO, CANADA: "I began introducing Wysong to my cat, adding only 3-4 tsp. to his other food at each feeding. Well, it has been only 3 days however; the change is almost astounding in my cat. His energy level has increased

---

* A super premium food, the identity of which we withhold to protect the guilty. To be fair, any pet can have a health problem eating any food (including ours) since pets are bound to be eating something when they become ill. But you can be sure that pets on properly designed diets as part of the Optimal Health Program (see pages 195-208) will have the best possible health.

greatly (he actually wants to play and socialize vs. sleep all the time). As a scientist, I want to be skeptical in attributing this change to the new food – but there is no other reasonable explanation. I am so very grateful."

TENNESSEE: "Muffin came to me shy and insecure and very much underweight... He's beginning to feel loved and somewhat secure and has gained weight. At your suggestion I'm also making a raw meat, rice and veggie formula."

WISCONSIN: "I am very pleased with my cat's health since I started using Wysong. She has maintained six to seven pounds for the last two years. Along with her weight, another problem she had was crystallization in her urine. That too is no longer a problem. When she was a kitten she was traumatized in the first home she lived in. When I took her in I noticed how touchy she was. I do not know how much her diet plays a part in this, but between my affection, devotion, safe home and healthy diet, she is no longer a terrified little cat. More than two years ago she could not be held, rubbed or anything. She would only hide in small dark places. It is hard to look back and remember exactly where the changes in her personality began, but I put it all back to when I began using Wysong. I felt the need to let you hear about one of your devoted clients. My cat is a wonderful, healthy cat...thank you."

INTERNET: "Love your food, my dog has never been happier!"

INTERNET: "My dog has been using your dog food for a long time and my pet is really happy. He's also very healthy. You are still the best dog food."

BETTER SKIN AND COAT HEALTH, AND STOPS ALLERGY

CALIFORNIA: "For once I found a food that helps my dog grow hair instead of lose it. I feel so good that I almost named my new pup 'Wysong'."

CALIFORNIA: "I cannot tell you how pleased I am with your food for allergies. I have used it for only one week but there is a big difference in my dogs."

CALIFORNIA: "I feed my 5 Golden Retrievers your dog food under the advice of my veterinarian. Besides my dogs liking the food, it seems to have cleared the skin problems they were having on (bleep)* pet foods."

CALIFORNIA: "I had a beautiful Irish Setter show dog given to me. He began to scratch and itch and quite frankly I found myself with a nearly nude Setter. My wonderful veterinarian did all he could do testing for allergies, using Cortisone as a desperate effort, all to no avail. I was administering anti-allergy shots to this poor dog nightly and still he did not respond. Of course, we tried many, many dog foods and preparations and still we had a miserable looking and feeling Setter. THEN WE FOUND WYSONG!!! Halfway through the first bag of Anergen™, the dog's itching stopped, he began to feel better and hair began to

---

* A super premium food, the identity of which we withhold to protect the guilty. To be fair, any pet can have a health problem eating any food (including ours) since pets are bound to be eating something when they become ill. But you can be sure that pets on properly designed diets as part of the Optimal Health Program (see pages 195-208) will have the best possible health.

grow...and grow...and grow. It was most remarkable! We are on our third bag of Wysong and singing its praises. The veterinarian is amazed and I am thrilled."

CALIFORNIA: "I have 2 cats and 1 dog. One of the cats, a 6-year-old Siamese, has had skin problems, dandruff and oily mess. After switching, his skin has cleared up and he now has a beautiful coat – after only 2 weeks on your food!"

CALIFORNIA: "I have been transitioning the animals off all their 'high end,' 'prescription,' and 'Veterinarian recommended' and went to Wysong's system. I am witnessing DRAMATIC results in my animals, i.e. ear secretions, fungus on the nail beds and in the ears, and the pruritic orange exudate that has been coming out of his entire body, mostly underneath and down all legs and feet, is all going away!!! For the first time in his lifetime, now eight, we can see white fur, and pink skin. The orange is turning yellow, and is just now on the tips of the hairs. The new growth is new growth! Every day of his life, he has suffered severely. He has endured daily scrubbings, ear cleanings, prescriptions, chemical washes in his ears, and everywhere else, so many visits to so many veterinarians, from dermatologists to acupuncture, to Bach's flower remedies, to hundreds of subcutaneous injections of allergy treatments, changes in diet, and he itched and itched and itched. Every time he would come to me for love, he would get poked, scraped, scrubbed, and rubbed, and then loved and smooched and hugged. Every day of his life I have shaken my head and wanted to cry for him. Months ago, I stopped injecting him. He said, "Please, I don't want anymore injections." Every night he hops beside my face on my pillow and licks himself to sleep. He licks, and I scratch him! Well, it is all going away! Day after day, I am watching it fade."

CALIFORNIA: "I just had to write to you and tell you what a remarkable product your C-Biotic™ is. My dog is an Airdale/Shepard mix and I got her at about 1½ years from an animal foundation. She is now 8½ and for her entire life she has chewed her back and has been on cortisone pills and shots – which I hated to give her. One of my clients raises Scottish Deerhounds and I was telling her about Benn, my dog, and she brought me in some C-Biotic and told me to try it. Well – after three months – my dog has a full growth of fur on her back and looks beautiful. No more pills, and maybe it's me, but she seems much spunkier. Being the skeptic that I am I would have never believed it but seeing is believing. All my friends are astounded at the way Benn looks – and I have sold a ton of your product through recommendation to them for their dogs. I should be a sales rep for you!! (Really Benn should be.) I'm only sorry I didn't find this sooner and I wish I had before and after pictures for you. Thank you so much!"

CALIFORNIA: "I would like to say that a few months ago I switched to Wysong Food for my dogs (upon the recommendation of a friend) and I absolutely love the results and the difference I see in their coats and general health. My Labradors never looked better! Many of my friends would like to switch to Wysong after seeing the results – even my Vet!"

CALIFORNIA: "My dog chews at his feet and I have noticed him *not* doing it after 4 weeks of dry Wysong."

DELAWARE: "My 2½-year-old German Shepherd was having an itching problem...my friend told me to try Wysong Diets...not a bit of itching – Praises be...thank you for all the concern and care you put into your products, I only wish every dog could be on it. I thank the day my friend told me about it."

FLORIDA: "Our dog's veterinarian has put our 'Hugo' on Wysong. Due to his food and many other allergies we had tried most every other food. He is doing fine on Wysong and loves it! Many good changes have taken place; less shedding, better coat and better stool habits."

LOUISIANA: "We've tried many other brands, but yours is definitely the best. Our Lab/Chow mix had a terrible dry, flaking skin with a dull coat. Since switching to Wysong, her coat is no longer dry and is full of luster. We also have a Sharpei. Known for their awful skin problems, our dog was no different. On Wysong, she no longer has any skin problems. Our Vet is astonished!"

MASSACHUSETTS: "My Collie was put on Wysong last January and the first positive result was he gained 10 lbs. in one month. He had always been very thin and could not put weight on no matter what he was fed. He put on a few more pounds and is now maintaining his weight. The next positive result was his allergies – which appeared every year in March (as the snow melted) and got progressively worse until November. The first 2 summers of his life he was put on potent antibiotics for the entire time, and the allergies got worse to the point that his entire body was affected. This is the Collie's 4th summer ...he is vastly improved and I attribute it to Wysong. Another 'miracle' is my mother's German Shepherd, whose coat was dull and dry; skin was red and in places actually bleeding; constantly biting at himself. The first vet shaved the dog in several places looking for fleas (he found none). Four months later, the dog still looked awful, still biting at himself constantly, but now he had bare patches where the vet had shaved him; not even a stubble had grown in. I took the dog to another vet to have thyroid tests done – he was normal. I then decided to put him on Wysong. Three weeks later he looked like a new dog: fur had grown in where there had been none, coat was shiny, no more dandruff, skin was nice and healthy looking – no more bleeding, and the dog no longer was biting at himself."

MICHIGAN: "It is WONDERFUL!! Our dog has major food allergies. Finally, something she can eat. Thank you so much."

MINNESOTA: "My husband and I were seriously considering having our 10-year-old West Highland White Terrier put to sleep because of her hysterical scratching from allergies. She has had numerous allergy tests and is allergic to almost all dog foods. At that time I was lucky enough to find Wysong at a pet food warehouse. Since that time her coat has grown back in thicker than it has ever been and her scratching is all but gone. This is after years of trying vets and medications, as well as every dog food on the market."

PENNSYLVANIA: "I just wanted to write and let you know I found your dog food through a breeder/friend and am eternally grateful to your company! We have two Shetland sheepdogs, which as everyone knows, can be easily affected by airborne or food borne allergies that affect their coat, skin and health in general. Shelties can be prone to many a varied problem, but are wonderful intelligent dogs. So, when our new Sheltie puppy had a bout with flea bite dermatitis (which took awhile to detect, since no fleas or flea related symptoms were present), which left him undernourished (he wouldn't eat) and with multiple skin and coat problems, we were advised by a Sheltie breeder that Wysong dog foods might help in getting this little pup back on his feet due to your superior/ healthy ingredients. We felt at this point that we had nothing to lose, and everything to gain by trying yet another dog food, as up to this point he was proving to be a 'non-eater' and was not healthy in our view. We had already tried (bleep)*, (bleep)*, (bleep)*, and a variety of other premium dog foods to no avail. Numerous trips to our vet included blood workups, skin scrapings, and other tests that proved negative and futile. So, we figured 'why not,' and gave your food a try. Well, no one was more amazed than us when our little boy not only ate the new Wysong dog food with gusto, but also actually started to thrive on it! Within three weeks of being on your Synorgon™ formula, he was a different puppy! He gained weight (in fact he doubled his weight within this period), skin and coat condition were remarkably better, and he was healthy once again! His vet has even been amazed at his quick recovery and lustrous new coat since putting him on this food. She admitted that the new food was helping him gain a whole new healthy self due to the high omega 3 content in this food and premium ingredients (chicken, ground brown rice, flaxseed), which in turn helped him regain a healthy immune system and overall health. I have started to recommend this food to all my Sheltie friends and acquaintances as both a normal maintenance diet and as a possible food source to help with Shelties who are also 'fussy eaters,' sick or convalescing. Everyone so far who has tried this food agrees that their Shelties gobble it up and for long term users, they have seen a marked improvement in overall health, coat and skin of their dogs. Again, thank you for making such a superior dog food that not only provides our dogs with a healthy, natural based nutritious diet, but giving us owners a little piece of mind as well. Our other Sheltie, who is almost a year old, is also on your Synorgon formula and has gained a wonderful coat and eagerly gobbles it up, which he had never done before on any other brand of premium dog food!"

VETERINARIAN, TENNESSEE: "An 8-month-old Old English Sheepdog was presented with intense pruritus...we started the dog on Wysong. One week later the owner reported that the pruritus had decreased significantly. At last report, the dog is doing well with no evidence of pruritus."

TEXAS: "I wanted to let you know how positively impressed I am with your Canine Diets. Feeding Wysong to my dogs has made a wonderful difference in their coats, and they are incredibly fit and healthy! I had not heard of your product until a friend of mine told me about it. I saw how beautiful and full of good health her Rottweiler was. She attributed her pet's health to Wysong. She couldn't sing its praises enough! That's when I decided to try it for my own dogs. I was indeed pleased. Thank you for making such a fine, high quality dog food. Eating well has shown to be the key to good health, and I'm glad I can provide that for my pets."

---

* A super premium food, the identity of which we withhold to protect the guilty. To be fair, any pet can have a health problem eating any food (including ours) since pets are bound to be eating something when they become ill. But you can be sure that pets on properly designed diets as part of the Optimal Health Program (see pages 195-208) will have the best possible health.

WASHINGTON: "...After two months, my beautiful Spaniel has hair over his whole body, and his dermatitis is much better, although still there. I recently added your Flaxseed Oil™ to his diet to give him a little extra help and he eats like he loves it. Even the Weimeraner benefited, she glows with health and her shedding is reduced, as is her waistline. I can now foresee my dog having a real Water Spaniel coat and going into the show ring again. Thank you for putting out such a superior product. I noticed the human products and plan to try some of them next. I am so grateful for what you have done to make my companions more healthy and comfortable. God bless you."

WASHINGTON: "My cat kept chewing the hair off her back and tail. She had been eating (bleep)* when this began. I changed her diet to (bleep)* which did not stop the chewing. Then I tried (bleep)*, and the chewing got worse. At one point, her body was ½ naked – the whole back half of her back, legs and 2 to 3 inches of her tail base. Then I discovered Wysong and her hair grew back completely!"

WASHINGTON: "I have a re-homed, year-old Irish Water Spaniel with allergies (bladder infection, inflamed sheath and flea dermatitis). By the time the original infections were cleared up, the poor guy had no hair on his back, belly, chest, paws, and rear legs. My husband, who is normally not too decisive on dog matters, made the choice then and there and bought a forty-pound box. We switched both dogs (we also have a Weimeraner) to Synorgon™ over the next week. They ate like animals and we haven't looked back."

WASHINGTON: "My tabby had skin scabs for 5 years and her hair was thin in places. She kept scratching her scabs until they bled. Finally Wysong came out and her scabs disappeared in 3 months and her fur is thick and shiny. Her fur has never looked this good!"

WASHINGTON: "We have used your Wysong Canine Diet for at least a year on a Doberman with allergies. His skin has been much better than with any other food, including lamb and rice diets. We had tried everything we could find, and this is the best for this dog. Thanks."

VETERINARIAN, WISCONSIN: "The pets on Wysong Diets seem healthier with better hair coat, improved growth in pups and kittens, and clients love it! Here is a typical case history: 6-year-old intact male Newfoundland has chronic (2 years) skin disease. The dog has been examined by four other veterinarians. Owner elected to try Wysong Maintenance™ Diet. At 30 days, itching had stopped. At 60 days, hair growth had become evident. At 90 days, skin and hair were normal."

INTERNET: "Attached is a picture of my Somali grand premiere. Take a look at that gorgeous coat! Thanks Wysong!"

INTERNET: "Both my cats have always had a bad case of dandruff. Then something extraordinary happened – I bought – just for the heck of it – your dry Vegan™

---

* A super premium food, the identity of which we withhold to protect the guilty. To be fair, any pet can have a health problem eating any food (including ours) since pets are bound to be eating something when they become ill. But you can be sure that pets on properly designed diets as part of the Optimal Health Program (see pages 195-208) will have the best possible health.

diet. I include a quarter of a can for each cat of Gourmet™ or the All Meat and Organ™ canned and in the evenings about half a cup each of dry. The result – no dandruff! I mean nothing, not a trace! Plus their shedding has been greatly reduced. Their fur is sleeker, softer, and shinier than I had ever seen it. What's in it? A magic bullet? I mean even my vet couldn't come up with anything! I thank you, thank you, thank you. A special meow from 2 happy felines."

INTERNET: "I adopted a 7-month-old cat from the local adopt-a-thon a few months ago. She had been cared for, spayed, etc., after being found roaming the streets. She was very thin and her coat was very dry and dull. She was eating (bleep)* when I got her and did not like to change her diet. She is the kind of cat that doesn't care what she eats, as long as we keep it consistent. But her coat is so shiny, it shimmers! This is GOOD food!"

INTERNET: "I am the owner of a 20-month Doberman female who was fed Wysong. She has done very well on your food and everyone who meets her comments on her overall appearance, but especially her coat."

INTERNET: "I recently changed to Wysong Synorgon™. I have one young Great Dane and two 10-year-old Italian Greyhounds. One of my Italian Greyhounds has had a thyroid problem most of his adult life and has been basically hairless except for a few spots here and there, and also has seizures every 4 to 6 months. Since Wysong, he has grown a full body of hair. I can't believe it, nor can anyone else who used to know Gabriel, the hairless. He is a beautiful soft silky golden fawn color. I have had him since he was three and I never knew what his true color was."

INTERNET: "I have been feeding my 11-year-old cat the Anergen™ formula – both the canned and dry – mixed together, as she has severe food allergies. She is absolutely thriving on it!"

INTERNET: "Just wanted to thank you from the bottom of my heart for your Wysong Anergen™ dog food. My Tommy (retired Greyhound) is better. After surgery to remove a broken infected leg, my Tommy developed an allergy and became red all around his mouth. He is white, so this was especially unnerving and sad. We tried everything, steroids, foods, vitamins, flax oil, etc. We also tried Benadryl™ and other antihistamines. Nothing worked and Tommy got progressively worse. I happened upon your dog food and ordered some. We are on our 5th week and Tommy is turning white again. It is a miracle. I love you all. Can you send it to me in 55-gallon drums?? It has been 18 months with no improvement until we tried your product. God bless you!!"

INTERNET: "My cats have been eating Wysong foods since they came to me at 5 months – my vet always exclaims about the gorgeousness of their coats."

INTERNET: "The breeder I got my cat from was feeding the mother Wysong before, during, and after she became pregnant. That cat's coat is gorgeous."

---

* A super premium food, the identity of which we withhold to protect the guilty. To be fair, any pet can have a health problem eating any food (including ours) since pets are bound to be eating something when they become ill. But you can be sure that pets on properly designed diets as part of the Optimal Health Program (see pages 195-208) will have the best possible health.

INTERNET: "We cannot sing your praises loudly enough! I feed my guide dog Wysong and add in the C-Biotic™. She is doing splendidly. I am on a mailing list for guide dog users and I just got this in the mail after referring a person to Synorgon™ about six months ago. Here you go: 'I don't know if you remember me, but I asked about food for dogs with bad allergies on G-Dog list and you were kind enough to suggest Wysong Synorgon™. I am the one with the pet Border Collie shepherd cross who loses all his hair in the spring. Couver is allergic to grass, corn, and a multitude of other things. I am writing because I just returned from the vet with the terrific news that he shows no signs of any allergies. But even better after about 6 months on Wysong he also has gained 10 pounds. We have never been able to keep weight on him and now he looks wonderful. I can't thank you enough.' The list knows we feed Wysong, and they know why! My own dog is allergy-free as well, although she chewed herself raw on other foods."

INTERNET: "We recently put our 11-year-old Keeshond on Wysong. We noticed some really neat improvements from the (bleep)* we had been giving him. Such things as his eyes clearing from a bluish black tint back to their original brown, and not having allergic type symptoms such as watery eyes and itchy inner ears. Plus, increased energy and overall well-being. We are extremely grateful for this."

HEALS BONES AND JOINTS

KENNEL, NEW YORK: "During our last K-9 school I noticed a significant decrease in the number of K-9 Panosteitis related illnesses which have plagued our K-9 schools for years...our dogs have done quite well nutritionally with the Wysong."

NEW YORK: "Our Schnauzer, Pepper, had a very bad problem with her back left leg. She had reconstructive surgery on her knee but she was left with painful arthritis in the leg. There were days she could not put any pressure on the leg. She would limp and if touched, cried in pain. We were very concerned that nothing could be done to make her more comfortable. After seeing an article in my dog magazine about your food and its benefits we decided to give it a try. Well it has been almost two years now and we have noticed a marked improvement in Pepper's leg. She does not limp anymore, runs around playing like a puppy and has never seemed healthier. Our vet said for her age she is in excellent condition. Pepper will be 14 years old in November. We firmly believe that Wysong has been a definite factor in Pepper's improvement. I bless the day I saw the article and started her on your food."

VETERINARIAN, WISCONSIN: "A 1-year-old Fox Terrier was presented at our clinic with a distal radial ulnar fracture. By mid-February the fracture appeared healed on the radiograph. Three weeks later, he came back refractured in approximately the same location. Checking into his diet revealed he had been on

---

* A super premium food, the identity of which we withhold to protect the guilty. To be fair, any pet can have a health problem eating any food (including ours) since pets are bound to be eating something when they become ill. But you can be sure that pets on properly designed diets as part of the Optimal Health Program (see pages 195-208) will have the best possible health.

a 'grocery store special' brand of dog food. We applied an Edgewood splint and put him on Wysong Diets. His body condition just bloomed – he gained weight and his leg healed so well that when we finally x-rayed the leg in May – the fracture area was barely discernible! Since that time, Wysong is part of our post surgery, trauma regimen. The results have been gratifying!"

INTERNET: "My 10-year-old Bernese Mountain Dog, who has Class III elbow dysplasia takes no chemical drugs and is doing better than 4 years ago when I was knee-deep in my veterinarian's pharmaceutical programs for her. The difference has been outstanding."

HELPS DIGESTIVE PROBLEMS

BRITISH COLUMBIA, CANADA.: "I have a 6 year old soft-coated Wheaten Terrier. Since he was a pup, he has had problems with diarrhea (big time). Last summer, I started feeding Canine Maintenance and I can't believe the difference!! He hardly has the loose poops and hasn't had major diarrhea since. It is great and I just wanted you to know."

CALIFORNIA: "I have a 2½ lb. Chihuahua that has colitis very bad. The only food that she can tolerate is Wysong. I feed her the canned and dry. Her life depends on it...Thank you for making such a wonderful product."

CALIFORNIA: "I want to let you know that I am very happy to have found out about Wysong. I adopted a cat a year ago and he had a very sensitive stomach. He would vomit all the time and it was concerning me so I tried changing his diet. When he started on Wysong he suddenly stopped vomiting and I saw his health improve substantially. Great product! Keep it up."

CALIFORNIA: "I've been feeding my cat, Archie, your Vitality™ Feline Diet, and it is the only dry cat food which doesn't constipate him. All others do, including the ones I've gotten from his vet. Can't tell you how happy I am, for both Archie and me."

CALIFORNIA: "Since using the Wysong Diets, our English Springer looks great and no longer has gastric disturbances. We recommend this product highly."

CALIFORNIA: "Thank you for creating such a wonderful product. It took me six years to find it but now my dog is happy and healthy. He eats Wysong, but now he digests his food well and eliminates easily! Hooray!"

GEORGIA: "I have a sweet cat who had been sick for several months with diarrhea. I had gone to the vet twice with only temporary relief. She was losing weight and I was very concerned, when a friend of mine recommended your food. I picked up a bag at the health food store I regularly shop at. I mixed it as directed and then went to straight Wysong after a month. To my great delight, my cat's diarrhea is completely gone. It's been two months now and she's feeling so much better. Thanks for making such super, healthy food for my cats. My kitty and I love Wysong."

LOUISIANA: "I can't tell you what a difference this food has made in my dog's life. He has gained weight and his stools are firmer and his stomach problems gone. What's more, he loves it! Thanks so much...you are a cut above the rest."

MAINE: "I have two 11-year-old cats that gave up all commercial food 9 months ago. They have very noticeable differences [on Wysong] and one was prone to throwing up every couple of weeks and never does now. Thanks!"

NEW HAMPSHIRE: "For the past six months I have been feeding our 9-year-old cat your Feline Vitality™ food. This food has ended a life-long digestive problem for the cat, who used to vomit several times weekly. Over the years we have tried almost every commercial cat food available. Yours is the *only* one which alleviated this problem. Thank You!"

WISCONSIN: "...Best of all, no one has had any digestive upsets switching over to the Tundra. One of the older cats, Punki, came to us with IBS when he was a youngster. He did pretty well on our regular diet about two years ago when he was about 15-years-old, then he seemed to become sensitive to any food. We tried various diets, we worked with vets, and still couldn't find a way to get his IBS back under control. Well, after trying Tundra for the group and getting good results, we decided to try Tundra for Punki. Within two days his stools became totally formed. Punki has been eating Tundra for several weeks and he has gained weight, he's satisfied, and he's very happy! Thank you for creating such a wonderful product!"

INTERNET: "I have been feeding your Synorgon™ to two of my Aussie's for the past 6 months. My 8-year-old neutered male with Inflammatory Bowel Disease has improved greatly since changing from (bleep)* to your Synorgon."

INTERNET: "I would like to commend you on some wonderful pet products. One of our three dogs, an aging 'mostly golden' has inflammatory bowel disease (IBD) and almost died before we found that he could digest (and thrive) on a diet of boiled chicken breasts and Wysong Synorgon™. His weight dropped from a 'normal' weight of 60 lbs. down to about 47 lbs. We tried all kinds of prescription foods and diets and nothing worked until a friend gave us half a bag of Synorgon. He has slowly improved over the last year and now weighs about 62 lbs. He is looking almost pudgy but the vet just laughs and says to leave him alone with the weight. Our vet asked for an empty Synorgon wrapper and keeps it in Buster's file to show other owners."

INTERNET: "I am ecstatic with your Feline foods. My 18-year-old cat was very ill (digestive problems that the vet could not figure out). I was very frustrated at 'conventional' veterinary nutrition/health suggestions. I graduated to the dry (Vitality™) and canned. Also used the Pet Inoculant™ and F-Biotic™, as her system was very upset from antibiotics. She is now doing better than ever, loves the foods. I've been told she should be the Wysong 'Poster Kitty'. She truly embodies 'Vitality'. Regards and many thanks."

INTERNET: "Our mini Poodle was plagued with GI problems until we changed his diet to Wysong. He's doing very well and we're all extremely pleased."

---

* A super premium food, the identity of which we withhold to protect the guilty. To be fair, any pet can have a health problem eating any food (including ours) since pets are bound to be eating something when they become ill. But you can be sure that pets on properly designed diets as part of the Optimal Health Program (see pages 195-208) will have the best possible health.

INTERNET: "Wysong has been my dog's primary food since February and his health and stool have been great ever since. For the first 16 months I had him he did not digest food well and was constantly very loose. Your diets, meats, vegetables and the supplement take full credit."

INTERNET: "My adopted cat had what they thought was an infected anus. Despite antibiotics and salves, it never cleared up. Since he's been eating your food, his anus looks mostly normal, with black skin instead of moist pink like he had."

INTERNET: "My dog Boris is perhaps the ultimate Wysong dog. He had surgery to help correct an anomalous digestive system at age 7 months, and can survive most dog foods, but cannot survive on them. Yet on Wysong he thrives. He'll be six in July. That's starting to get up there for a Lab. He's not a puppy anymore. Yesterday, he and I were in the yard when a young Great Dane showed up across the street, spotted Boris, and came on over. If you would like to see a testimonial to the 'power' of your dry Canine Maintenance product, see a 78 pound Lab toss around a huge Great Dane!"

HELPS URINARY PROBLEMS

NEW YORK: "My veterinarian recently switched my dog's diet to Wysong. My dog is 12 years old and has decreased kidney function. Using Wysong has greatly improved her health. I am very satisfied."

TEXAS: "I just wanted to thank you for making Chicken Gourmet™ canned for cats... it saved my 5 year old Siamese blue short hair's life! His kidney disease has almost vanished due to your great food. Thanks so much."

BREEDER, INTERNET: "Been using your products for 4 years now and they are fantastic. Had a young female Lhasa with struvite urinary crystals and was on antibiotics constantly. After 4 years of your Wysong and Biotic pH™, she is still free of the urinary crystals and not one problem in 4 years! Thank you for everything. I am sending several breeders your way, they can't believe the wonderful condition my show dogs are in and haven't been to the vet for any heath issues since."

INTERNET: "Dylan developed urinary tract problems about six months ago, so I started feeding Uretic™ to both of them. Dylan's problems immediately went away."

INTERNET: "I am feeding your food for cats with urinary problems to our 2 males. To say they love it is an understatement. I'm not sure where I am going to store it because they search for it. Thank you for creating a healthy cat food."

INTERNET: "Thanks for your wonderful work. My kitty who had a creatinine of 3.0 is now down to 2.2. She loves your food. She was able to have 5 teeth removed after her numbers went down and now she is doing beautifully. Her coat is shiny; she is happy, and less irritable. All is well with her."

CANCER REVERSAL

OREGON: "I am writing to you today to express my delight not only in your products, but in your insightful information and inspiration. Two years ago our Keeshond was diagnosed with cancer after finding a tumor on his tonsils. At this point our vet told us to prolong his life we needed to poison him (his exact words), then take him home for the remaining 6 months of his life. Already into the alternative world of medicine for ourselves, we decided that this vet's narrow view of reality was not for us. After searching our area, we discovered a holistic vet who told us about your products...she prescribed a diet of raw meat and vegetables and supplements... Well, needless to say, our Keeshond, Goliath, is alive and well today. We kept him on a protocol of raw meat and veggies...and Wysong products. Today, when we take him somewhere, people always comment on what a cute "puppy" we have. When we tell them he's no puppy, he is in fact 12, no one believes us! Naturally, I use the opportunity to inform the lucky inquirer about Wysong and nutrition, for both their pets and themselves! Two months ago I acquired another puppy – a mastiff/shepherd. I almost choked when we arrived at the owner's home to find them giving the 6-week-old puppies a generous serving of (bleep)*. Well, of course, I immediately switched her over to Wysong and fresh, organic raw meat and veggies. Thank you Dr. Wysong for your wonderful products, and most of all, for caring. It's a rare trait these days!"

MINNESOTA: "Thank you for such a great product. I have four cats and all eat Wysong Vitality™. The reason I started using your product when my cat was diagnosed with lymphatic leukemia. The vet I'd been seeing with my boys recommended steroids, which can be hard on the cat and with results iffy at best. I took him to a holistic vet and with Chinese herbs and Wysong Vitality; he's doing remarkably well. Thank you guys so much. Everyone seems to be thriving. What more can a Mom ask."

RELIEF FOR SEIZURES

FLORIDA: "Since you recommended this diet, Missy has not had a seizure in over a year. I must admit I was skeptical but I was willing to try anything since she was having seizures every 2 to 4 months. I am so happy to be able to say that she appears to be seizure free and I thank you for that."

OHIO: "Dudley started having seizures about 6 weeks after going off the Wysong diet. The distributor for our area stopped carrying Wysong and we were told that (bleep)* was 'the same' and (bleep)* and others were 'just as good.' Sometime in the middle of all this we also tried (bleep)* and (bleep)*, but the seizures continued, sometimes a month or so apart and sometimes less than a week apart depending upon which diet he was on. He was also very lethargic, would never play or run and we had to call the vet because of occasional bouts

---

* A super premium food, the identity of which we withhold to protect the guilty. To be fair, any pet can have a health problem eating any food (including ours) since pets are bound to be eating something when they become ill. But you can be sure that pets on properly designed diets as part of the Optimal Health Program (see pages 195-208) will have the best possible health.

of unexplained lameness. There were a couple of times that he was in so much pain that my husband had to carry him outside because he wasn't able to walk. A few months after the seizures started he also developed chronic corneal erosion (bullous keratopathy) in his left eye. After many trips to a specialist, much medication and three surgical keratectomy procedures, there was no evidence of any healing. We were told that it was a metabolic disorder and that it could take months longer to heal. For about 3 months, Dudley was in pain, the ulcer continued to get larger, the eye was usually closed and the seizures continued on and off. That's when I finally called you guys. Dudley has only had one seizure since his change back to Wysong and his eye magically started healing 5 days after being switched back to Wysong. He no longer has those mysterious bouts of lameness and is frisky and eager to play with us and our other dog. The vet was amazed, to say the least."

KENNEL, WASHINGTON: "As a kennel owner I am given all sorts of products to give to clients' pets while they are being boarded or in training. Most of these don't seem to do the job, however, five years ago a dog was brought in for boarding and it had seizures unless C-Biotic™ was put on its food twice a day. I thought what a great product! I have told all of my friends about this product."

INTERNET: "...I think he, as well as all my dogs, feel a lot better than ever before. He has not had a seizure since he has been on Wysong and time will tell if this problem too has been corrected because of the change in diet to Wysong Synorgon. I am very pleased with this product."

INTERNET: "Within a very short time of putting him on Synorgon his seizures became less and less frequent. He had no seizures for 3½ months (he used to seizure every 5 days). He now only seizures when placed under a lot of stress. Also, his coat is shiny and healthy. The last time he was at the vet they commented on his healthy coat and asked what I was feeding."

RELIEF FOR ORGAN DISEASE

TEXAS: "I'm so excited. Sometime ago I had written Dr. Wysong and extolled the virtues of your products and foods, further explaining how it saved my Sheba's life…my testimonial is on your website! It's all true, and I have the bloodwork (lab results) to show how your foods and supplements reversed Sheba's liver failure. I don't care what lists of 'best foods' you may or may not be on because my girls are gorgeous and in perfect health because of your products. I will never switch! I also tell anyone who will listen about Wysong!"

INTERNET: "...my dog (English Springer Spaniel) about 2 months ago had a bad bout with pancreatitis. At the time she was on antibiotics as well, but after speaking to a few people I was told that the food could also be a source of the problem. So after doing some extensive research on the internet, I chose Wysong as my new food. And then, I printed almost everything from your website…and presented it to my vet. Well, the first question he asked is can you give me the link to all of this, I did one better I gave him all my research! Well, I switched my dogs' food. The older of the two, that had the pancreatitis, had a slight limp, it's been almost 2 months now they've been on the food, guess what, no more limp. Their coats are shinier, their breath is better, and their disposition is better! I have always had a weight issue with the two, very common in this breed; they're starting to shed a little weight with no compromise in their daily intake of food. Of course your food is a little more expensive, but I've always been a firm believer in you get what you pay for. I'm actually not spending any more money because a can of wet lasts 3 days now. And you want to know the best part of all this, I felt so terrible when my dog got pancreatitis, so helpless, now that I've switched to your food, and they're doing so well, I really feel good and know that all my research has paid off."

INTERNET: "My ten year old dog has had chronic pancreatitis most of his life. The enzyme powder I have been using on his food, which is very expensive, stopped working like it used to. My dog lost seven pounds, so I tried the Wysong C-Biotic™ and just five days later he has gained back two pounds and is like a puppy again. His energy level has increased and another plus is that his horrible smelling breath is gone! I took him to my vet today and he wrote down the product information to refer other owners of dogs in his practice with this condition to your product. He was extremely impressed with the results. I tried your product in desperation along with Synorgon™ dry food and I am just thrilled with the results already! Thank you!"

RELIEF FOR EAR PROBLEMS

PENNSYLVANIA: "Our standard Poodle, Nigel, has had constant ear infections since he was a puppy. Our vet suggested that this might be due to food allergy (after 4½ years of vet bills). Nigel was switched to Wysong. We had an appointment with the University of Pennsylvania Vet. School... He had both ears scoped and they were completely normal, without any inflammation. The vet was familiar with Wysong products and was very impressed with the amazing results. He advised we keep Nigel on Wysong the rest of his life. Thank you again for your advice and products. We also give him E.F.A.™ and C-Biotic™."

INTERNET: "At first I was skeptical, but I used your product because I trust my two black Labs' veterinarian. The dogs were fine. I changed their food only to find that they both got bad ear infections. My veterinarian insisted to change back, which I did, and their ears haven't been infected since switching back. The proof has sold me! Thank you for such a great product! My dogs in their own way also thank you!!"

BETTER TEETH

FLORIDA: "Your food is fantastic. Their teeth are so much cleaner now. Everything is great."

PENNSYLVANIA: "Another probable benefit of Wysong is better teeth. I have noticed that his teeth are looking very good. I have always brushed them, however, in the last few weeks, there is not tartar buildup and they look considerably cleaner. Actually, they look wonderful. He continues to do very well. His ears are cool and without any irritation. His eyes do not have the usual discharge. I wish I had tried Wysong years ago. It would have saved Nigel a lot of discomfort and us a lot of money and worry."

FLEA RELIEF

OHIO: "This is the first time I've written a product endorsement letter in 52 years. I'm so pleased with both the food and the F-Biotic™ supplement. I do wish that the animal doctors my pets see would have taken nutrition as a factor in my four cats' health problems. I've seen more improvement in the four months on Wysong than any other treatment. There is a wonderful 'side effect.' We are in the high flea area, but their fleas are almost gone, and during the most active flea season too! This is without collars, sprays or any other toxic treatment; just the improvement of a healthy diet. Thank you so much."

BEST OF ALL FERRET FOODS

FLORIDA: "Thank you for putting on the market a fabulous food which ferrets truly enjoy. Ferret Friends Indian River County International (FFIRCI) considers your Wysong Feline Diet to be the number one Ferret Food in the United States."

POT BELLY PIGS THRIVE

INTERNET: "Just a quick note to thank you. I have recently begun working at a pet supply store... As I bring my dog to work with me, the owner suggested I switch her food from (bleep)* to Wysong. I was skeptical, but did the research. I liked what I found, and your website is honest and straightforward. After seeing how well my dog did, I decided to consider your foods for my other pets. We also have 6 cats, now on Wysong. We also have a potbelly pig. Our pig had several problems. Chronically dry skin that flaked off in huge patches every day (even if I put lotion on him), and several bouts with piggy colic. The colic could kill him, and as he is only 9 months old and had collicked several times, I was worried. As potbellies have gone down in favor as pets, their supplies have limited choices. I could only find one food specifically made for potbelly pigs and it caused him to colic. I began researching what potbelly's need for a healthy diet. I decided to try a bag of your Vegan™ formula for dogs/cats. I checked the ingredients, and all looked very well for pigs. He has been on your food for three weeks. The change took very little time. His skin hardly flakes at all, and there has been no colic. In fact his stools are softer, and he has an easier time going potty. I know it is the food because we ran out for a few days. At the end of three days without Wysong the skin flakes appeared again. They disappeared after I gave him his Wysong back."

---

* A super premium food, the identity of which we withhold to protect the guilty. To be fair, any pet can have a health problem eating any food (including ours) since pets are bound to be eating something when they become ill. But you can be sure that pets on properly designed diets as part of the Optimal Health Program (see pages 195-208) will have the best possible health.

FOOD FOR THINKING PEOPLE

CALIFORNIA: "Thank you for the informative and excellent health letter. We take your advice and counsel. We have been using Synorgon™ for our Golden Retriever for the past two years. Our satisfaction is at 100%."

PET SHOP EMPLOYEE, CANADA: "I have worked in a pet supply shop for close to two years and I have come to the conclusion that the Wysong products and philosophy are the best out there. What you advocate is the truth, plain and simple. I have listened to dozens of companies perpetuate the false idea that everything in a bag (porous paper one for that matter) or in tin will sustain an animal in optimal health forever. I can't thank you enough for providing this information and sticking to your philosophy when we live in a world that at times can be so resistant to critical thought. It's amazing how many people believe that what is inside a bag of dog food is absolutely perfect for their animal, that feeding so called "table scraps" can only be damaging to the health. In my opinion, a lot of pet food manufacturers are no better than the tobacco companies, they rely on the public's ignorance and take advantage of that for profit. Thank you for your respect."

BREEDER, LOUISIANA (excerpt from Great Dane Quarterly magazine): "In all of my personal search to gain some perspective on these problems, I have never come across a company as 'visionary' as Wysong. The philosophy and approach to feeding offers hope for all Great Dane owners that are wanting to improve the quality of life and longevity for ourselves and this breed."

NEW YORK: "...You are doing a wonderful job! I have written to many a company in my quest for finding the best food for my kittens (nearly cats now) and do you know NOT ONE has replied! It's been over a month since I have written to each of the other companies – I think that is ample time to reply, no? I guess they did not like my in depth questions or either they just don't care. Regardless, I have found the best foods and 'program' and company that cares for my animals and will be sticking with it for their lifetimes and subsequent animals to follow. You are doing a great job, and again THANK YOU!"

NEW YORK: "I have never written a letter with such excitement about my pet's nutrition! I have never been so impressed with a pet food company in my life. What else can I say... I love your products and the philosophy behind The Wysong Theories and Company. I also loved Dr. Wysong's tape as it was very informational to me... I think I should look into taking as good care of myself as I do my cats. Thank you so very much."

SOUTH DAKOTA: "Thank you so much for your offer of a free *Health Letter*, 'the best health newsletter in the world,' no less! We are feeding – or treating our dog to your biscuits and she loves them. Your instructions say 'feed dry from the container' – so for a joke, mind you, we set it on the floor! Our sweet little girl took one ever so gently and then another and waited for us to say one more. It was terribly cute. Believe me if we had taken the instructions seriously they would have all been gone in 10 minutes. Thanks for thinking of pets too."

WISCONSIN: "I actually trust you enough as a company to tell me the truth! I have decided to go back to Wysong...the 'stars' as my husband calls you."

BREEDER, INTERNET: "I have been using your products for over 6 years now. I have referred over one hundred people because I believe in your philosophy and your products. I tour the world with my 'K-9's in Flight Frisbee Show.' It is the number one Frisbee show in the world. Thank you for your love for animals and your great products."

INTERNET: "Great site, great products, great philosophy. Thanks, to all of you."

INTERNET: "Hi, I have used your products for quite some time now with much success for our cats. Also some of the human products as well. What I'd like to share most is the fact that you provide the best in health information that I have ever encountered. Thank you for this."

INTERNET: "I enjoy your e-Health Letter very much. Thank you. My dogs enjoy your food and people always comment on their healthy coats. I wanted to let you know that when my female dog had four puppies in November they also did very well on your food. I supplement the food with meat, veggies, etc. as you suggest. Thanks for the great products!"

INTERNET: "I love the way you guys think!"

INTERNET: "I tell everyone I know with pets about your products. Other manufacturers may be leaning too much towards what pleases the owner, not what the *animal* needs. It also seems to me that one is fired upon much more when they are on a pedestal (a much deserved pedestal, because you are so far above everyone else)."

INTERNET: "I thoroughly enjoy all the info found on your website. Initially I was drawn to Wysong because I was told it was the best dog food. Through reading your statements and approaches, as well as witnessing thorough and honest responses to questions and controversies regarding your approach to healthy living, I came to understand that you are not supplying the best dog food, but more importantly, supplying the best insight."

INTERNET: "My cats love your products and I admire your philosophy of education and learning."

INTERNET: "Thank you, thank you, thank you. I was always skeptical of commercial pet foods, treats, and chews...etc. Since I got my dog almost 5 years ago, I have searched for the right way to feed and take care of her. I always believed in giving her 'real food,' but she would suffer digestive upsets and diarrhea. I started her on Wysong supplemented with meats a couple months ago and now I'm excited to add your other products to her diet. She is so full of life and energy we call her the 'Tasmanian Devil.' At her last vet check-up the assistant had trouble restraining her for a blood sample because she is so strong! Finding the truth is difficult and finding people who believe the truth is difficult. I'm grateful for your efforts and resolve to expose the truth. You've found yourself another believer and customer!"

INTERNET: "I want to sincerely thank you for the excellent customer service I have received. My e-mails have been answered thoroughly and promptly. Please know how much we not only value your products, but your kindness and service as well."

INTERNET: "You have some of the best products I have ever seen, and my interest in supplemented nutrition now spans 31 years. Your detailed product monographs, one for every product, are worth their weight in gold."

INTERNET: "I wish to say foremost that I applaud the principles the company works with. I was most impressed with the idea of a company manufacturing pet food (amongst other products) and yet acknowledging its own products' limitations by promoting a supplement of 'fresh and whole' foods."

BETTER HUMAN HEALTH

MICHIGAN: "I have never been so impressed by the common sense expressed in your recent catalog. My daughter is studying to become a doctor at U of M medical school... Her statement when I read the 'For Prevention and Health Optimization' was 'Mom, this is all true' and she is going to present this to all her patients."

INTERNET: "I just wanted to thank you for contributing so substantially to the well-being of myself and my Weimeraner, Reckless. He and I are both on a nutritional regimen of food and supplements that are endorsed and developed by your research team and facility. The unispecies vitamins and supplements have benefited both of us enormously. Reckless is just two years old and I want to help ensure optimum health and well-being for him. In doing my own research for a nutritional philosophy that seemed to make the most sense, I selected yours for its combination of whole, fresh foods and a Maintenance™ diet developed at your research center. I have had a history of anorexia and I finally began to realize that I needed to take good care of myself if I was going to take care of my dog. Thus, both he and I are the very fortunate benefactors of your wonderful work and products, as well as your continuing research. At a recent check-up with my physician, the results of the exam and the blood work indicated that I have never before been in such good health. My doctor related to me, 'Whatever you are doing, keep it up.' That is just what I intend to do, for both myself and my much-loved canine companion. He and I are most grateful to you for contributing so substantially to our collective well-being. Our lives have been greatly enhanced."

INTERNET: "I love cats, but my allergy to them would not allow me to have these wonderful pets in my home, and I had no furry companions for 10+ years. However, I stayed at the home of a friend who had a cat, and nothing happened. No allergic reactions! The cat was very friendly and sat on my lap, and still nothing. I know that allergies to the cat are to the dander and the saliva. I also know that a human's diet can affect the skin and organ function, so I took a chance and got a rescue cat and fed her what my friend fed her cat. Wysong. I suffered for three days with runny nose and asthma, but then it cleared. That old cat (10 years old) did very well on Wysong products. And I now have two cats...The important note is that people need to understand what they are doing to their companion animals when they feed them the grocery store food, and that if they are more particular, there may be no animal allergies in the home."

INTERNET: "I owe my good health to my dog, for once I started researching for the optimum nutrition for him, I decided that perhaps I should take just as good care of myself as well."

INTERNET: "Thanks for being there and providing the services you do. My two cats and myself have benefited tremendously with your products and literature."

APPENDIX C

MAKING THE TRUTH YOUR OWN-
EDUCATIONAL AIDS
CATALOGS

Truth Is A Pursuit,
Not A Destination

EDUCATIONAL AIDS
Publications by Dr. Wysong

WYSONG WEBSITE

"The Thinking Person's Internet Location," packed with product and educational information. Pages also include testimonials, controversies, questions and answers and a Forum for exchange of ideas and questions. (www.wysong.net)

WYSONG E-MAIL SUBSCRIPTION SERVICE

Short periodic e-mail postings containing provocative thoughts, new research findings, resources, new products, humor, health-related news... and more. Just e-mail us at wysong@tm.net and say "Subscribe." Easy to unsubscribe too. (Free)

• •

RATIONALE FOR ANIMAL NUTRITION

An interview format with Dr. Wysong. Explores the popular fallacies in pet feeding and the detrimental effects of food processing. The logic of feeding archetypal foods, those which an animal is genetically adapted to, is contrasted with the disease-producing modern one-processed-food-in-a-bowl practice. Evidence is presented proving that diet can have far more impact on health than most people would assume and more potential in preventing and reversing disease than all modern medical measures combined. 104 pp. illustrated, scientifically referenced, and indexed. Soft-cover $9.95/ Audio cassette $9.95

• •

WYSONG 30-MINUTE TELEVISION INTERVIEW

A 30-minute television interview with Dr. Wysong. He explains the underlying science and health logic in his human and animal product development. Video cassette $14.95

• •

HOW TO OPTIMIZE YOUR PET'S HEALTH

A 60-minute audio cassette or CD. An entertaining and thought provoking relook at how pet health should be approached. Dr. Wysong wipes away all the modern assumptions on feeding and health and with a clean slate logically rebuilds proper thinking. If you would like to take control of your pet's health destiny and know you are doing the right thing, this is the place to start. Cassette $9.95/CD $12.95

• •

HEALTHY PACKAGING

A seventeen page booklet explaining the importance of packaging and food preservation in nutrition and health. The many innovative packaging features Dr. Wysong has developed are described and the dangers of long shelf-life, "no preservatives," and common light- and oxygen-pervious packaging exposed. (Free)

• •

RADIO MESSAGE CD

29 radio messages presenting short, thought-provoking ideas on nutrition and health. (Free)

TESTIMONIAL CD

A 70-minute CD presenting 99 unsolicited testimonials. Read by the Wysong staff. (Free)

WYSONG MONOGRAPH BOOK

Wysong Monograph Book

Details the extensive research that goes into each of the potent, safe and effective Wysong nutritional supplements. Includes clinical evidence, biochemical mechanisms of action, and the rationale for using each ingredient. Scientifically referenced and illustrated. Soft-cover $9.95

• •

LIPID NUTRITION

Dr. Randy L. Wysong

LIPID NUTRITION: UNDERSTANDING FATS AND OILS IN HEALTH AND DISEASE

Explains how fats and oils can be both villains and heroes in the search for health for both humans and animals. This is a complex subject which Dr. Wysong simply explains without sacrificing technical correctness. You'll learn why the current "fat free" craze is dangerous, what is so special about omega-3 fatty acids and other essential fats, how to increase the good fats in the diet and reduce the bad, and how to change the diet so the powerful preventive and healing effects of fats and oils can perform as they are naturally designed to. 170 pp. illustrated, scientifically referenced, and indexed. Soft cover $12.95, Hard-cover $14.95

• •

THE SYNORGON DIET: HOW TO ACHIEVE HEALTHY WEIGHT IN A WORLD OF EXCESS

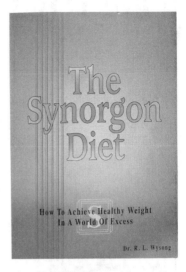

Provides a fundamental, unique understanding for why excess weight in people and animals is a modern epidemic. Weight control is never a problem in wild animals or human populations untouched by modern civilization. It is a disease created by food manipulation and modern life-style. The cure is as simple as rediscovering our genetic roots, our intimate link with our environment, and reconnecting. No problem can ever be truly solved without correct fundamental understanding. In this book you will come to learn not only the roots of obesity but disease itself. With that understanding you can take control of your own weight and health destiny. 270 pp. illustrated, scientifically referenced, and indexed. Soft-cover $12.95

• •

WYSONG HEALTH LETTER BOUND VOLUMES

The Wysong Health Letter explores current health and nutrition research as well as Dr. Wysong's thoughts on environmental, political, social, and philosophical topics. This is a thinking person's resource. Scientifically referenced, illustrated and cartooned. Each volume is a year's compilation of Wysong Health Letters in hard cover bound, indexed and cross-referenced form. Available in Volumes VII, VIII, IX and X. $19.95 each. ($59.95 for the complete set of 4.)

• •

THE CREATION-EVOLUTION CONTROVERSY

A provocative look at the study of origins. The careful logic Dr. Wysong uses in addressing this topic is the same as that used in his approach to health. The topic of origins is charged with emotion but can be approached with reason. Here you will learn the strengths and weaknesses of competing theories. You will be surprised that science and logic do not wholeheartedly support the notion that life can appear spontaneously from exploding stars. Evidence is presented from the fields of biochemistry, probability, genetics, geology, philosophy, archeology, astronomy, embryology and natural history. An enormous work that is still current some 30 years after its first writing. 455 pp. illustrated, scientifically referenced, and indexed. In its ninth printing. Soft-cover $12.95

● ●

WYSONG DIRECTORY OF ALTERNATIVE RESOURCES

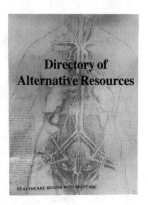

Guide to alternative sources of health care, self-improvement, environmental improvement and much more. Over 335 Resources. This is where you turn when you have a problem that is not being solved, want an alternative medical second opinion, and want help getting control of your own health destiny. 32 pp. $15.00

● ●

CATALOGS

WYSONG PRODUCT CATALOG
Hundreds of products for thinking people and their companion animals. (Free)

• •

BOOK STORE CATALOG
Listing of over 350 specially selected books, audios and videos covering all areas of personal and planetary transformation. (Free on website or $3.00 for a hard copy mailed.)

• •

VETERINARY CATALOG
Hundreds of medical/surgical and nutritional products (available to licensed veterinarians only.) (Free)

• •

ORDER FORM

Name: _____

Business: _____

Address: _____

City: _____

State: _____ Zip: _____

Phone: _____

E-mail: _____

Method of Payment

❏ Money Order/Cashier's Check

❏ Personal Check   ❏ Visa   ❏ M/C   ❏ Discover

Account Number: _____

Exp.Date: _____ Signature: _____

ORDER BY:

Mail: Wysong Corporation
         1880 N. Eastman Rd.
         Midland, MI 48642-7779

Telephone (orders only): 1-800-748-0188

(9:00 a.m. - 5:00 p.m. EST, please have your order ready)

Fax: 1-989-631-8801

Website: www.wysong.net

ITEM	QUANTITY	COST	TOTAL

MERCHANDISE TOTAL _____

MI RESIDENTS ADD 6% SALES TAX _____

*SHIPPING _____

GRAND TOTAL _____

*Shipping is $4.00 regardless of number of selections made.
Postage is free on those items indicated.